PALMS ON THE MIDDLE AMAZON.

THE ANDES AND THE AMAZON;

OR,

ACROSS THE CONTINENT OF SOUTH AMERICA.

By JAMES ORTON, M.A.,

PROFESSOR OF NATURAL HISTORY IN VASSAR COLLEGE, POUGHKEEPSIE, N. Y., AND CORRESPONDING MEMBER OF THE ACADEMY OF NATURAL SCIENCES, PHILADELPHIA.

WITH A NEW MAP OF EQUATORIAL AMERICA AND NUMEROUS ILLUSTRATIONS.

NEW YORK:

HARPER & BROTHERS, PUBLISHERS,

FRANKLIN SQUARE.

1870.

TO

CHARLES DARWIN, M.A., F.R.S., F.L.S., F.G.S.,

WHOSE PROFOUND RESEARCHES

HAVE THROWN SO MUCH LIGHT UPON EVERY DEPARTMENT OF SCIENCE,

AND

WHOSE CHARMING "VOYAGE OF THE BEAGLE" HAS SO PLEASANTLY

ASSOCIATED HIS NAME WITH OUR SOUTHERN CONTINENT,

THESE SKETCHES OF THE ANDES AND THE AMAZON ARE, BY PERMISSION,

MOST RESPECTFULLY

Dedicated.

"Among the scenes which are deeply impressed on my mind, none exceed in sublimity the primeval forests undefaced by the hand of man; whether those of Brazil, where the powers of Life are predominant, or those of Terra del Fuego, where Death and Decay prevail. Both are temples filled with the varied productions of the God of Nature: no one can stand in these solitudes unmoved, and not feel that there is more in man than the mere breath of his body."—DARWIN'S *Journal*, p. 503.

PREFACE.

This volume is one result of a scientific expedition to the equatorial Andes and the river Amazon. The expedition was made under the auspices of the Smithsonian Institution, and consisted of the following gentlemen besides the writer: Colonel Staunton, of Ingham University, Leroy, N. Y.; F. S. Williams, Esq., of Albany, N. Y.; and Messrs. P. V. Myers and A. Bushnell, of Williams College. We sailed from New York July 1, 1867; and, after crossing the Isthmus of Panama and touching at Paita, Peru, our general route was from Guayaquil to Quito, over the Eastern Cordillera; thence over the Western Cordillera, and through the forest on foot to Napo; down the Rio Napo by canoe to Pebas, on the Marañon; and thence by steamer to Pará.*

Nearly the entire region traversed by the expedition is strangely misrepresented by the most recent geographical

* Another division, consisting of Messrs. H. M. Myers, R. H. Forbes, and W. Gilbert, of Williams College, proceeded to Venezuela, and after exploring the vicinity of Lake Valencia, the two former traversed the llanos to Pao, descended the Apuré and ascended the Orinoco to Yavita, crossed the portage of Pimichin (a low, level tract, nine miles wide, separating the waters of the Orinoco from those of the Amazon), and descended the Negro to Manáos, making a vogage by canoe of over 2000 miles through a little-known but deeply-interesting region. A narrative of this expedition will soon be given to the public.

works. On the Andes of Ecuador we have little besides the travels of Humboldt; on the Napo, nothing; while the Marañon is less known to North Americans than the Nile.

Many of the following pages first appeared in the New York *Evening Post.* The author has also published "Physical Observations on the Andes and the Amazon" and "Geological Notes on the Ecuadorian Andes" in the *American Journal of Science*, an article on the great earthquake of 1868 in the Rochester *Democrat*, and a paper *On the Valley of the Amazon* read before the American Association at Salem. These papers have been revised and extended, though the popular form has been retained. It has been the effort of the writer to present a condensed but faithful picture of the physical aspect, the resources, and the inhabitants of this vast country, which is destined to become an important field for commercial enterprise. For detailed descriptions of the collections in natural history, the scientific reader is referred to the various reports of the following gentlemen, to whom the specimens were committed by the Smithsonian Institution:

Volcanic Rocks................	Dr. T. Sterry Hunt, F.R.S., Montreal.
Plants............................	Dr. Asa Gray, Cambridge.
Land and Fresh-water Shells.	M. Crosse, Paris, and Thomas Bland, Esq., New York.
Marine Shells......................	Rev. Dr. E. R. Beadle, Philadelphia.
Fossil "	W. M. Gabb, Esq., Philadelphia.
Hemiptera........................	Prof. P. R. Uhler, Baltimore.
Orthoptera......................	S. H. Scudder, Esq., Boston.
Hymenoptera and Nocturnal Lepidoptera..................	Dr. A. S. Packard, Jr., Salem.
Diurnal Lepidoptera..........	Tryon Reakirt, Esq., Philadelphia.
Coleoptera......................	George D. Smith, Esq., Boston.
Phalangia and Pedipalpi......	Dr. H. C. Wood, Jr., Philadelphia.
Fishes............................	Dr. Theodore Gill, Washington.
Reptiles..........................	Prof. E. D. Cope, Philadelphia.

Birds	John Cassin, Esq.,* Philadelphia.
Bats	Dr. H. Allen, Philadelphia.
Mammalian Fossils	Dr. Joseph Leidy, Philadelphia.

Many of the type specimens are deposited in the museums of the Smithsonian Institution, the Philadelphia Academy of Natural Science, the Boston Society of Natural History, the Peabody Academy of Science, and Vassar College; but the bulk of the collection was purchased by Ingham University, Leroy, New York.

The Map of Equatorial America was drawn with great care after original observations and the surveys of Humboldt and Wisse on the Andes, and of Azevedo, Castlenau, and Bates on the Amazon.† The names of Indian tribes are in small capitals. Most of the illustrations are after photographs or drawings made on the ground, and can be relied upon. The portrait of Humboldt, which is for the first time presented to the public, was photographed from the original painting in the possession of Sr. Aguirre, Quito. Unlike the usual portrait—an old man, in Berlin—this presents him as a young man in Prussian uniform, traveling on the Andes.

We desire to express our grateful acknowledgments to the Smithsonian Institution, Hon. William H. Seward, and Hon. James A. Garfield, of Washington; to Cyrus W. Field, Esq., and William Pitt Palmer, Esq., of New York; to C. P. Williams, Esq., of Albany; to Rev. J. C. Fletcher,

* This eminent ornithologist died in the midst of his examination. Mr. George N. Lawrence, of New York, has identified the remainder, including all the hummers.

† We have retained the common orthography of this word, though *Amazons*, used by Bates, is doubtless more correct, as more akin to the Brazilian name *Amazonas*.

now United States Consul at Oporto; to Chaplain Jones, of Philadelphia; to Dr. William Jameson, of the University of Quito; to J. F. Reeve, Esq., and Captain Lee, of Guayaquil; to the Pacific Mail Steamship, Panama Railroad, and South Pacific Steam Navigation companies; to the officers of the Peruvian and Brazilian steamers on the Amazon; and to the eminent naturalists who have examined the results of the expedition.

NOTE.—Osculati has alone preceded us, so far as we can learn, in obtaining a vocabulary of Záparo words; but, as his work is not to be found in this country, we have not had the pleasure of making a comparison.

INTRODUCTION

BY

REV. J. C. FLETCHER,

AUTHOR OF "BRAZIL AND BRAZILIANS."

IN this day of many voyages, in the Old World and the New, it is refreshing to find an untrodden path. Central Africa has been more fully explored than that region of Equatorial America which lies in the midst of the Western Andes and upon the slopes of these mountain monarchs which look toward the Atlantic. In this century one can almost count upon his hand the travelers who have written of their journeys in this unknown region. Our own Herndon and Gibbon descended—the one the Peruvian and the other the Bolivian waters—the affluents of the Amazon, beginning their voyage where the streams were mere channels for canoes, and finishing it where the great river appears a fresh-water ocean. Mr. Church, the artist, made the sketches for his famous "Heart of the Andes" where the headwaters of the Amazon are rivulets. But no one whose language is the English has journeyed down and described the voyage from the *plateaux* of Ecuador to the Atlantic Ocean until Professor Orton and his party accomplished this feat in 1868. Yet it was over this very route that the King of Waters (as the Amazon is called by the aborigines) was originally discovered. The *auri sacra fames*, which in 1541 urged the adventurous Gonzalo Pizarro to hunt for the fabled city of *El Dorado* in the depths of the South American forests, led to the descent of the great river by Orellana, a knight of Truxillo. The fabled women-warriors were said to have been seen in this notable voyage, and hence the name of the river *Amazon*, a name which in Spanish and Portuguese is in the plural. It was not until nearly one hundred years after Orellana was in his grave that a voyage of discovery ascended the river. In 1637 Pedro Teixeira started from Pará with an expedition of nearly two thousand (all but seventy of whom were natives), and with varied experiences, by water and by land, the explorer in eight months reached the city of Quito, where he was received with distinguished honor. Two hundred years ago the result of this expedition was published.

The Amazon was from that time, at rare intervals, the highway of Spanish and Portuguese priests and friars, who thus went to their distant charges among the Indians. In 1745 the French academician De la Condamine descended from Quito to Pará, and gave the most accurate idea of the great valley which we had until the first quarter of this century.

The narrow policy of Spain and Portugal was most unfruitful in its results to South America. A jealous eye guarded that great region, of which it can be so well said there are

> "Realms unknown and blooming wilds,
> And fruitful deserts, worlds of solitude,
> Where the sun smiles and seasons teem in vain."

Now, the making known to the world of any portion of these "fruitful deserts" is performing a service for the world. This Professor Orton has done. His interesting and valuable volume hardly needs any introduction or commendation, for its intrinsic merit will exact the approbation of every reader. Scientific men, and tourists who seek for new routes of travel, will appreciate it at once; and I trust that the time is near at hand when our mercantile men, by the perusal of such a work, will see how wide a field lies before them for future commercial enterprise. This portion of the tropics abounds in natural resources which only need the stimulus of capital to draw them forth to the light; to create among the natives a desire for articles of civilization in exchange for the crude productions of the forest; and to stimulate emigration to a healthy region of perpetual summer.

It seems as if Providence were opening the way for a great change in the Valley of the Amazon. That immense region drained by the great river is as large as all the United States east of the States of California and Oregon and the Territory of Washington, and yet it has been so secluded, mainly by the old monopolistic policy of Portugal, that that vast space has not a population equal to the single city of Rio de Janeiro or of Brooklyn. Two million five hundred thousand square miles are drained by the Amazon. Three fourths of Brazil, one half of Bolivia, two thirds of Peru, three fourths of Ecuador, and a portion of Venezuela are watered by this river. Riches, mineral and vegetable, of inexhaustible supply have been here locked up for centuries. Brazil held the key, but it was not until under the rule of their present constitutional monarch, Don Pedro II., that the Brazilians awoke to the necessity of opening this glorious region. Steamers were introduced in 1853, subsidized by the government. But it is to a young Brazilian statesman, Sr. A. C. Tavares Bastos, that belongs the credit of having agitated, in the press and in the national parliament, the opening of the Amazon, until public opinion, thus acted upon, produced the desired result. On another occasion, in May, 1868, I gave several indices of a more enlightened policy in Brazil, and stated that the opening of the Amazon, which occurred on the 7th of September, 1867, and by which the great river is free to the flags of all nations, from the Atlantic to Peru, and the abrogation of the monopoly of the coast-trade from the Amazon to the Rio Grande do Sul, whereby 4000 miles of Brazilian sea-coast are open to the vessels of every country, can not fail not only to develop the resources of Brazil, but will prove of great benefit to the bordering Hispano-American republics and to the maritime nations of the earth. The opening of the Amazon is the most significant indication that the leaven of the narrow monopolistic Portuguese conservatism has at last worked out. Portugal would not allow Humboldt to enter the Amazon Valley in Brazil. The result of the new policy is beyond the most sanguine expectation. The exports and imports for Pará for October and November, 1867, were double those of 1866. This is but the beginning. Soon it will be found that it is cheaper for Bolivia, Peru, Ecuador, and New Granada, east of the Andes, to receive their goods from, and to export their India-rubber, cinchona, etc., to the United States and Europe, *via* the great water highway which discharges into the Atlantic, than by the long, circuitous route of Cape Horn or the trans-Isthmian route of Panama.

CONTENTS.

CHAPTER I.

Guayaquil. — First and Last Impressions. — Climate. — Commerce. — The Malecon.—Glimpse of the Andes.—Scenes on the Guayas.—Bodegas.—Mounted for Quito.—La Mona.—A Tropical Forest ....Page 25

CHAPTER II.

Our Tambo.—Ascending the Andes.—Camino Real.—Magnificent Views.—Guaranda.—Cinchona.—The Summit.—Chimborazo.—Over the Andes.—Chuquipoyo the Wretched.—Ambato.—A Stupid City.—Cotopaxi.—The Vale of Machachi.—Arrival at Quito 40

CHAPTER III.

Early History of Quito.—Its Splendor under the Incas.—Crushed by Spain.—Dying now.—Situation.—Altitude.—Streets.—Buildings 56

CHAPTER IV.

Population of Quito.—Dress.—Manners.—Character.—Commerce.—Agriculture.—Manufactures.—Arts.—Education.—Amusements.— Quito Ladies 68

CHAPTER V.

Ecuador.—Extent.—Government.—Religion.—A Protestant Cemetery in Quito.—Climate.—Regularity of Tropical Nature.—Diseases on the Highlands 85

CHAPTER VI.

Astronomic Virtues of Quito.—Flora and Fauna of the Valley of Quito.—Primeval Inhabitants of the Andes.—Quichua Indians 97

CHAPTER VII.

Geological History of South America.—Rise of the Andes.—Creation of the Amazon.—Characteristic Features of the Continent.—Andean Chain.—The Equatorial Volcanoes... 114

CHAPTER VIII.

The Volcanoes of Ecuador.—Western Cordillera.—Chimborazo.—Iliniza.—Corazon.—Pichincha.—Descent into its Crater ....Page 127

CHAPTER IX.

The Volcanoes of Ecuador.—Eastern Cordillera.—Imbabura.—Cayambi.—Antisana.—Cotopaxi.—Llanganati.—Tunguragua.—Altar.—Sangai. 143

CHAPTER X.

The Valley of Quito.—Riobamba.—A Bed of "Fossil Giants."—Chillo Hacienda.—Otovalo and Ibarra.—The Great Earthquake of 1868........ 152

CHAPTER XI.

"The Province of the Orient," or the Wild Napo Country.—The Napos, Zaparos, and Jívaros Indians.—Preparations to cross the Continent...... 164

CHAPTER XII.

Departure from Quito.—Itulcachi.—A Night in a Bread-tray.—Crossing the Cordillera.—Guamani.—Papallacta.—Domiciled at the Governor's.—An Indian Aristides.—Our Peon Train.—In the Wilderness............... 177

CHAPTER XIII.

Baeza.—The Forest.—Crossing the Cosanga.—Curi-urcu.—Archidona.—Appearance, Customs, and Belief of the Natives.—Napo and Napo River.. 187

CHAPTER XIV.

Afloat on the Napo.—Down the Rapids.—Santa Rosa and its mulish Alcalde.—Pratt on Discipline.—Forest Music.—Coca.—Our Craft and Crew.—Storm on the Napo.. 200

CHAPTER XV.

Sea-Cows and Turtles' Eggs.—The Forest.—Peccaries.—Indian Tribes on the Lower Napo.—Anacondas and Howling Monkeys.—Insect Pests.—Battle with Ants.—Barometric Anomaly.—First View of the Amazon.—Pebas.. 215

CHAPTER XVI.

Down the Amazon.—Steam on the Great River.—Loreto.—San Antonio.—Tabatinga.—Brazilian Steamers.—Scenery on the Amazon.—Tocantins.—Fonte Boa.—Ega.—Rio Negro.—Manáos.................................. 230

CHAPTER XVII.

Down the Amazon.—Serpa.—Villa Nova.—Obidos.—Santarem.—A Colony of Southerners.—Monte Alegre.—Porto do Moz.—Leaving the Amazon. —Breves.—Pará River.—The City of Pará.—Legislation and Currency. —Religion and Education.—Nonpareil Climate......................Page 247

CHAPTER XVIII.

The River Amazon.—Its Source and Magnitude.—Tributaries and Tints.—Volume and Current.—Rise and Fall.—Navigation.—Expeditions on the Great River.. 264

CHAPTER XIX.

The Valley of the Amazon.—Its Physical Geography.—Geology.—Climate.—Vegetation.. 280

CHAPTER XX.

Life within the Great River.—Fishes.—Alligators.—Turtles.—Porpoises and Manatís.. 295

CHAPTER XXI.

Life around the Great River.—Insects.—Reptiles.—Birds.—Mammals. 300

CHAPTER XXII.

Life around the Great River.—Origin of the Red Man.—General Characteristics of the Amazonian Indians.—Their Languages, Costumes, and Habitations.—Principal Tribes.—Mixed Breeds.—Brazilians and Brazil. 315

CHAPTER XXIII.

How to Travel in South America.—Routes.—Expenses.—Outfit.—Precautions.—Dangers.. 325

CHAPTER XXIV.

In Memoriam.. 334

APPENDICES.

APPENDIX A.

Barometrical Measurements across South America....................Page 338

APPENDIX B.

Vocabularies from the Quíchua, Záparo, Yágua, and Cámpas Languages 340

APPENDIX C.

Commerce of the Amazon... 344

ADDENDA... 347

INDEX... 349

ILLUSTRATIONS.

Palms on the Middle Amazon..*Frontispiece.*
Cathedral of Guayaquil. ....Page 27
Equipped for the Andes.. 37
Ascending the Andes.. 42
Quito from the North.. 61
Water-carriers.. 62
Street in Quito.. 63
Capitol at Quito.. 66
Indian Dwellings.. 78
Washerwomen.. 83
Ecclesiastics.. 88
Profiles of Ecuadorian Volcanoes.. 123
Crater of Pichincha.. 135
Humboldt in 1802.. 156
Ibarra.. 158
Napo Peon.. 184
Autograph of an Indian.. 185
Papaya-tree.. 202
Trapiche, or Sugar-mill.. 208
Our Craft on the Napo.. 211
Hunting Turtle-eggs.. 217
A Howler.. 223
Kitchen on the Amazon.. 238
Natives on the Middle Amazon.. 241
A Siesta.. 244
Santarem.. 250
Pará.. 255
Fruit-peddlers.. 259
Igarape, or Canoe-path.. 265
Coca-plant.. 293
Iguana.. 305
Toucans.. 307

Brazilian Hummers..Page 309
Capybara. 310
Jaguar.. 311
Native Comb.. 317
Colonel Staunton..*To face page* 334
Map of Equatorial America... *End.*

THE ANDES AND THE AMAZON.

CHAPTER I.

Guayaquil. — First and Last Impressions. — Climate. — Commerce. — The Malecon.—Glimpse of the Andes.—Scenes on the Guayas.—Bodegas.—Mounted for Quito.—La Mona.—A Tropical Forest.

LATE in the evening of the 19th of July, 1867, the steamer "Favorita" dropped anchor in front of the city of Guayaquil. The first view awakened visions of Oriental splendor. Before us was the Malecon, stretching along the river, two miles in length—at once the most beautiful and the most busy street in the emporium of Ecuador. In the centre rose the Government House, with its quaint old tower, bearing aloft the city clock. On either hand were long rows of massive, apparently marble, three-storied buildings, each occupying an entire square, and as elegant as they were massive. Each story was blessed with a balcony, the upper one hung with canvas curtains now rolled up, the other protruding over the sidewalk to form a lengthened arcade like that of the Rue de Rivoli in imperial Paris. In this lower story were the gay shops of Guayaquil, filled with the prints, and silks, and fancy articles of England and France. As this is the promenade street as well as the Broadway of commerce, crowds of Ecuadorians, who never do business in the evening, leisurely paced the magnificent arcade; hatless ladies sparkling with fire-flies* instead of

* The *Pyrophorus noctilucus*, or "cucujo," found also in Mexico and the West Indies. It resembles our large spring-beetle. The light proceeds from two eye-like spots on the thorax and from the segments underneath. It feeds

diamonds, and far more brilliant than koh-i-noors, swept the pavement with their long trains; martial music floated on the gentle breeze from the barracks or some festive hall, and a thousand gas-lights along the levee and in the city, doubling their number by reflection from the river, betokened wealth and civilization.

We landed in the morning to find our vision a dissolving view in the light of the rising sun. The princely mansions turned out to be hollow squares of wood-work, plastered within and without, and roofed with red tiles. Even the "squares" were only distant approximations; not a right angle could we find in our hotel. All the edifices are built (very properly in this climate) to admit air instead of excluding it, and the architects have wonderfully succeeded; but with the air is wafted many an odor not so pleasing as the spicy breezes from Ceylon's isle. The cathedral is of elegant design. Its photograph is more imposing than Notre Dame, and a Latin inscription tells us that it is the Gate of Heaven. But a near approach reveals a shabby structure, and the pewless interior is made hideous by paintings and images which certainly must be caricatures. A few genuine works of art imported from Italy alone relieve the mind of the visitor. Excepting a few houses on the Malecon, and not excepting the cathedral, the majority of the buildings have a tumble-down appearance, which is not altogether due to the frequent earthquakes which have troubled this city; while the habitations in the outskirts are exceedingly primitive, floored and walled with split cane and thatched with leaves, the first story occupied by domestic animals and the second by their owners. The city is quite regularly laid out, the main streets

on the sugar-cane. On the Upper Amazon we found the *P. clarus*, *P. pellucens*, and *P. tuberculatus*. At Bahia, on the opposite coast, Darwin found *P. luminosus*, the most common luminous insect.

running parallel to the river. A few streets are rudely paved, many are shockingly filthy, and all of them yield grass to the delight of stray donkeys and goats. A number of mule-carts, half a dozen carriages, one omnibus, and a hand-car on the Malecon, sum up the wheeled vehicles of Guayaquil. The population is twenty-two thousand, the same for thirty years past. Of these, about twenty are from the United States, and perhaps twenty-five can command $100,000. No foreigner has had reason to complain

Cathedral of Guayaquil.

that Guayaquilians lacked the virtues of politeness and hospitality. The ladies dress in excellent taste, and are proverbial for their beauty. Spanish, Indian, and Negro blood mingle in the lower classes. The city supports two small papers, *Los Andes* and *La Patria*, but they are usually issued about ten days behind date. The hourly cry of the night-watchman is quite as musical as that of the muezzin in Constantinople. At eleven o'clock, for example, they sing "*Ave Maria purissima! los once han dedo, noche clara y serena. Viva la Patria!*"

The full name of the city is Santiago de Guayaquil.* It is so called, first, because the conquest of the province was finished on the 25th of July (the day of St. James), 1533; and, secondly, after Guayas, a feudatory cacique of Atahuallpa. It was created a city by Charles V., October 6, 1535. It has suffered much in its subsequent history by fires and earthquakes, pirates and pestilence. It is situated on the right bank of the River Guayas, sixty miles from the ocean, and but a few feet above its level. Though the most western city in South America, it is only two degrees west of the longitude of Washington, and it is the same distance below the equator—Orion sailing directly overhead, and the Southern Cross taking the place of the Great Dipper. The mean annual temperature, according to our observations, is 83°. There are two seasons, the wet, or *invierno*, and the dry, or *verano*. The *verano* is called the summer, although astronomically it is winter; it begins in June and terminates in November.† The heavy rains come on about Christmas. March is the rainiest month in the year, and July the coldest. It is at the close of the *invierno* (May) that fevers most abound. The climate of Guayaquil during the dry season is nearly perfect. At daybreak there is a cool easterly breeze; at sunrise a brief lull, and then a gentle variable wind; at 3 P.M. a southwest wind, at first in gusts, then in a sustained current; at sunset the same softened down to a gentle breeze, increasing about 7 P.M., and dying away about 3 A.M. Notwithstanding heaps of filth and green-mantled pools, sufficient to start a pes-

* The ancient name was *Culenta.*

† The continuity of the dry season is broken by a rainy fit commencing a few days after the autumnal equinox, and called *el Cordonazo de San Francisco.* "Throughout South America (observes Mr. Spruce) the periodical alternations of dry and rainy weather are laid to the account of those saints whose 'days' coincide nearly with the epochs of change. But if the weather be rainy when it ought to be fair, or if the rains of winter be heavier than ordinary, the blame is invariably laid on the moon."

tilence if transported to New York, the city is usually healthy, due in great part, no doubt, to countless flocks of buzzards which greedily wait upon decay. These carrion-hawks enjoy the protection of law, a heavy fine being imposed for wantonly killing one.* It is during the rainy season that this port earns the reputation of being one of the most pestiferous spots on the globe. The air is then hot and oppressive, reminding the geologist of the steaming atmosphere in the carboniferous period; the surrounding plains are flooded with water, and the roads, even some of the streets of the city, become impassable; intolerable musquitoes, huge cockroaches, disgusting centipedes, venomous scorpions, and still more deadly serpents, keep the human species circumspect, and fevers and dysenteries do the work of death.

The Guayas is the largest river on the Pacific coast; and Guayaquil monopolizes the commerce of Ecuador, for it is the only port. Esmeraldas and Peylon are not to be mentioned. Through its custom-house passes nearly every import and export. The green banks of the Guayas, covered with an exuberant growth, are in strong contrast with the sterile coast of Peru, and the possession of Guayaquil has been a coveted prize since the days of Pizarro. Few spots between the tropics can vie with this lowland in richness and vigor of vegetation. Immense quantities of cacao—second only to that of Caracas—are produced, though but a fraction is gathered, owing to the scarcity of laborers, so many Ecuadorians have been exiled or killed in senseless revolutions. Twenty million pounds are annually exported, chiefly to Spain; and two million pounds of excellent coffee, which often finds its way into New York under the name of "pure Java." There are three or four kinds of

* The turkey-buzzard, the "John Crow" of the West Indies, is not a social bird, though a score are often seen together: each comes and goes by himself.

indigenous cacao on this coast, all richly deserving the generic title *Theobroma*, or "food for the gods." The best grows in Esmeraldas, as it contains the largest amount of oil and has the most pleasant flavor. But very little of it is exported, because it rots in about six months. The *cacao de arriba*, from up the River Guayas, is the best to export, as it keeps two years without damage. Next in order is the *cacao de abajo*, from down the river, as Machala, Santa Rosa, Balao, and Manabi, below Guayaquil. A still richer nut is the mountain cacao, but it is never cultivated. It is small and white, and almost pure oil. This oil, called cacao-butter, is used by the natives for burns, sores, and many cutaneous diseases. Cacao contributes more to the commerce of the republic than any other production of its soil. The flowers and fruit grow directly out of the trunk and branches. "A more striking example (says Humboldt) of the expansive powers of life could hardly be met with in organic nature." The fruit is yellowish-red, and of oblong shape, and the seeds (from which chocolate is prepared) are enveloped in a mass of white pulp. The tree resembles our lilac in size and shape, and yields three crops a year—in March, June, and September. Spain is the largest consumer of cacao. The Mexican *chocolalt* is the origin of our word chocolate. Tucker gives the following comparative analysis of unshelled beans from Guayaquil and Caracas:

	Guayaquil.	Caracas.
Theobromine	0.63	0.55
Cacao-red	4.56	6.18
Cacao-butter	36.38	35.08
Gluten	2.96	3.21
Starch	0.53	0.62
Gum	1.58	1.19
Extractive matter	3.44	6.22
Humic acid	8.57	9.28
Cellulose	30.50	28.66
Ash	8.03	2.91
Water	6.20	5.58
	98.38	99.48

The coffee-tree is about eight feet high, and has dark green leaves, white blossoms, and green, red, and purple berries at the same time. Each tree yields on an average two pounds annually.

The other chief articles of exportation are hides, cotton, "Panama hats," manufactured at Indian villages on the coast, cinchona bark, caucho, tobacco, orchilla weed, sarsaparilla, and tamarinds.* The hats are usually made of the "Toquilla" (*Carludovica palmata*), an arborescent plant about five feet high, resembling the palm. The leaf, which is a yard long, is plaited like a fan, and is borne on a three-cornered stalk. It is cut while young, the stiff parallel veins removed, then slit into shreds by whipping it, and immersed in boiling water, and finally bleached in the sun. The same "straw" is used in the interior. The "Mocora," which grows like a cocoa-nut tree, with a very smooth, hard, thorny bark, is rarely used, as it is difficult to work. The leaves are from eight to twelve feet in length, so that the "straws" will finish a hat without splicing. Such hats require two or three months, and bring sometimes $150; but they will last a lifetime. They can be packed away in a vest pocket, and they can be turned inside out and worn, the inside surface being as smooth and well finished as the outside. "Toquilla" hats are whiter than the "mocora."

The exports from Guayaquil bear no proportion to the capabilities of the country; Ecuador has no excuse for being bankrupt. Most of the imports are of English origin; lard comes from the United States, and flour from Chile.

The Malecon and river present a lively scene all the year round; the rest of the city appears deserted in com-

* In 1867 there were exported to Europe of cacao, 197,260 quintals; cotton, 10,247 do.; caucho, 8911 do.; sarsaparilla, 149 do.; orchilla, 10,247 packages; quinine, 5000 do.; tobacco, 2000 do.; coffee, 1611 do.; tamarinds, 65 bbls.; sides of leather, 22,514; hats, 8397.

parison. The British steamers from Panama and Payta arrive weekly; Yankee steam-boats make regular trips up and down the Guayas and its tributaries; half a dozen sailing vessels, principally French, are usually lying in the stream, which is here six fathoms deep; and hundreds of canoes are gliding to and fro. But the *balsas* are the most original, and, therefore, the most attractive sight. These are rafts made of light balsa wood, so buoyant as to be used in coasting voyages. They were invented by the old Peruvians, and are the homes of a literally floating population. By these and the smaller craft are brought to the mole of the Malecon, besides articles for exportation, a boundless variety of fruits—pine-apples (whose quality has made Guayaquil famous), oranges, lemons, limes, plantains, bananas, cocoa-nuts, alligator pears, papayas, mangos, guavas, melons, etc.; many an undescribed species of fish known only to the epicure, and barrels or jars of water from a distant point up the river, out of the reach of the tide and the city sewers. Ice is frequently brought from Chimborazo, and sold for $1 per pound. A flag hoisted at a favorite café announces that snow has arrived from the mountains, and that ice-cream can be had. The market, held every morning by the river side, is an animated scene. The strife of the half-naked fishmongers, the cry of the swarthy fruit-dealers—"Pinas!" "Naranjas!" etc., and the song of the itinerant dulce-peddler—"Tamales!" mingled with the bray of the water-bearing donkeys as they trot through the town, never fail to arrest the attention of every traveler.

But there is another sight more attractive still—one worth a long voyage, for Nature nowhere else repeats the picture. From the balconies of Guayaquil can be seen on a clear day the long, towering range of the Andes. We may forget all the incidents in our subsequent journey, but the impression produced by that glorious view is unfading. The sun had nearly touched the Pacific when the clouds, which for days had wrapped the Cordilleras* in misty robes, suddenly rose like a curtain. There stood, in inconceivable grandeur, one of the stupendous products of the last great revolution of the earth's crust, as a geologist would say, but, in the language of history, the lofty home of the Incas, made illustrious by the sword of Pizarro and the pen of Prescott. On the right a sea of hills rose higher and higher, till they culminated in the purple mountains of Assuay. Far to the left, one hundred miles northeasterly, the peerless Chimborazo lifted its untrodden and unapproachable summit above its fellows—an imposing background to lesser mountains and stately forests. The great dome reflected dazzlingly the last blushes of the west, its crown of snow fringed with black lines, which were the steep and sharp edges of precipitous rocks. It was interesting to watch the mellowing tints on the summit as the shadows crept upward: gold, vermilion, violet, purple, were followed by a momentary "glory;" then darkness covered the earth, and a host of stars, "trembling with excess of light," burst suddenly into view over the peaks of the Andes.

Bidding "adios" to our Guayaquilian friends, we took passage in one of Captain Lee's little steamers to Bodegas, seventy miles up the river. The Ecuadorian government, strange to say, does not patronize these steamers, but carries the Quito mail in a canoe. The Guayas is a sluggish stream, its turbid waters starting from the slope of the

* *Cordillera* (pronounced Cor-de-yér-ra), literally a long ridge, is usually applied to a longitudinal subdivision of the Andes, as the east and west cordilleras inclosing the valley of Quito; *Sierra* (from the Spanish for saw or Arabic *sehrah*, an uncultivated tract) is a jagged spur of the Andes; *Cerro*, "a hog-backed hill." *Paramo* (a desert) is the treeless, uninhabited, uncultivated rolling steppes just below the snow-limit.

Andes, and flowing through a low, level tract, covered with varied forms of vegetable life. Forests of the broad-leaved plantain and banana line the banks. The fruit is the most common article of food in equatorial America, and is eaten raw, roasted, baked, boiled, and fried. It grows on a succulent stem formed of sheath-like leaf-stalks rolled over one another, and terminating in enormous light green, glossy blades nearly ten feet long by two feet wide, so delicate that the slightest wind will tear them transversely. Each tree (vulgarly called "the tree of paradise") produces fruit but once, and then dies. A single bunch often weighs 60 or 70 pounds; and Humboldt calculated that 33 pounds of wheat and 99 pounds of potatoes require the same space of ground as will produce 4000 pounds of bananas. They really save more labor than steam, giving the greatest amount of food from a given piece of ground with the least labor. They are always found where the palm is; but their original home is the foot of the Himalayas. The banana (by some botanists considered a different species from the plantain) is about four inches long, and cylindrical, and is eaten raw. The plantain is twice as large and prismatic, and uncooked is unhealthy. There is another variety, *platanos de Otaheite*, which resembles the banana in size and quality, but is prismatic.

A belt of jungle and impenetrable brushwood intervenes, and then cacao and coffee plantations, vast in extent, arrest the eye. Passing these, the steamer brings you alongside of broad fields covered with the low, prickly pine-apple plant; the air is fragrant with a rich perfume wafted from a neighboring grove of oranges and lemons; the mango spreads its dense, splendid foliage, and bears a golden fruit, which, though praised by many, tastes to us like a mixture of tow and turpentine; the exotic bread-tree waves its fig-like leaves and pendent fruit; while high over all the beautiful cocoa-palm lifts its crown of glory.* Animal life does not compare with this luxuriant growth. The steamer-bound traveler may see a few monkeys, a group of *gallinazos*, and many brilliant, though songless birds; but the chief representative is the lazy, ugly alligator. Large numbers of these monsters may be seen on the mud-bank basking in the hot sun, or asleep with their mouths wide open.

Eight hours after leaving the Malecon we arrived at Bodegas, a little village of two thousand souls, rejoicing in the synonym of Babahoyo. This has been a place of deposit for the interior from the earliest times. In the rainy season the whole site is flooded, and only the upper stories are habitable. Cock-fighting seems to be the chief amusement. We breakfasted with the governor, a portly gentleman who kept a little dry-goods store. His excellency, without waiting for a formal introduction, and with a cordiality and courtesy almost confined to the Latin nations, received us into his own house, and honored us with a seat at his private table, spread with the choicest viands of his kingdom, serving them himself with a grace to which we can not do justice. Much as we find to condemn in tropical society, we can not forget the kindness of these simple-hearted people. Though we may portray, in the coming pages, many faults and failings according to a New York standard, we wish it to be understood that there is another side to the picture; that there are virtues on the Andes to which the North is well-nigh a stranger. "How many times (says an American resident of ten years) I have ar-

* The mango of Asia is superior in size and flavor to that of America. It is eaten largely in Brazil by negroes and cattle. The cocoa-palm is also of Asiatic origin, and is most abundant in Ceylon. It has a swollen stem when young, but becomes straight and tall when mature. The flowers burst into a long plume of soft, cream-colored blossoms. It is worthy of remembrance that the most beautiful forms of vegetation in the tropics are at the same time most useful to man.

rived at a miserable hut in the heart of the mountains, tired and hungry, after traveling all day without any other companion than the arriero, to receive a warm-hearted welcome, the best, perhaps the only chair or hammock offered to me, the fattest chicken in the yard killed on my account, and more than once they have compelled me by force to take the only good bed, because I must be tired, and should have a good night's rest. A man may travel from one end of the Andes to the other, depending altogether on the good people he meets."

At Bodegas travelers take to mules or horses for the mountains, hiring one set for Guaranda and another at that village for Quito; muleteers seldom allow their animals to pass from one altitude to the other. These *arrieros*, or muleteers, form a very important class in Ecuador. Their little caravans are the only baggage and express trains in the republic; there is not a single regularly established public conveyance in the land. The *arrieros* and their servants (*peons*) are Indians or half-breeds. They wear a straw or felt hat, a poncho striped like an Arab's blanket, and cotton breeches ending at the knees. For food they carry a bag of parched corn, another bag of roasted barley-meal (*mashka*), and a few red peppers. The beasts are thin, decrepit jades, which threaten to give out the first day; yet they must carry you halfway up the Andes. The distance to the capital is nearly two hundred miles. The time required is usually eight or nine days; but officials often travel it in four.

We left Bodegas at noon. It was impossible to start the muleteer a moment earlier, though he had promised to be ready at seven. Patience is a necessary qualification in a South American traveler. In our company were a Jesuit priest, with three attendants, going to Riobamba, and a young Quito merchant, with his mother—the mother of only twenty-five children. This merchant had traveled in the United States, and could not help contrasting the thrift and enterprise of our country with the beggary and lazi-

Equipped for the Andes.

ness of his own, adding, with a show of sincerity, "I am sorry I have Spanish blood in my veins." The suburbs of Bodegas reminded us of the outskirts of Cairo; but the road soon entered a broad savannah instead of a sandy desert. At 3 P.M. we passed through La Mona, a village of twenty-five bamboo huts, all on stilts, for in the rainy season the whole town is under water. Signs of indolence and neglect were every where visible. Idle men, with an uncertain mixture of European, Negro, and Indian blood; sad-looking Quichua women, carrying a naked infant or a red water-jar on the back; black hogs and lean poultry wandering at will into the houses—such is the picture of the motley life in the inland villages. Strange was the contrast between human poverty and natural wealth. We were on the borders of a virgin forest, and the overpowering beauty of the vegetation soon erased all memory of the squalor and lifelessness of La Mona. Our road—a mere path, suddenly entered this seemingly impenetrable forest, where the branches crossed overhead, producing a delightful shade. The curious forms of tropical life were all attractive to one who had recently rambled over the comparatively bleak hills of New England. Delight is a weak term to express the feelings of a naturalist who for the first time wanders in a South American forest. The superb banana, the great charm of equatorial vegetation, tossed out luxuriantly its glossy green leaves, eight feet in length; the slender but graceful bamboo shot heavenward, straight as an arrow; and many species of palm bore aloft their feathery heads, inexpressibly light and elegant. On the branches of the independent trees sat tufts of parasites, many of them orchids, which are here epiphytal; and countless creeping plants, whose long flexible stems entwined snake-like around the trunks, or formed gigantic loops and coils among the limbs. Beneath this world of foliage above, thick beds of mimosæ covered the ground, and a boundless variety of ferns attracted the eye by their beautiful patterns.* It is easy to specify the individual

* Ferns constitute one sixth of the flora of South America; Spruce counted

objects of admiration in these grand scenes, but it is not possible to give an adequate idea of the higher feelings of wonder, astonishment, and devotion which fill and elevate the mind. This road to the Andes is a paradise to the contemplative man. "There is something in a tropical forest (says Bates) akin to the ocean in its effects on the mind. Man feels so completely his insignificance, and the vastness of nature." The German traveler Burmeister observes that "the contemplation of a Brazilian forest produced on him a painful impression, on account of the vegetation displaying a spirit of restless selfishness, eager emulation, and craftiness." He thought the softness, earnestness, and repose of European woodland scenery were far more pleasing, and that these formed one of the causes of the superior moral character of European nations. Live and let live is certainly not the maxim taught in these tropical forests, and it is equally clear that selfishness is not wanting among the people. Here, in view of so much competition among organized beings, is the spot to study Darwin's "Origin of Species." We have thought that the vegetation under the equator was a fitter emblem of the human world than the forests of our temperate zone. There is here no set time for decay and death, but we stand amid the living and the dead; flowers and leaves are falling, while fresh ones are budding into life. Then, too, the numerous parasitic plants, making use of their neighbors as instruments for their own advancement, not inaptly represent a certain human class.

140 species within the space of three square miles. Their limits of growth are 500 and 7000 feet above the sea.

CHAPTER II.

Our Tambo.—Ascending the Andes.—Camino Real.—Magnificent Views.—Guaranda.—Cinchona.—The Summit.—Chimborazo.—Over the Andes.—Chuquipoyo the Wretched.—Ambato.—A Stupid City.—Cotopaxi.—The Vale of Machachi.—Arrival at Quito.

WE reached Savaneta at 5 P.M. This little village of hardly twenty houses becomes the Bodegas, or place of deposit for the mountains six months in the year, for in the *invierno* the roads are flooded, and canoes take the place of mules from Savaneta to Babahoyo. Even in the dry season the dampness of this wilderness is so great that the traveler's sugar and chocolate are melted into one, and envelopes seal themselves. We put up at a *tambo*, or wayside inn, a simple two-storied bamboo hovel, thatched with plantain leaves without and plastered with cobwebs within, yet a palace compared with what sheltered us afterward. The only habitable part was the second story, which was reached by a couple of notched bamboo sticks. A hammock, two earthen kettles, two plates, and a few calabashes constituted the household furniture. The dormitory was well ventilated, for two sides were open. Our lodging, however, cost us nothing; travelers only pay for *yerba* for their beasts. Though this has been the royal road to Quito for three centuries, there is but one *posada* between Guayaquil and Ambato, a distance of one hundred and fifty miles; travelers must carry their own bedding and provisions.

Leaving Savaneta at dawn, and breakfasting at a wayside hut owned by an old negro, we struck about noon the Rio Charriguajaco, dashing down the mountains in hot haste for the Guayas. It was refreshing to look upon living wa-

Ascending the Andes.

ters for the first time since leaving the hills of our native country. Fording this stream we know not how many times, and winding through the dense forest in narrow paths often blockaded by laden donkeys that doggedly disputed the passage, we soon found ourselves slowly creeping up the Andes. We frequently met mountaineers on their way to Bodegas with loads of potatoes, peas, barley, fowls, eggs, etc. They are generally accompanied by their wives or daughters, who ride like the men, but with the knees tucked up higher. On the slippery tracks which traverse this western slope, bulls are often used as beasts of burden, the cloven hoofs enabling them to descend with great security. But mules are better than horses or asses. "That a hybrid (muses Darwin) should possess more reason, memory, obstinacy, social affection, powers of muscular endurance, and length of life than either of its parents, seems to indicate that art has here outdone nature."

Toward evening the ascent became rapid and the road horrible beyond conception, growing narrower and rougher as we advanced. Indeed, our way had long since ceased to be a road. In the dense forest, where sunshine never comes, rocks, mud, and fallen trees in rapid alternation macadamize the path, save where it turns up the bed of a babbling brook. In the comparatively level tracts, the equable step of the beasts has worn the soil into deep transverse ridges, called *camellones*, from their resemblance to the humps on a camel's back. In the precipitous parts the road is only a gully worn by the transit of men and beasts for ages, aided by torrents of water in the rainy season. As we ascend, this changes to a rocky staircase, so strait that one must throw up his legs to save them from being crushed, and so steep that horse and rider run the risk of turning a somersault. It is fearful to meet in a narrow defile, or where the road winds around the edge of a precipice, a drove of reckless donkeys and mules descending the mountain, urged on by the cries and lashes of the muleteers behind. Yet this has been the highway of Ecuadorian commerce for three hundred years. In vain we tried to reach the little village of Camino Real on the crest of the ridge; but the night was advancing rapidly, and crawling up such a road by starlight was not a little dangerous. So we put up at a miserable tambo, Pogyos by name. It was a mud hut of the rudest kind, windowless and unfloored; very clean, if it had been left to nature, but man and beast had rendered it intolerably filthy. Our hostess, a Quichua woman, with tattered garments, and hair disheveled and standing up as if electrified, set a kettle on three stones, and, making a fire under it, prepared for us a calabash of chicken and *locro*. *Locro*, the national dish in the mountains, is in plain English simply potato soup. Sitting on the ground, we partook of this refreshment by the aid of fingers and wooden spoons, enticing our appetites by the reflection that potato soup would support life. The unkempt Indian by our side, grinning in conscious pride over her successful cookery, did not aid us in this matter. Fire is used in Ecuador solely for culinary purposes, not for warmth. It is made at no particular spot on the mud floor, and there is no particular orifice for the exit of the smoke save the chinks in the wall. There is not a chimney in the whole republic. As the spare room in the establishment belonged to the women, we gentlemen slept on the ground outside, or on beds made of round poles. The night was piercingly cold. The wished-for morning came at last, and long before the sun looked over the mountains we were on our march. It was the same terrible road, running zigzag, or "quingo" fashion, up to Camino Real, where it was suddenly converted into a royal highway.

We were now fairly out of the swamps of the lowlands,

and, though under the equator, out of the tropics too. The fresh mountain breeze and the chilly mists announced a change of climate.* Fevers and dysenteries, snakes and musquitoes, the plantain and the palm, we had left behind. Camino Real is a huddle of eight or ten dwellings perched on the summit of a sierra a thousand feet higher than the top of Mount Washington. The views from this standpoint compensate for all past troubles. The wild chaos of mountains on every side, broken by profound ravines, the heaps of ruins piled up during the lapse of geologic ages, the intense azure of the sky, and the kingly condor majestically wheeling around the still higher pinnacles, make up a picture rarely to be seen. Westward, the mountains tumble down into hills and spread out into plains, which, in the far distant horizon, dip into the great Pacific. The setting sun turns the ocean into a sheet of liquid fire. Long columns of purple light shoot up to the zenith, and as the last point of the sun sinks beneath the horizon, the stars rush out in full splendor; for at the equator day gives place to night with only an hour and twenty minutes of twilight. The mountains are Alpine, yet grander than the Alps; not so ragged as the granite peaks of Switzerland, but with rounder heads. The prospect down this occidental slope is diversified by deep valleys, landslides, and flowering trees. Magnificent are the views eastward,

> "Where Andes, giant of the western star,
> Looks from his throne of clouds o'er half the world."

The majestic dome of Chimborazo was entirely uncovered of clouds, and presented a most splendid spectacle. There it stood, its snow-white summit, unsullied by the foot of man, towering up twice as high as Etna. For many years

* The altitude of 7000 feet is the usual limit of the rain-line on the west slope of the Andes. The condensation which produces rain takes place at the equator two or three times higher than in our latitude.

it received the homage of the world as the highest point in America; but now the Aconcagua of Chile claims the palm. Still, what a panorama from the top of Chimborazo, could one reach it, for the eye would command ten thousand square miles!

Our road gently winds down the sierra, giving us at every turn sublime ideas of what nature can do in tossing up the thin crust of our globe. But sublimity is at a discount here—there is too much of it. Suddenly we are looking down into the enchanting valley of Chimbo. This romantic and secluded spot is one of those forgotten corners of the earth which, barricaded against the march of civilization by almost impassable mountains, and inhabited by a thriftless race, has been left far behind in the progress of mankind. Distance lends enchantment to the view. We are reminded of the pastoral vales of New England. Wheat takes the place of the sugar-cane, barley of cacao, potatoes of plantains, and turnips of oranges. Bamboo sheds have given way to neatly whitewashed villages, and the fields are fenced with rows of aloe. But, drawing nearer, we find the habitations are in reality miserable mud hovels, without windows, and tenanted by vermin and ragged poverty. There are herds of cattle and fields of grain; yet we shall not find a quart of milk or a loaf of bread for sale. The descent into the valley is very precipitous, and, after a rain, alarmingly slippery. Mules, drawing their legs together, slide down with startling velocity, and follow the windings with marvelous dexterity.

We arrived at Guaranda at 5 P.M. on the third day after leaving Bodegas. This is a desolate town of two thousand souls, dwelling in low dilapidated huts made of the most common building material in the Andes—*adobe*, or sun-dried blocks of mud mingled with straw.* The

* From *adoub*, an Egyptian word still used by the Copts; carried by the

streets are rudely paved, and pitch to the centre, to form an aqueduct, like the streets of old Sychar. The inhabitants are in happy ignorance of the outside world. They pass the day without a thought of work, standing on the Plaza, or in front of some public office, staring vacantly into space, or gossiping. A cock-fight will soonest rouse them from their lethargy. They seem to have no purpose in life but to keep warm under their ponchos and to eat when they are hungry. Guaranda is a healthy locality, lying in a deep valley on the west bank of the Chimbo, at an elevation, according to our barometer, of 8840 feet, and having a mean temperature slightly less than that of Quito. It is a place of importance, inasmuch as it is the resting-place before ascending or after descending the still loftier ranges, and much more because it is the capital of the region which yields the invaluable *cinchona*, or Peruvian bark.* This tree is indigenous to the Andes, where it is found on the western slope between the altitudes of two thousand and nine thousand feet, the species richest in alkaloids occupying the higher elevations, where the air is moist. Dr. Weddell enumerates twenty-one species, seven of which are now found in Ecuador, but the only one of value is the the *C. succirubra* (the *calisaya* has run out), and this is now nearly extinct, as the trees have been destroyed to obtain the bark. This species is a beautiful tree, having large, broadly oval, deep green, shining leaves, white, fragrant flowers, and red bark, and sometimes, though rarely, attains the height of sixty feet. A tree five feet in circumference

Moors to Spain, thence to America; and from America the word has gone to the Sandwich Islands.

* This celebrated febrifuge was first taken to Europe about the middle of the seventeenth century, and was named after the Countess of Chinchon, who had been cured of intermittent fever at Lima. Afterward, when Cardinal de Lugo spread the knowledge of the remedy through France, and recommended it to Cardinal Mazarin, it received the name of *Jesuits' Bark*. The French chemists, Pelletier and Caverton, discovered quinine in 1820.

will yield fifteen hundred pounds of green bark, or eight hundred of the dry. The roots contain the most alkaloid, though the branches are usually barked for commerce. The true cinchona barks, containing quinine, quinidine, and cinchonine, are distinguished from the false by their splintery-fibrous texture, the latter being pre-eminently corky. The cascarilleros begin to hunt for bark in August. Dr. Taylor, of Riobamba, found one tree which gave $3600 worth of quinine. The general yield is from three to five pounds to a quintal of bark. The tree has been successfully transplanted to the United States, and particularly to India, where there are now over a million of plants. It was introduced into India by Markham in 1861. The bark is said to be stronger than that from Ecuador, yielding twice as much alkaloid, or eleven per cent. The quinine of commerce will doubtless come hereafter from the slopes of the Himalayas instead of the Andes. In 1867 only five thousand pounds of bark were exported from Guayaquil. The Indians use the bark of another tree, the *Maravilla*, which is said to yield a much stronger alkaloid than cinchona. It grows near Pallatanga.

We left Guaranda at 5 A.M. by the light of Venus and Orion, having exchanged our horses for the sure-footed mule. It was a romantic ride. From a neighboring standpoint Church took one of his celebrated views of "The Heart of the Andes." But the road, as aforetime, was a mere furrow, made and kept by the tread of beasts. For a long distance the track runs over the projecting and jagged edges of steeply-inclined strata of slate, which nobody has had the energy to smooth down. At many places on the road side were human skulls, set in niches in the bank, telling tales of suffering in their ghastly silence; while here and there a narrow passage was blocked up by the skeleton or carcass of a beast that had borne its last burden. At nine o'clock we came out on a narrow, grassy ridge called the Ensillada, or Saddleback, where there were three straw huts, with roofs resting on the ground, and there we breakfasted on *locro*. During our stay the Indians killed a pig, and before the creature was fairly dead dry grass was heaped upon it and set on fire. This is the ordinary method of removing the bristles.

Still ascending, we lose sight of the valley of the Chimbo, and find ourselves in a wilderness of crags and treeless mountains clothed with the long, dreary-looking paramo grass called *paja*. But we are face to face with "the monarch of the Andes," and we shall have its company the rest of the day. The snowy dome is flooded with the golden light of heaven; delicate clouds of softest hues float around its breast; while, far below, its feet are wrapped in the baser mists of earth. We attained the summit of the pass at 11 A.M. All travelers strive to reach it early in the morning, for in the afternoon it is swept by violent winds which render it uncomfortable, if not dangerous. This part of the road is called the "Arenal," from the sand and gravel which cover it. It is about a league in length, and crosses the side of Chimborazo at an elevation of more than fourteen thousand feet. Chimborazo stands on the left of the traveler. How tantalizing its summit! It appears so easy of access; and yet many a valiant philosopher, from Humboldt down, has panted for the glory and failed. The depth of the snow and numerous precipices are the chief obstacles; but the excessively rarefied air is another hinderance. Even in crossing the Arenal, a native of the lowlands complains of violent headache, a propensity to vomit, and a difficulty of breathing. The Arenal is often swept by snow-storms; and history has it that some of the Spanish conquerors were here frozen to death. The pale yellow gravel is considered by some geologists as the moraine of a glacier. It is spread out like a broad gravel walk, so that, without exaggeration, one of the best roads in Ecuador has been made by Nature's hand on the crest of the Andes.

It was interesting to trace the different hypsometrical zones by the change of vegetation from Bodegas to this lofty spot. The laws of the decrease of heat are plainly written on the rapid slopes of the Cordilleras. On the hot, steaming lowlands of the coast reign bananas and palms. As these thin out, tree-ferns take their place. Losing these, we found the cinchona bedewed by the cool clouds of Guaranda; and last of all, among the trees, the polylepis. The twisted, gnarled trunk of this tree, as well as its size and silvery foliage, reminded us of the olive, but the bark resembles that of the birch. It reaches the greatest elevation of any tree on the globe. Then followed shrubby fuchsia, calceolaria, eupatoria, and red and purple gentians; around and on the Arenal, a uniform mantle of monocotyledonous plants, with scattered tufts of valeriana, viola, and geranium, all with rigid leaves in the characteristic rosettes of super-alpine vegetation; and on the porphyritic and trachytic sides of Chimborazo, lichens alone. Snow then covers the last effort of vegetable life.* The change in the architecture of the houses indicated, likewise, a change of altitude. The open bamboo huts, shingled with banana leaves, were followed by warmer *adobe* houses, and these, in turn, by the straw hovels of the mountain-top, made entirely of the long, wiry grass of the paramos.

* According to Sir J. Hooker, among the flowers which adorn the slopes of the Himalayas, rhododendrons occupy the most prominent place, and primroses next. There are no orchids, neither red gentians, but blue. Organic life ceases 3000 feet lower than on the Andes; yet it is affirmed that flowering plants occur at the height of 18,460 feet, which is equivalent to the summit of Chimborazo in point of temperature! The polylepis (*P. racemosa*) is one of the *Sanguisorbaceæ;* in Quichua it is *Sachaquinoa.*

Leaving the Arenal, we rapidly descended by the usual style of road—stone stairs. But down we went, as all the goods for Quito, "the grand capital," have done since the Spanish Conquest. The old road from Beirût to Damascus is royal in comparison. The general aspect of the eastern slope is that of a gray, barren waste, overgrown with *paja;* but now and then we crossed deep gulleys, whose sides were lined with mosses and sprinkled with calceolarias, lupines, etc. In our descent we had before us the magnificent Valley of Quito, and beyond it the eastern Cordillera. Below us was Riobamba, and far away to the right the deep gorge of the Pastassa. Nevertheless, this is one of the loneliest rides earth can furnish. Not a tree nor human habitation is in sight. Icy rivulets and mule-trains are the only moving objects on this melancholy heath. Even "Drake's Plantation Bitters," painted on the volcanic cliffs of Chimborazo, would be a relief.

At last we reached our rude accommodations for the night. It was a solitary mud tambo, glorying in the euphonious name of Chuquipoyo. The court-yard was a sea of mud and manure, for this is the halting-place for all the caravans between Quito and the coast. Our room was a horrid hole, dark, dirty, damp, and cold, without a window or a fire. There was one old rickety bedstead, but as that belonged to the lady in our party, the rest betook themselves to benches, table, and floor. We filled our stomachs with an unpalatable potato soup containing cheese and eggs, and laid down—to wait for the morning. Grass is the only fuel here; but this is not the chief reason why it is so difficult to make good tea or cook potatoes at this wretched tambo. Water boils at 190°, or before it is fairly hot: it is well the potatoes are small. The muleteers slept with their beasts outside, though the night was fearfully cold, for Chuquipoyo lies on the frigid side of

Chimborazo, at an elevation of over twelve thousand feet above the sea. As Johnson said to Boswell, "This is a dolorous place."

Gladly we left this cheerless tambo, though a cold, heavy mist was falling as we rode northward, over the seemingly endless paramo of Sanancajas. Here, as throughout the highlands of Ecuador, ditches are used for fences; so that, should the traveler wander from the path, he finds himself stopped by an impassable gulf. In two hours and a half we reached Mocha, a lifeless pueblo under the shadow of Carguairazo. Slowly descending from our high altitude, we gradually entered a more congenial climate—the zone of wheat and barley, till, finally, signs of an eternal spring were all around us—ripening corn on one side, and blossoming peas on the other.

Late in the afternoon the road led us through a sandy, sterile tract, till suddenly we came in sight of Ambato, beautifully situated in a deep ravine, eight thousand five hundred and fifty feet above the Pacific. The city ranks next to Quito in beauty. It is certainly an oasis, the green foliage of its numerous shade-trees and orchards contrasting with the barren hills around. It is two degrees warmer than Quito, and is famous for its fruit and fine climate. It is the Lynn of Ecuador, the chief articles of manufacture being boots and shoes—cheap, but of poor quality. It was destroyed by an earthquake in 1698. The houses are built of sun-dried brick, and whitewashed. The streets, with gutters in the centre, are at right angles, and paved, and adorned with numerous cypress-looking trees, called *sauce*, a species of willow. The Plaza, which contains a useful if not ornamental fountain, presents a lively scene on Sunday, the great market-day. The inn is a fair specimen of a public house in Spanish America. Around the court-yard, where the beasts are fed, are three or four rooms to let. They are ventilated only when opened for travelers. The floor is of brick, but alive with fleas; the walls are plastered, but veiled with cobwebs. The furniture, of primitive make and covered with dust, consists of a chair or two, a table, and a bed of boards covered with a thin straw mat. There is not a hotel in Ecuador where sheets and towels are furnished. The landlords are seldom seen; the entire management of the concern is left to a slovenly Indian boy, who is both cook and hostler. No amount of bribery will secure a meal in less than two hours. Ten years ago there was not a posada in the country; now there is entertainment for man and beast at Guayaquil, Guaranda, Mocha, Ambato, Tacunga, Machachi, and Quito. Riobamba has a billiard saloon, but no inn.

Leaving Ambato, we breakfasted at Cunchebamba, an Indian village of half a dozen straw huts. Thence the road for a long distance winds through vast deposits of volcanic *débris*, the only sign of vegetation being hedges of aloe and cactus. Arid hills and dreary plains, covered with plutonic rocks and pumice dust, tell us we are approaching the most terrible volcano on the earth. Crossing the sources of the Pastassa, we entered Latacunga,* situated on a beautiful plain at the foot of Cotopaxi, seven hundred feet higher than Ambato. Its average temperature is 59°. The population, chiefly Indians, numbers about fifteen thousand. It is the dullest city in Ecuador, without the show of enterprise or business. Not even grass grows in the streets—the usual sign of life in the Spanish towns. It is also one of the filthiest; and though it has been many times thoroughly shaken by earthquakes, and buried under showers of volcanic dust, it is still the paradise of fleas, which have survived every revolution. Ida Pfeiffer says that, after a

* This is shortened in parlance to Tacunga. The full name, according to La Condamine, is *Llacta-cunga*, *llacta* meaning country, and *cunga*, neck.

night's rest in Latacunga, she awoke with her skin marked all over with red spots, as if from an eruptive disease. We can certify that we have been tattoed without the night's rest. The town has a most stupid and forlorn aspect. Half of it is in ruins. It was four times destroyed between 1698 and 1797. In 1756 the Jesuit church was thrown down, though its walls were five feet thick. The houses are of one story, and built of pumice, widely different from the palaces and temples which are said to have stood here in the palmy days of the Incas. Cotopaxi stands threateningly near, and its rumbling thunder is the source of constant alarm.

From Latacunga to Quito there is a very fine carriage road, the result of one man's administration—Señor G. Garcia Moreno. For many miles it passes over an uncultivated plateau, strewn with volcanic fragments. The farms are confined to the slopes of the Cordilleras, and, as every where else, the tumbling haciendas indicate the increasing poverty of the owner. Superstition and indolence go hand in hand. On a great rock rising out of the sandy plain they show a print of the foot of St. Bartholomew, who alighted here on a visit—surely to the volcanoes, as it was long before the red man had found this valley. Abreast of Cotopaxi the road cuts through high hills of fine pumice interstratified with black earth, and rapidly ascends till it reaches Tiupullo, eleven thousand five hundred feet above the sea. This high ridge,* stretching across the valley from Cotopaxi to Iliniza, is a part of the great water-shed of the continent—the waters on the southern slope flowing through the Pastassa and Amazon to the Atlantic, those on the north finding their way to the Pacific by the Rio Esmeraldas. At this bleak place we breakfasted on punch and guinea-pig.

* Sometimes called *Chisinche.*

As soon as we began to descend, the glittering cone of Cotopaxi, and the gloomy plain it has so often devastated, passed out of view, and before us was a green valley exceedingly rich and well cultivated, girt by a wall of mountains, the towers of which were the peaks of Corazon and Rumiñagui. Loathsome lepers by the wayside alone disturbed the pleasing impression. Three hours more of travel brought us to the straggling village of Machachi, standing in the centre of the beautiful plain, at an altitude of nine thousand nine hundred feet. Nature designed this spot for a home of plenty and comfort, but the habitations of the wretched proprietors are windowless adobe hovels, thatched with dried grass, and notorious for their filth.

We must needs make one more ascent, for the ridge of Tambillo hides the goal of our journey. The moment we reached the summit, views unparalleled in the Andes or any where else met our astonished vision whithersoever we looked. Far away to the south stretched the two Cordilleras, till they were lost in the mist which enshrouded Chimborazo and Tunguragua. Turning to the north, we beheld the city of Quito at our feet, and Pichincha and Antisana standing like gallant sentinels on either side of the proud capital. Beautiful were the towering mountains, and almost as delightful now are the memories of that hour. A broad, well-traveled road, gentlemen on horseback clad in rich ponchos, droves of Indians bowed under their heavy burdens, and long lines of laden donkeys hurrying to and fro, indicate our approach to a great city. Winding with the road through green pastures and fields of ripening grain, and crossing the Machángara by an elegant bridge, we enter the city of the Incas.

CHAPTER III.

Early History of Quito.—Its Splendor under the Incas.—Crushed by Spain.—Dying now.—Situation.—Altitude.—Streets.—Buildings.

QUITO is better known than Ecuador. Its primeval history, however, is lost in obscurity. In the language of Prescott, "the mists of fable have settled as darkly round its history as round that of any nation, ancient or modern, in the Old World." Founded, nobody knows when, by the kings of the Quitus, it was conquered about the year 1000 by a more civilized race, the Cara nation, who added to it by conquest and alliance. The fame of the region excited the cupidity of the Incas of Peru, and during the reign of Cacha (1475), Huayna-Capac the Great moved his army from Cuzco, and by the celebrated battle of Hatuntaqui, in which Cacha was killed, Quito was added to the realm of the Incas. Huayna-Capac made Quito his residence, and reigned there thirty-eight years—the most brilliant epoch in the annals of the city. At his death his kingdom was divided, one son, Atahuallpa,* reigning in Quito, and Huascar at Cuzco. Civil war ensued, in which the latter was defeated, and Atahuallpa was chosen Inca of the whole empire, 1532. During this war Pizarro arrived at Tumbez. Every body knows what followed. Strangled at Caxamarca, the body of Atahuallpa was carried to Quito, the city of his birth, in compliance with his dying wish, and buried there with imposing obsequies. Refounded by Benalcazar

* The son of his Quito love. The name was first written *Atauhuallpa*, meaning fortunate in war; after the fratricide, he was called *Atahuallpa*, or game-cock. He was the Boabdil of this occidental Granada. He is called traitor by Peruvian writers, and is not admitted by them into the list of their Incas.

in 1534, Quito was created an imperial city by Charles V. seven years later. It formed part of Peru till 1710; then of Santa Fé till 1722; and again of Peru till its independence. The power of Spain in South America was destroyed at the battle of Ayacucho, Dec. 9, 1824. In 1830 Venezuela separated from Colombia, and Ecuador followed the same year. The first Congress was held in Riobamba; but Quito has ever since been the political focus. The first president was General Flores.

Under the diadem of the Incas, Quito assumed a magnificence which it never saw before and has not displayed since. It was the worthy metropolis of a vast empire stretching from the equator to the desert of Atacama, and walled in by the grandest group of mountains in the world. On this lofty site, which amid the Alps would be buried in an avalanche of snow, but within the tropics enjoys an eternal spring, palaces more beautiful than the Alhambra were erected, glittering with the gold and emerald of the Andes. But all this splendor passed away with the sceptre of Atahuallpa. Where the pavilion of the Inca stood is now a gloomy convent, and a wheat-field takes the place of the Temple of the Sun.

The colonial history of this favored spot is as lifeless as the history of Sahara. Not a single event occurred of which even Spain can be proud; not a monument was raised which reflects any credit upon the mother country. Every thing was prescribed by law, and all law emanated from a tribunal five thousand miles distant. There was no relation of private life with which the government did not interfere: what the colonist should plant and what trade he should follow; where he should buy and where he should sell; how much he should import and export; and where and when he should marry, were regulated by the "Council of the Indies" and the Inquisition. In the words of a native writer, "The great majority of the people knew nothing of sciences, events, or men. Their religion consisted of outward observances, and an imperfect knowledge of the papal bulls; their morality, in asceticism and devotion to their king; their philosophy, in the subtleties of Aristotle; their history, in the history of the mother country; their geography, in the maps of Spanish America and of Spain; their press, in what sufficed to print bill-heads and blank forms; their commerce, in an insignificant coasting trade; their ambition and highest aspirations, in titles of nobility; their amusements, in bull-fights. The arrival of a mail was an event of great moment, and with ringing of bells was received the *cajon de España* which announced the health of the sovereigns. Thus, while Europe was passing through the stormy times of Louis XIV.; while the philosophical writings of the illustrious men of those times found their way into the remotest corners of the globe; while the English colonies of North America conquered their independence; while the Old World was drenched in blood to propagate the ideas which the French Revolution had proclaimed, the Presidency of Quito, walled in by its immense cordilleras and the ocean, and ruled by monkish ignorance and bigotry, knew as little of men and events as we now know of men and events in the moon."*

From an iron despotism which existed for three centuries, Quito passed to a state of unbridled licentiousness. Without any political experience whatever, the people attempted to lay the foundation of a new system of government and society. With head and hearts perverted by monkish superstition and Spanish tyranny, yet set on fire by the French Revolution, what did they know of liberty!

* *Geografia de la Republica del Ecuador, por Dr. Villavicencio.* This work abounds with erroneous and exaggerated statements, but it is nevertheless a valuable contribution to Ecuadorian literature.

Endless civil wars have followed independence. "Political ambition," says a late United States minister, "personal jealousies, impracticable theories, official venality, reckless disregard of individual rights and legal obligations, foolish meddling and empirical legislation, and an absolute want of political morality, form the principal features of their republican history."* To-day they tread on the dust of an ancient race whose government was in every respect a most complete contrast to their own.

At the foot of volcanic Pichincha, only five hours' travel from its smoking crater, lies "the city above the clouds," "the navel of the world," "magnificent Quito." On the north is the plain of Rumibamba, the battle-field where Gonzalo Pizarro routed the first viceroy of Peru, and the scene, two centuries later, of the nobler achievements of La Condamine, which made it the classic ground of astronomy. On the southern edge of the city rises Panecillo, reminding one of Mount Tabor by its symmetrical form, and overlooking the beautiful and well-watered plain of Turubamba. On the east flows the Rio Machángara, and just beyond it stand the Puengasi hills hiding the Chillo valley, while the weary sun goes early to rest behind the towering peaks of Pichincha. So encircled is this sequestered spot, the traveler, approaching by the Guayaquil road, sees only a part of it, and is disappointed; and even when standing on Panecillo, with the entire city spread out before him, he is not wholly satisfied. Buried between treeless, sombre sierras, and isolated from the rest of the world by impassable roads and gigantic cordilleras, Quito appears to us of the commercial nineteenth century as useless as the old feudal towns perched on the mountains of Middle Europe.

* *Four Years among Spanish Americans, by Hon. F. Hassaurek:* a truthful work, to which we refer the reader for details, especially concerning Ecuadorian life and manners.

Not a chimney rises above the red-tiled roofs, telling of homely hearths beneath. No busy hum greets the ear; there are bugles instead of spindles, and jingling church bells in place of rattling carriages. The wandering eye does not look for a railroad or a telegraph, for even the highways, such as they are, seem deserted, and, save the music made for soldiers and saints, all is silent. The very mountains, too, with their snow-mantled heads, and their sides scarred by volcanic eruptions and ruptured by earthquake shocks, have a melancholy look. In the words of a great artist, "They look like a world from which not only the human, but the spiritual presences had perished, and the last of the archangels, building the great Andes for their monuments, had laid themselves down to eternal rest, each in his snow-white shroud."

But let us enter. Passing the ruined chapel "Del Señor del buen pasaje," and crossing by a substantial stone bridge the little Machángara hastening to pay tribute to the Pacific, we leave behind us the dirty, dilapidated suburbs of the capital. Soon we cross another bridge—the Bridge of Buzzards—spanning a deep ravine, and gallop through the Plaza de Santo Domingo. Very different are the sights and sounds from the stir and style of Central Park. The scene has a semi-oriental cast—half Indian, half Egyptian, as if this were the confluence of the Marañon and Nile. Groups of men—not crowds, for there is plenty of elbow-room in Ecuador—in gay ponchos stand chatting in front of little shops, or lean against the wall to enjoy the sunshine; beggars in rags or sackcloth stretch forth their leprous hands for charity; monks in white, and canons in black, walk in the shade of immense hats; shoeless soldiers saunter to and fro; Indians from the mountains in every variety of costume cluster around heaps of vegetables for sale; women in red, brown, and blue frocks are peddling

Quito, from the North.

oranges and alligator pears, or bearing huge burdens on their heads; children, guiltless of clothing, and obtuse donkeys, wander whithersoever they will; and water-carriers, filling their jars at the fountain, start off on a dog-trot.

We cross the Plaza diagonally, pass down the Calle de San Fernando, up the Calle del Algodon, and through the busy Calle del Correo, till we reach the *Casa Frances*, opposite the mansion of the late General Flores. This is our hotel—owned by a Frenchman, but kept by an Indian. We ride under the low archway, bowing with ill grace, like all republicans unaccustomed to royalty, tie our beasts in the court-yard, ascend to our spacious quarters on the second floor, and, ordering coffee, seat ourselves in the beautiful balcony to talk of Quito and Quitonians.

Water-carriers.

Quito, though not the highest city on the globe, is two thousand feet higher than the Hospice of Great St. Bernard on the Alps, which is the only permanent place of abode in Europe above six thousand five hundred feet. When Mr. Hassaurek was appointed United States Minister to Ecuador, he thanked Mr. Lincoln for conferring upon him the *highest* gift in his power. The mean result of our numerous observations with Green's standard barometer places the Grand Plaza nine thousand five hundred and twenty feet above the sea, or fifty feet lower than the calculation of Humboldt. Water boils at 194°.5. Cuzco and Potosi may surpass it in altitude, but there is not a city in the world which can show at once such a genial climate, such magnificent views, and such a checkered history. It is unique likewise in its latitude, lying only fifteen miles below the equator; no other capital comes within three hundred miles of the equinoctial line.

Street in Quito.

Whatever may have been the plan of Quito in the days of Huayna-Capac, it is evident that the Spanish founders were guided more by the spurs of Pichincha than by astronomy. The streets make an angle of forty-five degrees with the meridian, so that not a single public building faces any one of the four cardinal points of the compass. Two deep ravines come down the mountain, and traverse the city from west to east. They are mostly covered by arches, on which the houses rest; but where they are open, they disclose as fit representatives of the place of torment as the Valley of Hinnom. The outline of the city is as irregular as its surface. It incloses one square mile. Twenty streets, all of them straiter than the apostolic one in Damascus, cross one another very nearly at right angles. None of them are too wide, and the walks are painfully narrow; but, thanks to Garcia Moreno, they are well paved. The inequality of the site, and its elevation above the Machángara, render the drainage perfect.* The streets are dimly lighted by tallow candles, every householder being obliged to hang out a lantern at 7 P.M., unless there is moonshine. The candles, however, usually expire about ten o'clock. There are three "squares"—Plaza Mayor, Plaza de San Francisco, and Plaza de Santo Domingo. The first is three hundred feet square, and adorned with trees and flowers; the others are dusty and unpaved, being used as market-places, where Indians and donkeys most do congregate. All the plazas have fountains fed with pure water from Pichincha.

Few buildings can boast of architectural beauty, yet Quito looks palatial to the traveler who has just emerged

* The following quotation, however, is true to the letter, and will apply equally well to Guayaquil and to Madrid—the mother of them both: "There is another want still more embarrassing in Quito than the want of hotels—it is the want of water-closets and privies, which are not considered as necessary fixtures of private residences. Men, women, and children, of all ages and colors, may be seen in the middle of the street, in broad daylight, making privies of the most public thoroughfares; and while thus engaged, they will stare into the faces of passers-by with a shamelessness that beggars description."—*Hassaurek.*

from the dense forest on the coast, "crossing bridgeless rivers, floundering over bottomless roads, and ascending and descending immense mountains." He is astonished to find such elegant edifices and such a proud aristocracy in this lofty lap of the Andes. The Indian habitations which girdle the city have no more architectural pretensions than an Arab dwelling. They are low mud hovels, the scene within and without of dirt and disorder.

As we approach the Grand Plaza, the centre of the city, the buildings increase in size, style, and finish. The ordinary material is adobe, not only because it is cheap, but also because it best resists earthquake shocks. Fear of a *terremoto* has likewise led to a massiveness in construction which is slightly ludicrous when we see the poverty which it protects; the walls are often two or three feet thick. The ground floor is occupied by servants, whose rooms—small enough to be called niches — surround the paved court-yard, which is entered from the street by a broad doorway. Within this court is sometimes a fountain or flower-plot. Around it are arches or pillars supporting a gallery, which is the passage-way to the apartments of the second story. All the rooms are floored with large square bricks. With few exceptions, the only windows are folding glass doors leading to balconies overhanging the pavement. The tiled roofs project far over into the street, and from these project still further uncouth water-spouts, such as used to be seen in Rio Janeiro, but have now been banished to the antiquarian museum. Only three or four private residences rise above two stories. The shops are small affairs—akin to the cupboards of Damascene merchants; half a dozen modern ladies can keep out any more customers. The door serves as entrance, exit, window, and show-case. The finest structures cluster around the plazas. Here are the public buildings, some of them dating back to the times of Philip II. They are modeled after the old Spanish style; there is scarcely a fragment of Gothic architecture. They are built of large brick, or a dark volcanic stone from Pichincha.

The Government House, which serves at once as "White House" and Capitol, is an imposing edifice fronting the

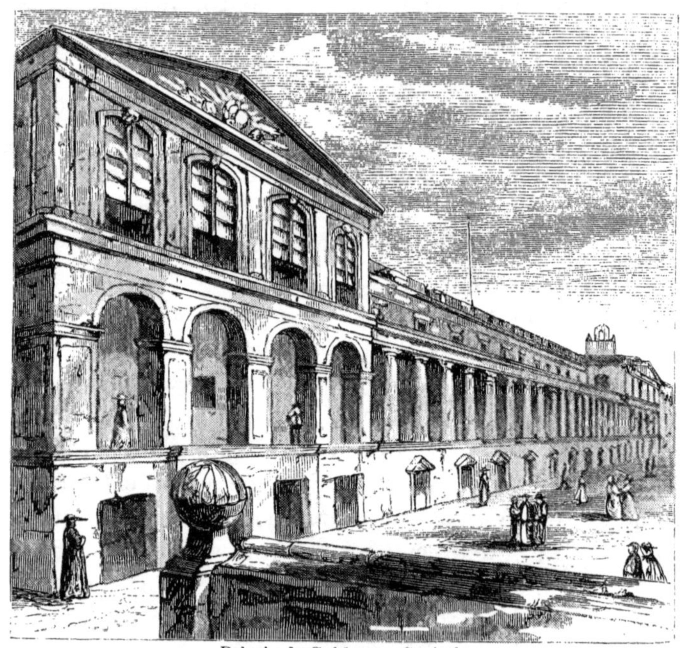

Palacio de Gobierno—Capitol.

Grand Plaza, and adorned with a fine colonnade. On its right rises the cathedral; on the left stands the unpretending palace of the nuncio. The former would be called beautiful were it kept in repair; it has a splendid marble porch, and a terrace with carved stone balustrade. The view above was taken from this terrace. The finest façade is presented by the old Jesuit church, which has an elaborate front of porphyry. The Church of San Francisco, built by the treasures of Atahuallpa, discovered by an Indian named Catuna, is the richest. It is surmounted by two lofty towers, and the interior is a perfect blaze of gilding. The monastery attached to it is one of the largest in the world, but the greater part of it is in ruins, and one of the wings is used as a barrack. Those unsightly, unadorned convents, which cling to every church save the cathedral, have neutralized nearly all architectural effect.

CHAPTER IV.

Population of Quito.—Dress.—Manners.—Character.—Commerce.—Agriculture. —Manufactures.—Arts.—Education.—Amusements.—Quito Ladies.

QUITONIANS claim for their capital eighty thousand inhabitants; but when we consider that one fourth of the city is covered with ecclesiastical buildings, and that the dwelling-houses are but two stories high, we see that there is not room for more than half that number. From thirty thousand to forty thousand is the estimate of the venerable Dr. Jameson, who has resided here for a generation.* Census taking is as difficult as in Constantinople; the people hide themselves to escape taxation. The women far outnumber the men. The white population — a stiff aristocracy of eight thousand souls—is of Spanish descent, but not more than half a dozen can boast of pure blood. The coarse black hair, prominent cheek-bones, and low foreheads, reveal an Indian alliance. This is the governing class; from its ranks come those uneasy politicians who make laws for other people to obey, and hatch revolutions when a rival party is in power. They are blessed with fair mental capacity, quick perception, and uncommon civility; but they lack education and industry, energy and perseverance. Their wealth, which is not great, consists mainly in *haciendas*, yielding grain, cotton, and cattle. The Aguirre family is one of the noblest and wealthiest in the city; their

* Spanish rhetoric is given to exaggeration. "All their geese are swans." A Peruvian assured us that Cuzco contained 200,000 souls. It is, in fact, about as large as Quito; Gibbon says 20,000.

mansion is on the Grand Plaza, facing the Capitol. The pure Indians of Quito number perhaps 10,000; not all those seen in the city are citizens, as many *serranos*, or mountaineers, come in to sell produce. They are the serfs that do the drudgery of the republic; they are the tillers of the soil, and beasts of burden. Many sell themselves for money in advance, and then are ever kept in debt. Excepting a few Zambos (the children of Indians and Negroes), and a very few foreigners and Negroes, the remainder, constituting the bulk of the population, are Cholos—the offspring of whites and Indians. They are not strictly half-breeds, for the Indian element stands out most prominent. Though a mixed race, they are far superior to their progenitors in enterprise and intelligence. They are the soldiers, artisans, and tradesmen who keep up the only signs of life in Quito. "I know not the reason," says Darwin, "but men of such origin seldom have a good expression of countenance." This may be true on the pampas, but Quito, where there is every imaginable mixture of Indian and Spaniard, is wonderfully free from ugly features. It may be owing to the more peaceful and civilized history of this mountain city.

As to dress, black is the color of etiquette, but is not so national as in Madrid. The upper class follow *la mode de Paris*, gentlemen adding the classic cloak of Old Spain. This modern toga fits an Ecuadorian admirably; it favors habits of inactivity, preventing the arms from doing any thing, and covers a multitude of sins, especially pride and poverty. The *poncho*, so peculiar to the West Coast and to the Gauchos of Buenos Ayres, is a piece of cloth of divers colors, with a slit in the centre, through which the head is passed. It is the only variable article of the wardrobe. It is an excellent riding habit, and is made of heavy woolen for mountain travel, and of silk or cotton for warmer altitudes. No gentleman will be seen walking in the streets of Quito under a poncho. Hence citizens are divided into men with ponchos, and gentlemen with cloaks. The pañuelon is the most essential article of female gear. It answers to the mantilla of the mother country, though it is not worn so gracefully as on the banks of the Tagus. Andean ladies are not troubled with the distressing fluctuations in the style of hats; a bonnet in Quito is as much out of place as a turban in New York. When the daughter of our late minister resident appeared in the cathedral with one, the innovation was the subject of severe remark. The Spanish hair is the glory of the sex. It is thick and black (red, being a rarity, is considered a beauty), and is braided in two long tresses. A silk dress, satin shoes, and fancy jewelry complete the visible attire of the belles of Quito.

The ordinary costume of the Indians and Cholos consists of a coarse cotton shirt and drawers, and silk, cotton, or woolen poncho of native manufacture, the females adding a short petticoat, generally of a light blue or "butternut" color, belted around the waist with a figured woolen belt woven by themselves. The head, arms, legs, and feet are often bare, but, by those who can afford it, the head is covered with a straw or white felt broad-brim, and the feet protected by sandals, called *alpargates*, made of the fibres of the aloe. They are very fond of bracelets and necklaces. Infants are usually swathed from neck to feet with a broad strip of cloth, so that they look like live mummies.

Quitonians put us to shame by their unequaled courtesy, cordiality, and good-nature, and are not far below the grave and decorous Castilian in dignified politeness.*

* "I must express my admiration at the natural politeness of almost every Chileno. We met, near Mendoza, a little and very fat negress, riding astride on a mule. She had a *goître* so enormous that it was scarcely possi-

Rudeness, which some Northerners fancy is a proof of equality and independence, we never met with, and duels and street quarrels are almost unknown. We detected none of the touchy sensitiveness of the punctilious Spanish *hidalgos*. Their compliments and promises are without end; and, made in the magnificent and ceremonious language of Spain,* are overwhelming to a stranger. Thus a fair Quitonian sends by her servant the following message to another lady: "Go to the Señorita Fulana de Tal, and tell her that she is my heart and the dear little friend of my soul; tell her that I am dying for not having seen her, and ask her why she does not come to see me; tell her that I have been waiting for her more than a week, and that I send her my best respects and considerations; and ask her how she is, and how her husband is, and how her children are, and whether they are all well in the family; and tell her she is my little love, and ask her whether she will be kind enough to send me that pattern which she promised me the other day."† This highly important message the servant delivers like a parrot, not omitting a single compliment, but rather adding thereto.

A newly-arrived foreigner is covered with promises: houses, horses, servants, yea, every thing is at his disposal. But, alas! the traveler soon finds that this ceremony of words does not extend to deeds. He is never expected to call for the services so pompously proffered. So long as

ble to avoid gazing at her for a moment; but my two companions almost instantly, by way of apology, made the common salute of the country by taking off their hats. Where would one of the lower or higher classes in Europe have shown such feeling politeness to a poor and miserable object of a degraded race?"—*Darwin's Naturalist's Voyage.*

* The Spanish tongue is the manly son of the Latin, as the Italian is the fair daughter; a language in which, as Charles V. said, "God ought alone to be addressed in prayer." It is spoken in America with an Andalusian rather than Toledan pronunciation.

† We are indebted to Mr. Hassaurek for this capital illustration. Every lady, married or unmarried, is addressed *Señorita*, or Miss.

he stays in Quito he will not lose sight of the contrast between big promise and beggarly performance. This outward civility, however, is not hypocritical; it is mere mechanical prattle; the speaker does not expect to be taken at his word. The love of superlatives and the want of good faith may be considered as prominent characteristics. "The readiness with which they break a promise or an agreement (wrote Colonel Hall forty years ago) can only be equaled by the sophistical ingenuity with which they defend themselves for having done so." The Quitonians, who are sensible of their shortcomings, have this standing apology: "Our vices we owe to Spain; our virtues to ourselves."*

Such is the mutual distrust, partnerships are almost unknown; we do not remember a single commercial firm, save a few made up of brothers, or father and son. With this moral debility is joined the procrastinating spirit of the oriental. *Mañana* (to-morrow), like the *Boukra* of the Arabs, is the universal winding up of promises. And very often, if one promises a thing to-morrow, he means the day after that. It is impossible to start a man into prompt compliance; he will not commence a piece of work when you wish nor when he promises. No amount of cajolery, bribery, or threats will induce a Quitonian to do any thing or be any where in season. If there were a railroad in Ecuador, every body would be too late for the first train. There are only one or two watch-tinkers in the great city, and, as may be inferred, very few watches are in running order. As a consequence, the people have very little idea of time. But this is not the sole reason for their

* "When speaking of these countries, the manner in which they have been brought up by their unnatural parent, Spain, should always be borne in mind. On the whole, perhaps, more credit is due for what has been done, than blame for that which may be deficient."—*Darwin's Journal of Researches*, p. 158.

dilatoriness; they are indifferent. Nobody seems to want to make money (though all are in sad need of it); nobody is in a hurry; nobody is busy save the tailors, who manifest a commendable diligence. Contempt for labor, a Spanish inheritance, and lack of energy, are traits which stand out in *alto relievo*.

One can form his own judgment of the spiritless people from the single statement which we have from Dr. Jameson, that during the last forty years not ten Quitonians have visited the grand crater of Pichincha, though it is possible to ride horseback to its very edge. Plenty of gentlemen by profession walk the streets and cathedral terrace, proud as a Roman senator under his toga, yet not ashamed to beg a cup of coffee at the door of a more fortunate fellow-citizen. Society is in a constant struggle between ostentation and want.

Nature has done more for Ecuador than for Ecuadorians. She laid out this beautiful valley for an Elysian field; "de Quito al Cielo" (from Quito to Heaven) is not an empty adage; and it is painful to look upon tottering walls and impassable roads, upon neglected fields and an idle population—poor as poverty in the lap of boundless natural wealth. The only really live man in the republic is the president, Señor G. Garcia Moreno, a man of wide views and great energy, standing in these respects head and shoulders above his fellow-citizens. Quito and Quito Valley owe nearly all their improvements to this one man.

It is easy to say what would be the industry of a people who spend much of their time repeating traditions of treasures buried by the Incas, and stories of gold deposits in the mountains. Of commerce there is scarcely enough to deserve the name. Quito is an ecclesiastical city, and is nearly supported by Guayaquil. Without capital, without energy, without business habits, Quitonians never embark in grand commercial schemes and industrial enterprises. There is not a highway for commerce in any direction, only a natural path (called by the innocent natives a road), which rises to the altitude of fourteen thousand feet, by which the beasts of burden pick their way over the Cordillera. And this is open only six months in the year. Should a box designed for Quito arrive at Guayaquil at the beginning of the rainy season, it must tarry half a year till *Nature* makes the road passable.

The unstable condition of the country does not encourage great undertakings; all business is periodically paralyzed by revolution. Merchants generally buy their goods in Lima, to which city and Guayaquil the fabrics of England and France are brought by foreigners in foreign ships. The shops of Quito, as we have remarked, are very small, without windows, and with only one wooden door. The door is double, and is fastened by a ponderous padlock. They are open from 7 A.M. till sunset, excepting between nine and ten and between three and four, when the stores are closed for breakfast and dinner; the merchants never trusting their clerks, even when they have any, which is not usually the case. They have no fixed price, but get what they can. The majority know nothing of wholesale, and refuse to sell by the quantity, fearing a cheat. An Indian woman will sell you a real's worth of oranges any number of times, but she would object to parting with a dollar's worth—her arithmetic can not comprehend it.

In the *portals* or arcades of the Aguirre mansion and the nuncio's palace are the stalls of the haberdashers. Articles are not wrapped in paper; customers must get them home the best way they can. Ladies of the higher class seldom go out shopping, but send for samples. It is considered disgraceful to either sex to be seen carrying any thing through the streets of Quito. The common people buy only for immediate wants—a dose of medicine, or a handful of potatoes at a time. Nearly all liquids, kerosene as well as wine, are sold by the bottle.

There was no bank in Quito in 1867, but an attempt has just been made to establish one. The paper money of Guayaquil is often at nine per cent. discount in the capital. The currency is silver adulterated with one third of copper. The smallest coin, the calé, is worth about two and a half cents. Above that are medios (five cents), reals (ten cents), two, four, and eight reals. Eight reals make a soft dollar ($0 80); ten reals, a hard dollar ($1 00). There is no copper coin—oranges and loaves of bread are sometimes used to make change; and nearly all the gold in circulation are New Granada *condors* and Peruvian *onzas*. Many of the silver pieces have large holes cut in the centre, so that they resemble rings. Government set the example (and the people followed) on the plea that it would prevent the exportation of coin. The plan has succeeded, for it does not pass out of the valley.

Nearly the only sign of progress is the late introduction of the grape and silk-worm; and these give so much promise of success that the threadbare nobility have already begun to count their coming fortunes. Husbandry is more pastoral than agricultural. Thousands of cattle are raised on the paramos, but almost wholly for beef. "A dislike to milk (observes Humboldt), or at least the absence of its use before the arrival of Europeans, was, generally speaking, a feature common to all nations of the New Continent, as likewise to the inhabitants of China." Some cheese (mostly unpressed curd) and a little butter are made, but in the patriarchal style. Only one American churn is in operation; the people insist upon first boiling the milk and then stirring with a spoon. Custom is omnipotent here, and its effects hereditary. Milking is done at any hour of the day, or whenever milk is wanted. The operation is a formidable one to these bull-fighting people. Stopping at a hacienda near Peliléo for a drink of milk, we were eye-witness of a comical sight. A mild-looking cow was driven up to the door; the woman, evidently the bravest member of the household, seized the beast by the horns; a boy tied the hind legs with a long rope, and held on to one end of it at a respectful distance; while the father, with outstretched arms, milked into a calabash.

Agricultural machinery is not in use. The first threshing-machine Quito ever saw was made in 1867 by some California miners, but it remained unsold when we last saw it. The spade is not known; the nearest approach to it is a crowbar flattened at one end. Hoes are clumsy and awkward. Yankee plows are bought more as curiosities than for use. Many a crooked stick is seen scratching the land, as in Egypt, which the cattle drag by their horns. Sometimes a number of sharp-nosed hogs are tied together and let into a field, and driven from place to place till the whole is rooted up. Corn is planted by making holes in the ground with a stick, and dropping in the seed. The soil and climate of Ecuador, so infinitely varied, offer a home to almost every useful plant. The productions of either India could be naturalized on the lowlands, while the highlands would welcome the grains and fruits of Europe. But intertropical people do not subdue nature like the civilized men of the North; they only pick up a livelihood.

Spanish Americans, like Castilians on the banks of the Tagus, have a singular antipathy to trees. When Garcia Moreno made a park of the dusty Plaza Mayor, he was ridiculed, even threatened. To plant a fruit or shade tree (a thing of foresight and forethought for others) in a land where people live for self, and from hand to mouth, is considered downright folly in theory and practice. A large portion of the valley, left treeless, is becoming less favorable for cultivation.

Yet, as it is, the traveler is charmed by the emerald verdure of the coast, and by "evergreen Quito"—more beautiful than the hanging gardens of Babylon—suspended far above the ordinary elevation of the clouds. In the San Francisco market we find wheat, barley, maize, beans, peas, potatoes, cabbages, beets, salads, pine-apples, chirimoyas, guavas, oranges, lemons, pears, quinces, peaches, apricots, melons, and strawberries—the last all the year round. Most of these are exotics; the early discoverers found not a cereal grain of the Old World, not an orange or apple, no sugar-cane or strawberries.*

There is but little manufacturing industry in the interior of Ecuador, but much more than on the coast. The chief articles manufactured are straw hats, shoes, baskets, carpets, embroidery, tape, thread, ponchos, coarse woolen and cotton cloth, saddles, sandals, soap, sugar, cigars, aguardiente, powder, sweetmeats, carved images, paints, and pottery. Wines, crockery, glassware, cutlery, silks, and fine cloth are imported. There are three cotton mills in the country; one in Chillo (established by Señors Aguirre in 1842), another in Otovalo (built by Señor Parija in 1859), and a third in Cuenca (1861). The machinery of the Chillo factory came from England; that of Otovalo from Patterson, N. J. The latter was utterly destroyed in the late great earthquake, and the proprietor killed. The cotton is inferior to that of New Orleans; it is not "fat," as mechanics say; the seeds yield only two per cent. of oil. But it is whiter than American cotton, though coarse, and can

* The vase is still shown in which Father Rixi brought the first wheat from Europe. It was sown in what is now the San Francisco Plaza, the chief market-place of the city.

be used only for very ordinary fabrics. The average length is five eighths of an inch. One pod will produce on an average three pennyweights. The mills of Chillo and Otovalo consume 425,000 pounds annually. The first sugar-mill was erected by the Aguirres in 1840 at Nanegal.

Quito is more than a century behind this age of steam and lightning. To form an adequate idea of the mechanic and fine arts in that "city of the kings," we must transport ourselves to the Saxon period of European civilization. Both the material and the construction of the houses would craze Sir Christopher Wren. With fine quarries close at hand, they must build with mud mixed with stones, or plastered on wattles, like the Druses of Mount Lebanon. Living on the equatorial line and on the meridian so accurately measured by the highest mathematics of France and Spain, Quitonians must needs leave out every right angle or straight line in the walls, and every square beam and rafter. Except on the grand road from Quito to Ambato, commenced by President Moreno, there is not a wheelbarrow to be seen; paving-stones, lime, brick, and dirt, are

Indian Dwellings.

usually carried on human backs. Saint Crispin never had the fortitude to do penance in the shoes of Quito, and the huge nails which enter into the hoofs of the quadrupedants remind one of the Cyclops. There are not six carts in Quito. If you wish to move, you must coax a dozen Indians, who care little for your money or your threats. Horse-hire, peonage, and most mechanical work must be paid for in advance. Carriages—antique vehicles, of which there are two or three in the city—are drawn by mules. The first was introduced by Señor Aguirre so late as 1859, and he was fined by the police for the privilege of riding in it. Quitonians are not a traveling people, and they are painfully ignorant of their own country. The most enterprising merchant ignores every thing but Quito and the road to Guayaquil.

We can not praise the musical talent of Spanish Americans; their intonation is too nasal, while in their jumpings and chirpings they take after the grasshopper. A resident Englishman, who has traveled in many countries, and sings the songs of nearly every nation, told us he could not remember one of Ecuador. Pianos they have brought over the mountains at great expense; but they are more at home with the guitar. The embroidery and lace, wood carving and portrait painting of Quito, are commendable; but the grandeur of the Andes, like the beauty of the Alps, was never sketched by a native.

Ecuador boasts of one University and eleven colleges; yet the people are not educated. Literature, science, philosophy, law, medicine, are only names. Nearly all young gentlemen are doctors of something; but their education is strangely dwarfed, defective, and distorted; and their knowledge, such as they have, is without power, as it is without practice. The University of Quito has two hundred and eighty-five students, of whom thirty-five are pursuing law, and eighteen medicine. There are eleven professors. They receive no fees from the students, but an annual salary of $300. The library contains eleven thousand volumes, nearly all old Latin, Spanish, and French works. The cabinet is a bushel of stones cast into one corner of a lumber-room, covered with dust, and crying out in vain for a man in the University to name them. The College of Tacunga has forty-five students; a fine chemical and philosophical apparatus, but no one to handle it; and a set of rocks from Europe, but only a handful from Ecuador. The College of Riobamba has four professors, and one hundred and twenty students. In the common schools, the pupils study in concert aloud, Arab fashion. There are four papers in the republic; two in Guayaquil, one in Cuenca, and one in Quito. *El Nacional*, of the capital, is an official organ, not a newspaper; it contains fourteen duodecimo pages, and is published occasionally by the Minister of the Interior. Like the *Gazeta* of Madrid, it is one of the greatest satires ever deliberately published by any people on itself. There is likewise but one paper in Cuzco, *El Triumfo del Pueblo*.

The amusements of Quito are few, and not very amusing. Indo-Castilian blood runs too slowly for merry-making. There are no operas or concerts, no theatres or lectures, no museums or menageries. For dramas they have revolutions; for menageries, bull-baitings. A bull-bait is not a bull-fight. There is no coliseum or amphitheatre; no *matador* gives the scientific death-wound. Unlike their fraternity in the ring of Seville, where they are doomed to die, the animals are only doomed to be pothered; they are "scotched, not killed." They are teased and tormented by yelling crowds, barking dogs, brass bands, red ponchos, tail-pulling, fire-crackers, wooden lances, and such like. The Plaza de Toros is the Plaza de San Francisco. This sport is reserved for the most notable days in the calendar: Christmas, New Year's, Inauguration-day, and Independence-day—the 10th of August.

Cock-fights come next in popularity, and are *bona fide* fights. Often the roosters are so heroic that both leave their blood in the arena, and never crow again. Little knives are fastened to the natural spurs, with which the fowls cut each other up frightfully. The interesting scene takes place on Sundays and Thursdays, near the Church of Santa Catalina, and is regulated by a municipal tribunal. The admission fee of five cents, and the tax of two per cent. on bets, yield the city a monthly revenue of $100.

Other pastimes are carnivals and masquerades. Carnival is observed by pelting one another with eggs and sprinkling with water. Whoever invented this prelude to Lent should be canonized. Masquerades occur during the holidays, when all classes, in disguise or fancy dress, get up a little fun at each other's expense. The monotony of social life is more frequently disturbed by fashionable funerals than by these amusements; and, as the principal families are inter-related, the rules of condolence keep the best part of society in mourning, and the best pianos and guitars silent for at least six months in the year.

A word about the ladies of Quito. We concur in the remark of our minister, Mr. Hassaurek, that "their natural dignity, gracefulness, and politeness, their entire self-possession, their elegant but unaffected bearing, and the choiceness of their language, would enable them to make a creditable appearance in any foreign drawing-room." Their natural talents are of a high order; but we must add that the señoras are uneducated, and are incapable of either great vices or great virtues. Their minds, like the soil of their native country, are fertile, but uncultivated; and their hearts, like the climate, are of a mean temperature. Prayer-books and French novels (imported, as wanted, for there is not a book-store in the city) are the alpha and the omega of their literature; Paris is considered the centre of civilization. They are comely, but not beautiful; Venus has given her girdle of fascination to few. Sensible of this, they paint.

Holinski gives his impressions by contrasting the fair Quitonians with the fairer Guayaquilians: "Les yeux vifs et ardent, le pied fine et mignon, les teintes chaudes et dorées" distinguish the latter. In the ladies of the high capital there is nothing of this: "Les yeux ne lancent pas de flammes, le pied est sans gentillesse, l'epiderme ne refléte pas les rayons du soliel." The ladies on the coast take all possible pains to preserve the small size of the foot; a large foot is held in horror. Von Tschudi once overheard some ladies extolling in high terms the beauty of an English lady; all their praise, however, ending with this exclamation, "But what a foot! Good heavens! it is like a great boat!" Gibbon is continually talking of beautiful señoras and señoritas on the Andes; surely the lieutenant is in sport.*

The ladies of Quito give few entertainments for lack of ready money. They spend much of their time in needlework and gossip, sitting like Turkish sultanas on divans or the floor. They do not rise at your entrance or departure. They converse in a very loud, unmusical voice. We never detected bashfulness in the street or parlor. They go to mass every morning, and make visits of etiquette on Sundays. They take more interest in political than in domestic affairs. Dust and cobwebs are unmistakable signs of indifference. Brooms are rarities; such as exist are besoms

* "The young ladies of Cuzco are, in general, very beautiful, with regular features, fresh olive complexions, bright eyes full of intelligence, furnished with long lashes, and masses of black hair plaited in two tails."—*Markham.*

made of split stick. Since our return, we have sent to a Quitonian gentleman, by request, a package of broom-corn seed, which, we trust, will be the forerunner of a harvest of brooms and cleaner floors in the high city. Not only the lords, but also the ladies, are inveterate smokers. Little mats are used for spittoons.

Washerwomen.

Perhaps Quitonian ladies have too many Indian servants about them to keep tidy; seven or eight is the average number for a family. These are married, and occupy the ground floor, which swarms with nude children. They are cheap, thievish, lazy, and filthy. No class, pure-blood or half-breed, is given to ablution, though there are two public baths in the city. Washerwomen repair to the Machángara, where they beat the dirty linen of Quito over the smooth rocks. We remember but two or three table-cloths which entirely covered the table, and only one which was clean. There are but two daily meals; one does not feel the need of more; they are partaken at nine and three, or an hour earlier than in Guayaquil. When two unwashed, uncombed cooks bend over a charcoal fire, which is fanned by a third unkempt individual, and all three blinded by smoke (for there is no chimney), so that it is not their fault if capillaries and something worse are mingled with the stew, with onions to right of them, onions to left of them, onions in front of them, and *achote* already in the pot in spite of your repeated anathemas and expostulations —*achote*, the same red coloring matter which the wild Indians use for painting their bodies and dyeing their cloth—and with several aboriginal wee ones romping about the kitchen, keen must be the appetite that will take hold with alacrity as the dishes are brought on by the most slovenly waiter imagination can body forth.* The aim of Ecuadorian cookery is to eradicate all natural flavor; you wouldn't know you were eating chicken except by the bones. Even coffee and chocolate somehow lose their fine Guayaquilian aroma in this high altitude, and the very pies are stuffed with onions. But the beef, minus the garlic, is most excellent, and the *dulce* unapproachable.

* We noticed at Riobamba a custom which formerly prevailed also at Quito. As soon as the guests have finished, and before they have risen, the Indian waiter kneels devoutly down beside the table, and offers thanks in a very solemn, touching tone.

CHAPTER V.

Ecuador.—Extent.—Government.—Religion.—A Protestant Cemetery in Quito.—Climate.—Regularity of Tropical Nature.—Diseases on the Highlands.

THE republic of Ecuador looks like a wedge driven into the continent between the Marañon and the Putumayo. It has 1200 miles of Pacific coast, and an area of about two hundred thousand square miles, including the Galápagos Islands. Peru, however, claims the oriental half, drawing her northern boundary from Tumbez through Canélos and Archidona; and she is entitled to much of it, for she has established a regular line of steamers on the Marañon, while the Quito government has not developed an acre east of the Andes. Ecuador is hung between and upon two cordilleras, which naturally divide it into three parts: the western slope, the Quitonian valley, and the Napo region. The fluvial system is mainly made up of the Napo, Pastassa, and Santiago, tributaries of the Marañon, and the Mira, Esmeraldas, and Guayaquil, flowing westward into the Pacific. There are no lakes proper, but the natives enumerate fifty-five lagunes, the largest of which, Capucuy, is not over five miles long.

Villavicencio tells the world that his country has a total population of 1,308,042. But Dr. Jameson believes it does not exceed 700,000. The government is based on the Constitution of 1845, amended in 1853. The president is chosen by a plurality of votes, holds his office for four years, and has a salary of $12,000. He can not be re-elected,* nor can he exercise his functions more than twenty-five miles from the capital. But the law is often set aside by those in power. During the administration of Garcia Moreno, prominent citizens were shot or banished by his order, without trial by jury. To every plea for mercy the stern president replied, that as he could not save the country according to the Constitution, he should govern it according to his own views of public necessity.

Congress assembles on the 15th of September every other year, and consists of eighteen senators and thirty representatives. The chambers are small, and literally barren of ornament. The members sit in two rows facing each other, have no desks, and give an affirmative vote by a silent bow. Politics has less to do with principles and parties than with personalities. Often it has a financial aspect; and the natural expression on learning of a revolution is, "Somebody is out of money." The party in feathers its nest as fast as possible; there is scarcely a public officer who is not open to bribery. The party out plots a premature resurrection to power by the ladders of corruption, slander, and revolution.† Revolution has so rapidly followed revolution that history has ceased to count them; and it may be said of them what Milton wrote of the wars of the Saxon Heptarchy, "that they are not more worthy of being recorded than the skirmishes of crows and kites." The Grand Plaza, the heart where all the great arteries of circulation meet and diverge, is where the high tides of Quito affairs ebb and flow.

* Since this was written, Garcia Moreno has been re-elected to the presidency and the Constitution revised.

† Government has more than once paid its debts by repudiation. Congress lately voted to pay only seven per cent. of the claims against the state which are dated prior to a certain year. Among the sufferers is the venerable Dr. Jameson, a distinguished foreigner, who has served this country faithfully for forty years, first as assayer, then as director of the mint, and always by his scientific position.

The Supreme Court consists of five judges. Criminal cases only are tried by jury; and an attorney is not permitted to question a witness. There are no penitentiaries: second-class criminals are made to work for the public, while political offenders are banished to the banks of the Napo, or to Peru. Here, as in no other country, every man's house is his castle. No search-warrants are allowed; a policeman can be shot dead on the threshold. The person and property of a foreigner are safe; and no native in the employ of a foreigner can be taken by the government for military purposes. All, except pure Indians, can vote if over twenty-one, and can read and write. A man's signature is without value if it lacks his flourish—a custom of Spanish origin.

The permanent army consists of two regiments. The soldiers are mostly half-breeds, and are generally followed by their wives. They are poorly paid; and as they are impressed into the service, they carry out the principle by helping themselves wherever they go. In marching, they have a quicker step than Northern soldiers. The chief expenditure of the republic is for the army, about $500,000; the next is for the payment of the national debt, $360,000. The foreign debt is £1,470,374. Ecuadorians claim a revenue of a million and a half, of which one half is from the custom-house, and one fiftieth from the post-office.

One would suppose that the people who breathe this high atmosphere, and enjoy this delightful climate, and are surrounded by all that is truly grand and beautiful, would have some corresponding virtues. But we find that Nature, here as every where, has mingled base and noble elements. The lofty mountains, bearing in their steadfastness the seal of their appointed symbol—"God's righteousness is like the great mountains"—look down upon one of the lowest and most corrupt forms of republican government on earth;*

* Asking the late Chilian minister for his view of the rank of the different

their snowy summits preach sermons on purity to Quitonian society, but in vain; and the great thoughts of God written all over the Andes are unable to lift this proud capital out

Ecclesiastics.

of the mud and mire of mediæval ignorance and superstition. The established religion is the narrowest and most intolerant form of Romanism. Mountains usually have a

South American states, he gave us this order: Chile, Brazil, Argentine Republic, Venezuela, New Granada, Central America, Mexico, Peru, Bolivia, Ecuador.

more elevating, religious influence than monotonous plains. The Olympian mythology of the Greek was far superior to the beastly worship on the banks of the Nile. And yet at the very feet of glorious Chimborazo and Pichincha we see a nation bowing down to little images of the rudest sculpture with a devotion that reminds us of the Middle Ages.

The belief is called *La Fe*, or the only true one. The oath of a Protestant is not regarded in courts of law. One fourth of Quito is covered by convents and churches. The convents alone number fifty-seven, and are very extensive, sometimes spreading over eight or nine acres. The Church revenue amounts to $800,000. There are more than four hundred priests, monks, and nuns in the capital. The native ecclesiastics are notorious for their ignorance and immorality. "It is a very common thing (says Dr. Terry) for a curate to have a whole flock of orphan nephews and nieces, the children of an imaginary brother." There is one ex-president who has the reputation of tying a spur on the leg of a game-cock better even than a curate. The imported Jesuits are the most intelligent and influential clergy. They control the universities and colleges, and education generally. Active and intellectual, though not learned, they have infused new life into the fat indolence of the Spanish system. Men of this world rather than the next, they have adopted a purely mundane policy, abjured the gloomy cowl, raised gorgeous temples, and say, "He that cometh unto us shall in no wise lose heaven." Their chief merit, however, is the discovery of the turkey and quinine.

The Protestant in Quito is annoyed by an everlasting jingling of bells and blowing of bugles night and day. The latter are blown every third hour. The bells are struck by boys, not rung. A bishop, returning from a visit to London, was asked if there were any good bells in England. "Very fine," he replied, "but there is not a man there who knows how to ring them." Foreign machinery is sprinkled with holy water to neutralize the inherent heresy; but a miller, for example, will charge more for his flour after the baptism.

Lotteries are countenanced by both Church and State, and in turn help support them; we saw one "grand scheme" carried out on the cathedral terrace and defended by bayonets.

At half past nine in the morning all Quito is on its knees, as the great bell of the cathedral announces the elevation of the Host. The effect is astonishing. Riders stop their horses; foot-passengers drop down on the pavement; the cook lets go her dishes and the writer his pen; the merchant lays aside his measure and the artisan his tool; the half-uttered oath (*carájo!*) dies on the lips of the Cholo; the arm of the cruel Zambo, unmercifully beating his donkey, is paralyzed; and the smart repartee of the lively donna is cut short. The solemn stillness lasts for a minute, when the bell tolls again, and all rise to work or play. Holidays are frequent. Processions led by a crucifix or wooden image are attractive sights in this dull city, simply because little else is going on. Occasionally a girl richly dressed to represent the humble mother of God is drawn about in a carriage, and once a year the figures of the Virgin belonging to different churches are borne with much pomp to the Plaza, where they bow to each other like automatons.

"This is a bad country to live in, and a worse one to die in," said Dr. Jameson. But times have changed, even in fossil Quito. Through the efforts of our late minister, Hon. W. T. Coggeshall, the bigoted government has at last consented to inclose a quarter of an acre outside the city for the subterranean burial of heretics. The cemetery is on the edge of the beautiful plain of Iñaquito, and on the right of the road leading to Guápolo. "What a shame," said a Quitonian lady of position, "that there should be a place to throw Protestant dogs!"

On St. Nathaniel's day died Colonel Phineas Staunton, Vice-Chancellor of Ingham University, New York. An artist by profession, and one of very high order, Colonel Staunton joined our expedition to sketch the glories of the Andes, but he fell a victim to the scourge of the lowlands one week after his arrival in Quito. We buried him at noonday* in the new cemetery, "wherein was never man laid," and by the act consecrated the ground. Peace to his ashes; honor to his memory. That 8th of September, 1867, was a new day in the annals of Quito. On that day the imperial city beheld, for the first time in three centuries, the decent burial of a Protestant in a Protestant cemetery. Somewhere, mingled with the ashes of Pichincha, is the dust of Atahuallpa, who was buried in his beloved Quito at his own request after his murder in Caxamarca. But dearer to us is that solitary grave; the earth is yet fresh that covers the remains of one of nature's noblemen.

Turn we now to a more delightful topic than the politics and religion of Quito. The climate is perfect. Fair Italy, with her classic prestige and ready access, will long be the land of promise to travelers expatriated in search of health. But if ever the ancients had reached this Andean valley, they would have located here the Elysian Fields, or the seat

* This was a new thing under the sun. Quitonians "bury at dead of night, with lanterns dimly burning." The dirges sung as the procession winds through the streets are extremely plaintive, and are the most touching specimens of Ecuadorian music. The corpse, especially of a child, is often carried in a chair in a sitting posture. The wealthy class wall up their dead in niches on the side of Pichincha, hypothetically till the resurrection, but really for two years, when, unless an additional payment is made, the bones are thrown into a common pit and the coffin burnt. To prevent this, a few who can afford it embalm the deceased. One of the most distinguished citizens of Quito keeps his mummified father at his hacienda, and annually dresses him up in a new suit of clothes!

of "the blessed, the happy, and long-lived" of Anacreon.* No torrid heat enervates the inhabitant of this favored spot; no icy breezes send him shivering to the fire. Nobody is sun-struck; nobody's buds are nipped by the frost. Stoves and chimneys, starvation and epidemics, are unknown. It is never either spring, summer, or autumn, but each day is a combination of all three. The mean annual temperature of Quito is 58°.8, the same as Madrid, or as the month of May in Paris. The average range in twenty-four hours is about 10°. The coldest hour is 6 A.M.; the warmest between 2 and 3 P.M. The extremes in a year are 45° and 70°; those of Moscow are −38° and 89°. It is a prevalent opinion that since the great earthquake of 1797 the temperature has been lower. "It was suddenly reduced (says the *Encycl. Metropolitana*) from 66° or 68° to 40° or 45°"—a manifest error. The natives say that since the *terremote* of 1859 the seasons have not commenced so regularly, nor are they so well defined; there are more rainy days in summer than before. It remains to be seen whether the late convulsion has affected the climate.

The mean diurnal variation of the barometer is only .084. So regular is the oscillation, as likewise the variations of the magnetic needle, that the hour may be known within fifteen minutes by the barometer or compass. Such is the clock-like order of Nature under the equator, that even the rains, the most irregular of all meteorological phenomena in temperate zones, tell approximately the hour of the day. The winds, too, have an orderly march—the ebb and flow of an aerial ocean. No wonder watch-tinkers can

* In the mountain-town of Caxamarca, farther south, there were living in 1792 seven persons aged 114, 117, 121, 131, 132, 141, and 147. One of them, when he died, left behind him eight hundred living descendants to mourn his loss. We confess, however, that we saw very few old persons in Quito. Foreigners outlive the natives, because they live a more regular and temperate life.

not live where all the forces in nature keep time. Nobody talks about the weather; conversation begins with benedictions or compliments.

The greatest variations of the thermometer occur in autumn, and the greatest quantity of rain falls in April.* While on the western side of the Andes, south of the equator, the dry season extends from June to January, on the eastern side of the Cordillera the seasons are reversed, the rain lasting from March to November. The climate of the central valley is modified by this opposition of seasons on either side of it, as also by the proximity of snowy peaks. Nine such peaks stand around Quito within a circle of thirty miles. The prevailing winds in summer are from the northeast; in the winter the southwest predominate.

There are only three small drug-stores in the great city of Quito. The serpent is used as the badge of apothecary art. Physicians have no offices, nor do they, as a general rule, call upon their patients. When an invalid is not able to go to the doctor, he is expected to die. Yellow fever, cholera, and consumption are unknown; while intermittent fevers, dysentery, and liver complaints, so prevalent on the coast, are uncommon. The ordinary diseases are catarrhal affections and typhoid fever. Cases of inflammation of the lungs are rare; more coughing may be heard during a Sunday service in a New England meeting-house than in six months in Quito. The diseases to which the monks of St. Bernard are liable are pulmonary, and the greater number become asthmatic. Asthma is also common in Quito, while phthisis increases as we descend to the sea. Individuals

* The mean annual fall of rain at Quito is 70 inches.
" " " " Charleston is 45.9 inches.
" " " " New York is 42.23 "
" " " " Albany is 40.93 "
" " " " Montreal is 36 "
" " " " Madrid is 10. "

are often seen with a handkerchief about the jaws, or bits of plaster on the temples; these are afflicted with headache or toothache, resulting from a gratified passion for sweetmeats, common to all ages and classes. Digestive disorders are somewhat frequent (contrary to the theory in Europe), but they spring from improper food and sedentary habits. The *cuisine* of the country does not tempt the stomach to repletion, and the climate is decidedly peptic. So the typhoid fever of Quito is due to filth, poor diet, and want of ventilation. Corpulency, especially among the men, is astonishingly rare.

According to Dr. Lombard, mountain districts favor the development of diseases of the heart; and contagious diseases are not arrested by the atmosphere of lofty regions. This is true in Quito. But while nervous diseases are rare in the inhabited highlands of Europe, in Quito they are common. Sleep is said to be more tranquil and refreshing, and the circulation more regular at high altitudes; but our experience does not sustain this. Goître is quite common among the mountains. It is a sign of constitutional weakness, for the children of goîtred parents are usually deaf and dumb, and the succeeding generation idiots. Boussingault thinks it is owing to the lack of atmospheric air in the water; but why is it nearly confined to the women? In the southern provinces about Cuenca, cutaneous affections are quite frequent. In the highlands generally, scrofulous diseases are more common than in the plains. There are three hospitals for lepers; one at Cuenca with two hundred patients, one at Quito with one hundred and twelve patients, and one at Ambato. Near Riobamba is a community of dwarfs.

D'Orbigny made a *post-mortem* examination of some Indians from the highest regions, and found the lungs of extraordinary dimensions, the cells larger and more in number. Hence the unnatural proportion of the trunk, which is plainly out of harmony with the extremities. The expanded chest of the mountaineers is evidently the result of larger inspirations to secure the requisite amount of oxygen, which is much less in a given space at Quito than on the coast. This is an instance, observes Prichard, of long-continued habit, and the result of external agencies modifying the structure of the body, and with it the state of the most important functions of life. We tried the experiment of burning a candle one hour at Guayaquil, and another part of the same candle for the same period at Quito. Temperature at Guayaquil, 80°; at Quito, 62°. The loss at Guayaquil was 140 grains; at Quito, 114, or 26 grains less at the elevation of 9500 feet. Acoustics will also illustrate the thinness of the air. M. Godin found (1745) that a nine-pounder could not be heard at the distance of 121,537 feet; and that an eight-pounder at Paris, at the distance of 102,664 feet, was louder than a nine-pounder at Quito at the distance of 67,240 feet.

According to Dr. Archibald Smith, the power of muscular exertion in a native of the coast is greatly increased by living at the height of 10,000 feet. But it is also asserted by observing travelers that dogs and bulls lose their combativeness at 12,000 feet, and that hence there can never be a good bull-fight or dog-fight on the Sierras. This is literally true: the dogs seem to partake of the tameness of their masters. Cats do not flourish at all in high altitudes; and probably the lion, transplanted from the low jungle to the table-lands, would lose much of his ferocity. Still, cock-fights seem to prosper; and the battle of Pichincha was fought on an elevation of nearly 11,000 feet. Bolivar and the Spaniards, also, fought like tigers on the high plain of Junin.*

* Gibbon states that the temperature of the blood of a young bull in Cuzco was 100°; air, 57°. At the base of the Andes a similar experiment resulted

The sickness felt by some travelers at great elevations —violent headache and disposition to vomit—is called *veta*; and the difficulty of breathing from the rarity of the air is termed *puna*. Gerard complained of severe headache and depression of spirits at the height of 15,000 feet on the Himalayas; Dr. Barry, in ascending Mont Blanc (15,700 feet), speaks of great thirst, great dryness and constriction of skin, loss of appetite, difficult breathing, tendency to syncope, and utter indifference. Baron Müller, in his ascent of Orizava (17,800 feet), found great difficulty in breathing, and experienced the sensation of a red-hot iron searing his lungs, and agonizing pains in the chest, followed by fainting-fits and torrents of blood from his mouth; Humboldt, in scaling Chimborazo, suffered from nausea akin to sea-sickness, and a flow of blood from the nose and lips; while Herndon, on the slope of Puy-puy (15,700 feet), said he thought his heart would break from his breast with its violent agitation. Though ascending the Andes to the height of 16,000 feet, and running up the last few rods, we experienced nothing of this except a temporary difficulty in respiration. We were exhilarated rather than depressed. The experience of Darwin on the Portillo ridge (14,000 feet) was only "a slight tightness across the head and chest." "There was some imagination even in this (he adds); for, upon finding fossil shells on the highest ridge, I entirely forgot the puna in my delight." De Saussure says truly: "The strength is repaired as speedily as it has been exhausted. Merely a cessation of movement for three or four minutes, without even seating one's self, seems to restore the strength so perfectly that, on resuming progress, one feels able to climb at a single stretch to the very peak of the mountain."

in 101° for the blood, air 78°. The lieutenant jocosely adds: "The Spaniards have forced the hog so high up on the Andes that he suffers every time he raises his bristles, and dies out of place."—Puna has been attributed to the presence of arsenical vapor.

CHAPTER VI.

Astronomic Virtues of Quito.—Flora and Fauna of the Valley of Quito.—Primeval Inhabitants of the Andes.—Quichua Indians.

QUITO, with a position unparalleled for astronomical purposes, has no observatory. The largest telescope in the city is about five feet long, but the astute professor of natural philosophy in the Jesuit College who has charge of it had not the most distant idea that an eclipse of the sun would occur on the 29th of August, and an eclipse of the moon fifteen days later. In ancient days this "holy city" had within it the Pillar of the Sun, which cast no shadow at noon, and a temple was built for the god of light. The title of the sovereign Inca was the Child of the Sun; but there was very little knowledge of astronomy, for, being the national religion, it was beyond the reach of scientific speculation.

The atmosphere of Quito is of transparent clearness. Humboldt saw the poncho of a horseman with the naked eye at a horizontal distance of ninety thousand feet. The sky is of a dark indigo color; the azure is less blended with white because of the extreme dryness of the air. The stars stand out with uncommon brilliancy, and the dark openings between them the great German compared to "tubes through which we look into the remotest depths of space." It is true at Quito, as Humboldt noticed at Cumana, that the stars do not twinkle when they are more than fifteen degrees high; "the soft planetary light" of the stars overhead is not mere rhetoric.

Living under the equatorial line, Quitonians enjoy the

peculiar privilege of beholding the stars of both hemispheres, the guiding stars of Ursa Major as well as the Magellanic Clouds and Southern Cross, not omitting that black spot near the latter, "the unappropriated region in the skies reserved by Manager Bingham for deposed American presidents."

The zodiacal light here appears in all its glory. This strange phenomenon has long puzzled philosophers, and they are still divided. It is generally considered to be produced by a continuous zone of infinitesimal asteroids. The majority place this zone beyond the orbit of the earth, and concentric with the sun. But Rev. George Jones, of Philadelphia, who has spent several years in observing this light, including eight months in Quito, considers it geocentric, and possibly situated between the earth and its satellite. At New York only a short pyramidal light, and this only at certain seasons, is to be seen; but here, an arch twenty degrees wide, and of considerable intensity, shoots up to the zenith, and Mr. Jones affirms that a complete arch is visible at midnight when the ecliptic is at right angles to the spectator's horizon. We have not been so fortunate as to see it pass the zenith; and Professor Barnard contends that it never does pass. We may remark that the main part of the zodiacal light shifts to the south side of the celestial equator as we cross the line. To us the most magnificent sight in the tropical heavens is the "Milky Way," especially near Sobieski's Shield, where it is very luminous. We observed that this starry tract divided at α Centauri, as Herschel says, and not at β, as many maps and globes have it. The brightest stars in the southern hemisphere follow the direction of a great circle passing through ε Orionis and α Crucis.

Another thing which arrests the attention of the traveler is the comparatively well-defined boundary-line between day and night. The twilight at Quito lasts only an hour and a half; on the coast it is still shorter. Nor is there any "harvest moon," the satellite rising with nearly equal intervals of forty-eight minutes.

From the stars we step down to the floral kingdom on the Andes, using as our ladder of descent the following sentence from Humboldt, at the age of seventy-five: "If I might be allowed to abandon myself to the recollections of my own distant travels, I would instance among the most striking scenes of nature the calm sublimity of a tropical night, when the stars—not sparkling, as in our Northern skies—shed their soft and planetary light over the gently heaving ocean; or I would recall the deep valleys of the Cordilleras, where the tall and slender palms pierce the leafy veil around them, and wave on high their feathery and arrow-like branches."

Father Velasco praises Ecuador as "the noblest portion of the New World." Nature has doubtless gifted it with capabilities unsurpassed by those of any other country. Situated on the equinoctial line, and embracing within its limits some of the highest as well as lowest dry land on the globe, it presents every grade of climate, from the perpetual summer on the coast and in the Orient to the everlasting winter of the Andean summits, while the high plateau between the Cordilleras enjoys an eternal spring. The vegetable productions are consequently most varied and prolific. Tropical, temperate, and arctic fruits and flowers are here found in profusion, or could be successfully cultivated. As the Ecuadorian sees all the constellations of the firmament, so Nature surrounds him with representatives of every family of plants. There are places where the eye may embrace an entire zone, for it may look up to a barley-field and potato-patch, and down to the sugar-cane and pineapple.

Confining our attention to the Quito Valley, we remark that the whole region from Pichincha to Chimborazo is as treeless as Palestine. The densest forest is near Baños. The most common tree is the "Aliso" (*Betula acuminata*). Walnut is the best timber. There are no pines or oaks.* The slopes of the mountains, between twelve and fifteen thousand feet, are clothed with a shrub peculiar to the high altitudes of the Andes, called *Chuquiragua*. This is a very valuable shrub; the twigs are used for fuel, and the yellow buds as a febrifuge. The castor-oil-tree grows naturally by the road side, sometimes to the height of twelve feet.

A very useful as well as the most ordinary plant in the valley is the American aloe, or "Century Plant."† It is the largest of all herbs. Not naturally social, it imparts a melancholy character to the landscape as it rises solitary out of the arid plain. Most of the roads are fenced with aloe hedges. While the majority of tropical trees have naked stems with a crown of leaves on the top, the aloe reverses this, and looks like a great chandelier as its tall peduncle, bearing greenish-yellow flowers, rises out of a graceful cluster of long, thick, fleshy leaves. When cultivated, the aloe flowers in much less time than a century; but, exhausted by the efflorescence, it soon dies. Nearly every part serves some purpose; the broad leaves are used by the poorer class instead of paper in writing, or for thatching their huts; sirup flows out of the leaves when tapped, and, as

* On the Himalayas are oaks, birches, pines, chestnuts, maples, junipers, and willows; no tree-ferns, bamboos, or palms.

† The *Agava Americana* of botanists, *cabulla* of Ecuadorians, *maguey* of Venezuelans, and *metl* of Mexicans. It is an interesting fact, brought to light by the researches of Carl Neuman, that the Chinese in the fifth century passed over to America by way of the Aleutian Islands, and penetrated as far south as Mexico, which they called the land of *fusung*, that being the celestial name of the aloe. Terzozomoc, the high-priest of the ancient Mexicans, gave aloe leaves, inscribed with sacred characters, to persons who had to journey among the volcanoes, to protect them from injury.

they contain much alkali, a soap (which lathers with salt water as well as fresh) is also manufactured from them; the flowers make excellent pickles; the flower-stalk is used in building; the pith of the stem is used by barbers for sharpening razors; the fibres of the leaves and the roots are woven into sandals and sacks; and the sharp spines are used as needles. A species of yucca, resembling the aloe, but with more slender leaves and of a lighter green, yields the hemp of Ecuador.

The "crack fruit" of Quito, and, in fact, of South America, is the chirimoya.* Its taste is a happy mixture of sweetness and acidity. Hanke calls it "a masterwork of Nature," and Markham pronounces it "a spiritualized strawberry." It grows on a tree about fifteen feet high, having a broad, flat top, and very fragrant flowers. The ripe fruit, often attaining in Peru the weight of sixteen pounds, has a thick green skin, and a snow-white pulp containing about seventy black seeds. Other pomological productions are alligator pears, guavas, guayavas, granadillas, cherries (a small black variety), peaches (very poor), pears (equally bad), plums, quinces, lemons, oranges (not native), blackberries, and strawberries (large, but flavorless).† The cultivation of the grape has just commenced. Of vegetables there are onions (in cookery, "the first, and last, and midst, and without end"), beets, carrots, asparagus, lettuce, cabbages, turnips, tomatoes (indigenous, but inferior to ours), potatoes (also indigenous, but much smaller than their descendants),‡

* Bollaert derives the name from *chiri* (cold) and *muhu* (seed).

† Dr. Jameson has found the following species of *Rubus* in the valley of Quito: *macrocarpus*, *stipularis*, *glabratus*, *compactus*, *glaucus*, *rosæflorus*, *loxensis*, *urticæfolius*, *floribundus*, nd *nubigenus*. The common strawberry, *Fragaria vesca*, grows in the valley, as also the *Chilensis*.

‡ Lieutenant Gilliss praises the potatoes of Peru, but we saw no specimens in Ecuador worthy of note. The "Irish potato" is a native of the Andes. It was unknown to the early Mexicans. It grows as far south on this continent as lat. 50°. The Spaniards carried the potato to Europe from Quito early in

red peppers, peas (always picked ripe, while green ones are imported from France!), beans, melons, squashes, and mushrooms. The last are eaten to a limited extent; Terra del Fuego, says Darwin, is the only country in the world where a cryptogamic plant affords a staple article of food.

The most important grains are barley, red wheat, and corn, with short ears, and elongated kernels of divers colors. Near the coast three crops of corn a year are obtained; at Quito it is of slower growth, but fuller. The sugar-cane is grown sparingly in the valley, but chiefly on the Pacific coast. Its home is Polynesia. Quito consumes about one hundred and fifty barrels of flour daily. The best sells for four dollars a quintal. The common fodder for cattle is alfalfa, an imported lucerne. There is no clover except a wild, worthless, three-leaved species (*Trifolium amabile*). Nearly all in the above list are cultivated for home consumption only, and many valuable fruits and vegetables which would grow well are unknown to Quitonians. As Bates says of the Brazilians, the incorrigible nonchalance and laziness of the people alone prevent them from surrounding themselves with all the luxuries of a temperate as well as tropical country.

It would be an endless task to speak of the flowers. It must suffice to state that a *Synopsis Plantarum Æquatoriensium*, the life-work of the venerable Professor Jameson, of the University of Quito, has just been published by the tardy government. Botanists will find in these two small volumes many new species unknown to American

the sixteenth century. From Spain it traveled to Italy, Belgium, and Germany. Sir Walter Raleigh imported some from Virginia in 1586, and planted them on his estate near Cork, Ireland. It is raised in Asiatic countries only where Europeans have settled, and for their consumption. It is successfully grown in Australia and New Zealand, where there is no native esculent farinaceous root. Von Tschudi says there is no word in Quichua for potato. It is called *papa* by the Napos.

science, and others more correctly described by one who has dwelt forty years among the Andes. The last zone of vegetation nearest the snow-line consists chiefly of yellow-flowering *Compositæ.* In fact, this family includes one fourth of the plants in the immediate vicinity of Quito. The next most numerous family is the *Labiatæ*, and then follow *Leguminosæ* and *Gentians.* Although the *Rosaceæ* is represented, there is not one species of the genus *Rosa* not even in the whole southern hemisphere. The magnificent *Befaria*, found in the lower part of the valley, is called "the Rose of the Andes." Fuchsias may be considered characteristic of South America, since they are so numerous; only one or two kinds occur in any other part of the world. Flowers are found in Quito all the year round, but the most favorable months are December and May. Yellow is the predominating color. The higher the altitude, the brighter the hues of any given species. Thus the *Gentiana sedifolia* is a small, light blue flower in the lowlands, but on the Assuay it has bright blue petals three times as large and sensitive. This accords with Herschel's statement: "The chemical rays of the spectrum are powerfully absorbed in passing through the atmosphere, and the effect of their greater abundance aloft is shown in the superior brilliancy of color in the flowers of Alpine regions."

America is plainly the continent of vegetation; and wherever the vegetable element predominates, the animal is subordinated. We must not look, therefore, for a large amount or variety of animal life in the Ecuadorian forests. Time was when colossal megatheroids, mastodons, and glyptodons browsed on the foliage of the Andes and the Amazon; but now the terrestrial mammals of this tropical region are few and diminutive. They are likewise old-fashioned, inferior in type as well as bulk to those of the eastern hemisphere, for America was a finished continent long before Europe. "It seems most probable (says Darwin) that the North American elephants, mastodons, horse, and hollow-horned ruminants migrated, on land since submerged near Behring's Straits, from Siberia into North America, and thence, on land since submerged in the West Indies, into South America, where for a time they mingled with the forms characteristic of that southern continent, and have since become extinct.* The rise of the Mexican table-land split up the New World into two well-defined zoological provinces. A few species, as the puma, peccari, and opossum, have crossed the barrier; but South America is characterized by possessing a family of monkeys, the llama, tapir, many peculiar rodents, and several genera of edentates.

The tapir, the largest native quadruped, is sometimes found on the mountains, but never descends into the Quito Valley. A link between the elephant and hog, its true home is in the lowlands. The tapir and peccari (also found on the Andean slopes) are the only indigenous pachyderms in South America, while the llama† and deer (both abounding in the valley) are the only native ruminants; there is not one native hollow-horned ruminant on the continent. The llama is the only native domesticated animal; indeed, South America never furnished any other animal serviceable to man: the horse, ox, hog, and sheep (two, four, and

* *Journal of Researches*, p. 132.

† The llama, or "mountain-camel," is a beautiful animal, with long, slender neck and fine legs, a graceful carriage, pointed ears, soft, restless eyes, and quivering lips. It has a gentle disposition; but when angry it will spit, and when hurt will shed tears. We have seen specimens entirely white; but it is generally dark brown, with patches of white. It requires very little food and drink. Since the introduction of horses, asses, and mules, the rearing of llamas has decreased. They are more common in Peru. The llama, guánaco, alpaca, and vicuña were "the four sheep of the Incas:" the first clothing the common people, the second the nobles, the third the royal governors, the fourth the Incas. The price of sheep's wool in Quito was formerly four cents a pound; it is now twelve.

six-horned), are importations. Of these animals, which rendered such important aid in the early civilization of Asia and Europe, the genera even were unknown in South America four centuries ago; and to-day pure Indians with difficulty acquire a taste for beef, mutton, and pork. The llama is still used as a beast of burden; but it seldom carries a quintal more than twelve miles a day. The black bear of the Andes ascends as high as Mont Blanc, and is rarely found below three thousand five hundred feet. The puma, or maneless American lion, has an immense range, both in latitude and altitude, being found from Oregon to the Straits of Magellan, and nearly up to the limit of eternal snow. It is as cowardly as the jaguar of the lowlands is ferocious. It is a very silent animal, uttering no cry even when wounded. Its flesh, which is very white, and remarkably like veal in taste, is eaten in Patagonia. Squirrels, hares, bats (a small species), opossums, and a large guinea-pig (*Cuye del Monte*), are found in the neighborhood of Quito.

As only about sixty species of birds are common to North and South America, the traveler from the United States recognizes few ornithic forms in the Valley of Quito. Save the hummers, beautiful plumage is rare, as well as fine songsters. But the moment we descend the Eastern Cordillera into the interior of the continent, we find the feathered race in robes of richest colors. The exact cause of this brilliant coloring in the tropics is still a problem. It can not be owing to greater light and heat, for the birds of the Galápagos Islands, directly under the equator, are dull.*

* Mr. Gould, however, holds that the difference of coloration is due to the different degrees of exposure to the sun's rays, the brilliantly-colored species being inhabitants of the edges of the forest. Birds from Ucayali, in the centre of the continent, are far more splendid than those which represent them in countries nearer the sea, owing to the clearer atmosphere inland. But it is a fact, at least exceptional to this theory, that the "Cock of the Rock"

The males, both of birds and butterflies, are the most gaudily dressed. In the highlands the most prominent birds are the condor and the humming-bird. These two extremes in size are found side by side on the summit of Pichincha. The condor appears in its glory among the mountains of Quito. Its ordinary haunt is at the height of Etna. No other living creature can remove at pleasure to so great a distance from the earth; and it seems to fly and respire as easily under the low barometric pressure of thirteen inches as at the sea-shore. It can dart in an instant from the dome of Chimborazo to the sultry coast of the Pacific. It has not the kingly port of the eagle, and is a cowardly robber: a true vulture, it prefers the relish of putrescence and the flavor of death. It makes no nest, but lays two eggs on a jutting ledge of some precipice, and fiercely defends them. The usual spread of wings is nine feet. It does not live in pairs like the eagle, but feeds in flocks like its loathsome relative, the buzzard. It is said to live forty days without food in captivity, but at liberty it is very voracious. The usual method of capture is to kill an old mare (better than horse, the natives say), and allow the bird to gorge himself, when he becomes so sluggish as to be easily lassoed. It is such a heavy sleeper, it is possible to take it from its roost. The evidences in favor of and against its acute smelling powers are singularly balanced. For reasons unknown, the condor does not range north of Darien, though it extends its empire through clouds and storms to the Straits of Magellan. In the Inca language it was called *cuntur*, and was anciently an object of worship. The condor, gallinazo, turkey-buzzard, and caracara eagle (says Darwin) "in their habits well supply the place

(Rupicola) on the western side of the Andes (Esmeraldas) is of a richer, deeper color than the same species on the eastern slope (Napo). In keeping with Mr. Gould's theory is the statement by Mr. Bates, that the most gaudy butterflies (the males) flutter in the sunshine.

of our carrion crows, magpies, and ravens—a tribe of birds widely distributed over the rest of the world, but entirely absent in South America." The condor appears on the gold coins of New Granada and Chile. Of *Trochilidæ* there are hosts. The valley swarms with these "winged jewels" of varied hues, from the emerald green of Pichincha to the white of Chimborazo. They build long, purse-like nests by weaving together fine vegetable fibres and lichens, and thickly lining them with silk-cotton. In this delicate cradle, suspended from a branch, the female lays two eggs, which are hatched in about twelve days. The eggs are invariably white, with one exception, those of a species on the Upper Amazon, which are spotted. The young have much shorter bills than their parents. The humming-bird is exclusively American: the nearest form in the Old World is the nectarinia, or sunbird. Other birds most commonly seen in the valley are: *Cyanocitta turcosa* (Jay), *Pœcilothraupis atricrissa*, *Pheuticus chrysogaster*, *Chlorospingus superciliaris*, *Buthraupis chloronata*, *Tanagra Darwini*, *Dubusia selysia*, *Buarremon latinuchus*, and *B. assimilis*. The only geese in the valley are a few imported from Europe by Señor Aguirre, of Chillo, and these refuse to propagate.

Reptiles are so rare in the highlands the class can hardly be said to be represented. During a residence of nearly three months in the Quito Valley we saw but one snake.* Nevertheless, we find the following sentence in such a respectable book as Bohn's Hand-book of Modern Geography: "The inhabitants of Quito are dreadfully tormented by reptiles, which it is scarcely possible to keep out of the beds!" Of frogs there are not enough to get up a choir,

* *Herpetodryas carinatus*, which we observed also at Guayaquil and on the Marañon. We procured two or three species from the natives, and several new forms from Pallatanga, on the west slope.

and of fishes there is but one solitary species, about a finger long.* The entomology of Quito is also brief, much to the satisfaction of travelers from the insectiferous coast. Musquitoes and bedbugs do not seem to enjoy life at such an altitude, and jiggers† and flies are rare. Fleas, however, have the hardihood to exist and bite in the summer months, and if you attend an Indian fair you will be likely to feel something "gently o'er you creeping." But fleas and lice are the only blood-thirsty animals, so that the great Valley of Quito is an almost painless paradise. Of beetles and butterflies there are a few species, the latter belonging for the most part to the familiar North American genera *Pyrameis* and *Colias*. At Vinces, on the coast, we found the pretty brown butterfly, *Anartia Jatrophæ*, which ranges from Texas to Brazil. A light-colored coleopter is eaten roasted by the inhabitants. The cochineal is raised in the southern part of the valley, particularly in Guananda, at the foot of Tunguragua, where the small, flat-leaved cactus (*Opuntia tuna*), on which the insect feeds, is extensively cultivated. The male is winged, but the female is stationary, fixed to the cactus, and is of a dark brown color. It takes seventy thousand to make a pound, which is sold in the valley for from sixty cents to $3. The best cochineal comes from Teneriffe, where it was introduced from Honduras in 1835. The silk-worm is destined to work a revolution in the finances of Ecuador; Quito silk gained a gold medal at the Paris Exhibition. No bees are hived in the republic; the people seem to be content

* *Antelopus lævis* at Ambato, and *A. longirostris*, a new species from Antisana Hacienda, were the only frogs noticed. The little fish is *Pimelodes cyclopum* (preñadilla of the Spaniards, *imba* of the Indians), the same that was thrown out in the eruptions of Imbabura and Caraguairazo.

† The jigger, chigoe, or nigua (*Pulex penetrans* of science) is a microscopic flea that buries itself under the skin and lays a myriad eggs; the result is a painful tumor. Jiggers are almost confined to sandy places.

with treacle. The Italian species would undoubtedly thrive here. The bees of Ecuador, like all the bees of the New World, are inferior to those of the Old World. Their cells are not perfectly hexagonal, and their stings are undeveloped. They are seldom seen feeding on flowers. Mollusca in the Quito Valley are not great in number or variety. They belong principally to the genera *Bulimus*, *Cyclostoma*, and *Helix*. The first is as characteristic of the Southern Continent as *Helix* of the North and *Achatina* of Africa.

From the animal creation we mount by a short step to the imbruted Indian. When and by whom the Andes were first peopled is a period of darkness that lies beyond the domain of history. But geology and archæology are combining to prove that Sorata and Chimborazo have looked down upon a civilization far more ancient than that of the Incas, and perhaps coeval with the flint-flakes of Cornwall, and the shell-mounds of Denmark. On the shores of Lake Titicaca are extensive ruins which antedate the advent of Manco Capac, and may be as venerable as the lake-dwellings of Geneva. Wilson has traced six terraces in going up from the sea through the province of Esmeraldas toward Quito; and underneath the living forest, which is older than the Spanish invasion, many gold, copper, and stone vestiges of a lost population were found. In all cases these relics are situated below high-tide mark, in a bed of marine sediment, from which he infers that this part of the country formerly stood higher above the sea. If this be true, vast must be the antiquity of these remains, for the upheaval and subsidence of the coast is exceedingly slow.

Philology can aid us little in determining the relations of the primeval Quitonians, for their language is nearly obscured by changes introduced by the Caras, and afterward by the Incas, who decreed that the Quichua, the language of elegance and fashion three hundred years ago, should be the universal tongue throughout the empire.* Quichua is to-day spoken from the equator to 28° S. (except by the Aymará people), or by nearly a million and a half. We found it used, corrupted, however, by Spanish, at the mouth of the Napo. There are five dialects, of which the purest is spoken in Cuzco, and the most impure in Quito. The Indians of the northern valley are descendants of the ancient Quitus, modified by Cara and Peruvian blood. They have changed little since the invasion of Pizarro. They remember their glory under the Incas, and when they steal any thing from a white man, they say they are not guilty of theft, as they are only taking what originally belonged to them. Some see in their sacred care of Incarial relics a lingering hope to regain their political life. We noticed that the pure mountaineers, without a trace of Spanish adulteration, wore a black poncho underneath, and we were informed by one well acquainted with their customs that this was in mourning for the Inca. We attended an Indian masquerade dance at Machachi, which seemed to have an historical meaning. It was performed in full view of that romantic mountain which bears the name of the last captain of Atahuallpa. There is a tradition that after the death of his chief, Rumiñagui burned the capital, and, retiring with his followers to this cordillera, threw himself from the precipice. The masquerade at Machachi was evidently intended to keep alive the mem-

* "History (says Prescott) furnishes few examples of more absolute authority than such a revolution in the language of an empire at the bidding of a master." The pronunciation of Quichua requires a harsh, explosive utterance. Gibbon says the sound of it to him resembled Welsh or Irish; that of Aymará, English. The letters *b*, *d*, *f*, *g*, and *o* are wanting in the ancient tongue of Quito; *p* was afterward changed to *b*, *t* to *d*, *v* to *f*, *c* to *g*, and *u* to *o*; thus Chim-pu-razu is now Chimborazo. A few words bear a striking analogy to corresponding Sanscrit words; as *Ynti*, the Inca for sun, and *Indra*, the Hindoo god of the heavens.

ory of the Incas. Three Indians, fantastically adorned with embroidered garments, plumed head-dresses, and gold and silver tinsel, representing Atahuallpa and his generals, danced to music of the rudest kind, one individual pounding on a drum and blowing on a pipe at the same time. Before them went three clowns, or *diablos*, with masks, fit caricatures of the Spaniards. Like all other Indian feasts, this ended in getting gradually and completely drunk. During the ceremony a troop of horsemen, gayly dressed, and headed by one in regimentals with a cocked hat, galloped twice around the Plaza, throwing oranges at the people; after which there was a bull-bait.

The features of the Quichuans have a peculiar cast, which resembles, in D'Orbigny's opinion, no other American but the Mexican, and some ethnologists trace a striking similarity to the natives of Van Diemen's Land. They have an oblong head (longitudinally), somewhat compressed at the sides and occiput; short and very slightly arched forehead; prominent, long, aquiline nose, with large nostrils; large mouth, but not thick lips; beautiful enduring teeth; short chin, but not receding; cheek-bones not prominent; eyes horizontal, and never large; eyebrows long; thick, straight, coarse, yet soft jet black hair; little or no beard; a long, broad, deep, highly-arched chest; small hands and feet; short stature, seldom reaching five feet, and the women still shorter; a mulatto color (olive-brown says D'Orbigny, bronze says Humboldt), and a sad, serious expression. Their broad chests and square shoulders remind one of the gorilla; but we find that, unlike the anthropoid ape, they have very weak arms; their strength lies in their backs and legs. They have shrewdness and penetration, but lack independence and force. We never heard one sing.* Always submissive to your face, taking

* Their favorite musical instrument is the *rondador*, a number of reeds of

off his hat as he passes, and muttering, "Blessed be the altar of God," he is nevertheless very slow to perform. Soured by long ill treatment, he will hardly do any thing unless he is compelled. And he will do nothing well unless he is treated as a slave. Treat him kindly, and you make him a thief; whip him, and he will rise up to thank you and be your humble servant. A certain curate could never trust his Indian to carry important letters until he had given him twenty-five lashes. Servile and timid, superstitious and indolent, the Quichuans have not half the spirit of our North American Indians. It has passed into a proverb that "the Indian lives without shame, eats without repugnance, and dies without fear." Abject as they are, however, they are not wholly without wit. By a secret telegraph system, they will communicate between Quito and Riobamba in one hour. When there was a battle in Pasto, the Indians of Riobamba knew of it two hours after, though eighty leagues distant.

The civilization of South America three centuries ago was nearly confined to this Andean family, though they had attained only to the bronze period. In the milder character of their ancient religion and gentleness of disposition they are strongly distinguished from the nations that encircled the vale of Anahuac, the centre of civilization on the northern continent. But little of this former glory is now apparent. The Incas reached an astronomical knowledge which astonished the Spaniards, but the Quichuans of to-day count vaguely by moons and rains. Great is the contrast between the architecture of this century and that in the days of Huayna-Capac. There are few Incarial relics, however, in the Valley of Quito, for the Incas ruled there only half a century. The chief

different lengths tied in a row. The "plaintive national songs" which Markham heard at Cuzco are not sung in Ecuador.

monuments are the tolas or mounds (mostly at Cuenca), containing earthen vessels and bronze hatchets and ear-rings; the *Inga-pirrca*, or oval fortress, and the *Intihu-aicu*, or temple of the sun, near Cañar; the *Inga-chungana*, a massive stone resembling a sofa, where the Inca reposed to enjoy the delightful prospect over the Valley of Gulán; and remnants of causeways and roads.

CHAPTER VII.

Geological History of South America.—Rise of the Andes.—Creation of the Amazon.—Characteristic Features of the Continent.—Andean Chain.—The Equatorial Volcanoes.

THREE cycles ago an island rose from the sea where now expands the vast continent of South America. It was the culminating point of the highlands of Guiana. For ages this granite peak was the sole representative of dry land in our hemisphere south of the Canada hills. In process of time, a cluster of islands rose above the thermal waters. They were the small beginnings of the future mountains of Brazil, holding in their laps the diamonds which now sparkle in the crown of Dom Pedro II. Long protracted eons elapsed without adding a page to the geology of South America. The Creator seems to have been busy elsewhere. Decorating the north with the gorgeous flora of the carboniferous period, till, in the language of Hugh Miller, "to distant planets our earth must have shone with a green and delicate ray," he rubbed the picture out, and ushered in the hideous reptilian age, when monstrous saurians, footed, paddled, and winged, were the lords of this lower world. All the great mountain chains were at this time slumbering beneath the ocean. The city of New York was sure of its site; but huge dinotheria wallowed in the mire where now stand the palaces of Paris, London, and Vienna.

At length the morning breaks upon the last day of creation, and the fiat goes forth that the proud waves of the Pacific, which have so long washed the table-lands of Guiana and Brazil, shall be stayed. Far away toward the setting sun the white surf beats in long lines of foam against a low, winding archipelago—the western outline of the coming continent. Fierce is the fight for the mastery between sea and land, between the denuding power of the waves and the volcanic forces underneath. But slowly—very slowly, yet surely—rises the long chain of islands by a double process; the submarine crust of the earth is cooling, and the rocks are folded up as it shrivels, while the molten material within, pressed out through the crevices, overflows and helps to build up the sea-defiant wall. A man's life would be too short to count even the centuries consumed in this operation. The coast of Peru has risen eighty feet since it felt the tread of Pizarro: supposing the Andes to have risen at this rate uniformly and without interruption, seventy thousand years must have elapsed before they reached their present altitude. But when we consider that, in fact, it was an intermittent movement—alternate upheaval and subsidence—we must add an unknown number of millennia.

Three times the Andes sank hundreds of feet beneath the ocean level, and again were slowly brought up to their present height. The suns of uncounted ages have risen and set upon these sculptured forms, though geologically recent, casting the same line of shadows century after century. A long succession of brute races roamed over the mountains and plains of South America, and died out ages ere man was created. In those pre-Adamite times, long before the Incas ruled, the mastodon and megatherium, the horse and the tapir, dwelt in the high valley of Quito; yet all these passed away before the arrival of the aborigines: the wild horses now feeding on the pampas of Buenos Ayres were imported from Europe three hundred and thirty-three years ago.*

* At Paita, the most western point of South America, there is a raised

And now the Andes* stand complete in their present gigantic proportions, one of the grandest and most symmetrical mountain chains in the world. Starting from the Land of Fire, it stretches northward and mounts upward until it enters the Isthmus of Panama, where it bows gracefully to either ocean, but soon resumes, under another name, its former majesty, and loses its magnificence only where the trappers chase the fur-bearing animals over the Arctic plains. Nowhere else does Nature present such a continuous and lofty chain of mountains, unbroken for eight thousand miles, save where it is rent asunder by the Magellanic Straits, and proudly tossing up a thousand pinnacles into the region of eternal snow. Nowhere in the Old World do we see a single well-defined mountain chain, only a broad belt of mountainous country traversing the heart of the continent.

The moment the Andes arose, the great continental val-

beach three hundred feet high. The basal slate and sandstone rocks, dipping S. of E., are covered by conglomerate, sand, and a gypseous formation, containing shells of living species. Additional to those described by D'Orbigny we found here *Cerithium læviuscula*, *Ostrea gallus*, and *Ampullina Ortoni*, as determined by W. M. Gabb, Esq., of Philadelphia. Darwin found shells in Chile 1300 feet above the sea, covered with marine mud. President Loomis, of Lewisburg University, Pa., informs the writer that in 1853, after nearly a day's ride from Iquique, he came to a former sea-beach. "It furnished abundant specimens of *Patellæ* and other shells, still perfect, and identical with others that I had that morning obtained at Iquique with the living animal inhabiting them." This beach is elevated 2500 feet above the Pacific. The same observer says that near Potosi there is one uninterrupted mass of lava, having a columnar structure, not less than one hundred miles in length, fifty miles wide, and eight hundred feet thick. It overlies a bed of saliferous sandstone which has been worked for salt. Fifty feet within a mine, and in the undisturbed rock which forms its roof, the doctor found fragments of dicotyledonous trees with the bark on, undecomposed, uncharred, and fibrous.

* The name Andes is often derived from *anta*, an old Peruvian word signifying metal. But Humboldt says: "There are no means of interpreting it by connecting it with any signification or idea; if such connection exist, it is buried in the obscurity of the past." According to Col. Tod, the northern Hindoos apply the name Andes to the Himalayan Mountains.

ley of the Amazon was sketched out and moulded in its lap. The tidal waves of the Atlantic were dashing against the Cordilleras, and a legion of rivulets were busily plowing up the sides into deep ravines; the sediment produced by this incessant wear and tear was carried eastward, and spread out stratum by stratum, till the shallow sea between the Andes and the islands of Guiana and Brazil was filled up with sand and clay. Huge glaciers (thinks Agassiz), afterward descending, moved over the inclined plane, and ground the loose rock to powder.* Eddies and currents, throwing up sand-banks as they do now, gradually defined the limits of the tributary streams, and directed them into one main trunk, which worked for itself a wide, deep bed, capable of containing its accumulated flood. Then and thus was created the Amazon.

In South America Nature has framed her works on a gigantic scale. Where else combined do we see such a series of towering mountains, such a volume of river-water, and such wide-spreading plains? We have no proper conception of Andine grandeur till we learn that the top of the tallest mountain in North America is nearly a mile beneath the untrodden dome of Chimborazo; nor any just view of the vast dimensions of the Amazonian Valley till we find that all the United States could be packed in it without touching its boundaries; nor any adequate idea of the Amazon itself till we ascertain that it drains a million square miles more than the Mississippi.

South America is a triangular continent, with its axis, the Andes, not central, as in Europe, but lying on its extreme western edge, and in harmony with the well-known law that the highest mountains and the grandest volcanoes face the broadest ocean. The highlands of Brazil and

* On this point see Chapter XVII.

Guiana have neither volcanic nor snow-clad peaks.* Like all the dry land which first appeared, these primitive mountains on the Atlantic border trend east and west. The result of this position is a triple river system—the Orinoco, Amazon, and La Plata, draining three immense plains—the llanos of Venezuela, the sylvas of Brazil, and the pampas of the Argentine Republic. The continuity and extent of these vast depressions are more remarkable even than the height and length of the mountain chains.†

Such are the characteristic features of South America; they are not repeated in any other continent.‡ Not one feature could be changed without destroying those peculiarities of soil and climate which so remarkably distinguish South America. Its position on the equator places it in the path of the vapory trade winds, which continually sweep over it westward till they strike the Andes, which, like a great condenser, roll a thousand streams eastward again to feed the mighty Amazon. So effectual is that barrier, not a drop of moisture passes it, and the trade wind is not felt again on the Pacific till you are one hundred

* "The interior plateau of Brazil (says Dr. Lund) is composed of horizontal strata of the transition period, which are nowhere covered with the secondary or tertiary formations." The highest point in Brazil is 5755 feet. Darwin speaks of "some ancient submarine volcanic rocks (in the province of La Plata) worth mentioning, from their rarity on this eastern side of the continent." With the exception of the coast of Venezuela, the eastern system is little exposed to earthquakes.

† These three plains constitute four fifths of all South America east of the Andes. The west slope of the Ecuadorian Andes is about 275 feet per mile; on the east it is 125 feet.

‡ There is, however, a striking coincidence between the mountain and river systems of the northern and southern continents of this hemisphere. Thus,

The Andes represent the Rocky Mountains.
" Highland of Guiana represent the Canadian Mountains.
" " Brazil " Appalachian "
" Amazon " Saskatchewan.
" La Plata " Mississippi.
" Orinoco " Mackenzie.

and fifty miles from the coast. Were the Andes on the Atlantic side, South America would be turned into a vast Sahara. As it is, the interest which attaches to this continent, save a few relics of the Incas, is exclusively that of pure nature. Nowhere does Nature affect us more deeply with the feeling of her grandeur; nowhere does she exhibit wilder freaks or more startling contrasts; nowhere do we find such a theatre for the free development of vegetable and animal life.

The long and lofty chain of the Andes is certainly one of the grandest results of the plications and uplifts of the earth's crust. While the waves of the Pacific, from Panama to Patagonia, submissively kiss the feet of the Andes, and the showers that swell the Amazon fall within sight of the mariner on that peaceful ocean, the Rocky Mountains are situated five hundred miles from the sea. The space west of the Andes does not contain 20,000 square leagues, while the country east of it equals 424,600. While the compact Andes have an average width of only sixty miles,* the straggling mountain system beyond the Mississippi has the breadth of the Empire State; but the mean elevation of the latter would scarcely reach the bottom of the Quito Valley. The mountains of Asia may surpass the Cordilleras in height, but, situated beyond the tropics, and destitute of volcanoes, they do not present that inexhaustible variety of phenomena which characterizes the latter. The outbursts of porphyry and trachytic domes, so characteristic of the high crests of the Cordilleras, impart a physiognomy quite distinct from that presented by the mountains of Europe. The Andes offer, in the least space, the greatest possible variety of impressions.† There is near Huanca, Peru,

* The width of the chain south of the equator varies with that of the continent.

† "No mountains which I have seen in Hungary, Saxony, or the Pyrenees

a coal-bed lifted up to the enormous height of 14,700 feet, and on the side of Chimborazo there is a salt spring 13,000 feet above the sea. Marine shells have not been found in Europe above the summit of the Pyrenees, or 11,700 feet; but the Andes can show some a thousand feet higher. A strange sight, to see shells once crawling on the bottom of the ocean now resting at an elevation twice the height of Mount Washington!

Beneath the Southern Cross, out of a sea perpetually swept by fearful gales, rise the rocky hills of Terra del Fuego. It is the starting-point of that granite chain which winds around the earth in a majestic curve, first northwesterly to the Arctic Sea, thence by the Aleutian and Japanese Isles to Asia, crossing the Old World southwesterly from China to South Africa.

Skirting the bleak shores of Patagonia in a single narrow sierra, the Andes enter Chile, rising higher and higher till they culminate in the gigantic porphyritic peak of Aconcagua. At the boundary-line of Bolivia, the chain, which has so far followed a precise meridional direction, turns to the northwest, and, at the same time, separates into two Cordilleras, inclosing the great table-land of Desaguadero. This wonderful valley, the Thibet of the New World, has four times the area of New York State, and five times the elevation of the Catskill Mountain House. At one end of the valley, perched above the clouds, is silvery Potosí, the highest city in the world; at the other stands the once golden capital of Cuzco. Between them is Lake Titicaca*

are as irregular as the Andes, or broken into such alternate substances, manifesting such prodigious revolutions of nature."—*Helms.* "More sublime than the Alps by their *ensemble*, the Andes lack those curious and charming details of which Nature has been so lavish in the old continent."—*Holinski.*

* This lake is the largest fresh-water accumulation in South America. It has diminished within the historic period. Its surface is 12,795 feet above the Pacific, or higher than the highest peaks of the Pyrenees.

(probably an ancient crater), within which is an island celebrated as the cradle of the strange empire of Peru, which, though crushed by Pizarro in its budding civilization, ranks as the most extraordinary and extensive empire in the annals of American history. The Cordillera, of which Sahama, Sorata, and Illimani are the pinnacles, so completely inclose this high valley that not a drop of water can escape except by evaporation. At the silver mines of Pasco the Andes throw off a third cordillera, and with this triple arrangement and a lower altitude, enter the republic of Ecuador. There they resume the double line, and surpass their former magnificence. Twenty volcanoes, presided over by the princely Chimborazo and Cotopaxi, rise out of a sublime congregation of mountains surrounding the famous valley of Quito. In New Granada there is a final and unique display of Andine grandeur: the Cordilleras combine just above the equator into one dizzy ridge, and then spread out like a fan, or, rather, like the graceful branches of the palm. One sierra bends to the east, holding in its lap the city of Bogota, and, rolling off a thousand streams to swell the Orinoco, terminates in the beautiful mountains of Caracas; the central range culminates in the volcanic Tolima,* but is soon lost in the Caribbean Sea; the western chain turns to the left, humbling itself as it threads the narrow isthmus, and expands into the level table-land of Mexico. You may cross Mexico from ocean to ocean in a carriage, but no wheeled vehicle ever crossed South America.

We will now speak more particularly of the Andes of the equator. The mountain chain is built up of granite, gneissoid, and schistose rocks, often in vertical position, and

* This is the loftiest summit of the Andes in the northern hemisphere, being 18,200 feet. It is also remarkable for being situated farther from the sea (120 miles) than any other active volcano.

capped with trachyte and porphyry.* Large masses of *solid* rock are rarely seen; every thing is cracked, calcined, or triturated. While in Bolivia the Eastern Cordillera shows a succession of sharp, ragged peaks, in contrast with the conical summits of the Cordillera of the coast, there is no such distinction in the Andes of the equator.† The Eastern Cordillera has a greater mean height, and it displays more volcanic activity. Twenty volcanic mountains surround the valley, of which twelve are in the oriental chain. Three of the twenty are now active (Cotopaxi, Sangai, and Pichincha), and five others are known to have erupted since the Conquest (Chiles, Imbabura, Guamani, Tunguragua, and Quirotoa). The truncated cone of Cotopaxi, the jagged, Alpine crest of ruined Altar, and the dome of Chimborazo, are the representative forms of the volcanic summits. The extinct volcanoes usually have double domes or peaks, while the active peaks are slender cones. Antisana and Cayambi are fashioned after Chimborazo, though the latter is table-topped rather than convex; Caraguairazo, Quirotoa, Iliniza, Sincholagua, Rumiñagui, and Corazon, resemble Altar; Tunguragua, Sangai, Llanganati, Cotocachi, Chiles, and Imbabura, imitate Cotopaxi; Pichincha, Atacatzo, and Guamani are irregular. The Ecuadorian volcanoes have rarely ejected liquid lava, but chiefly water, mud, ashes, and fragments of trachyte and porphyry. Cotopaxi alone produces

* "As a general rule, whenever the mass of mountains rises much above the limit of perpetual snow, the primitive rocks disappear, and the summits are trachyte or trappean porphyry."—*Humboldt.* In general, "the great Cordilleras are formed of innumerable varieties of granites, gneiss, schists, hornblende, chloritic slates, porphyries, etc., and these rocks alternate with each other in meridional bands, which in the ridges frequently present the appearance of a radiated or fan-shaped structure, and under the plains are more or less vertical."—*Evan Hopkins, F.G.S.*

† Von Tschudi makes the incorrect statement that "throughout the whole extent of South America there is not a single instance of the Western Cordillera being intersected by a river." Witness the Esmeraldas.

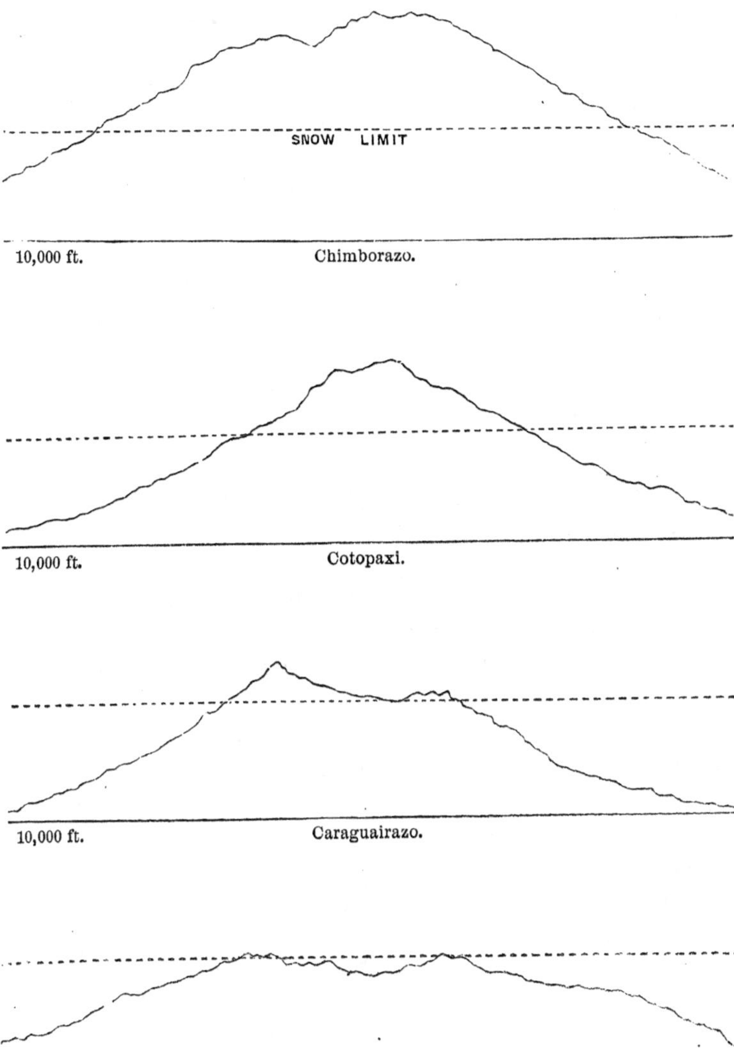
SNOW LIMIT
10,000 ft.
Chimborazo.
10,000 ft.
Cotopaxi.
10,000 ft.
Caraguairazo.
10,000 ft.
Pichincha.

pure, foam-like pumice, and glossy, translucent obsidian.* The paucity of quartz, and the absence of basalt, are remarkable. Some of the porphyroids are conglomerate, but the majority are true porphyries, having a homogeneous base. Dr. T. Sterry Hunt calls them porphyroid trachytes. They have a black, rarely reddish, vitreous, or impalpable base, approaching obsidian, with a specific gravity of 2.59 in pure specimens, and holding crystals or crystalline grains of glassy feldspar, and sometimes of pyroxene and hematite. They differ from the Old World porphyries in containing no quartz, and seldom mica.† D'Orbigny considers the porphyries of the Andes to have been ejected at the close of the cretaceous period, and formed the first relief of the Cordillera. The prevalence of trachyte shows that the products have cooled under feeble pressure.

From the deluges of water lately thrown out have resulted deep furrows in the sides; and from the prevalence of the east wind, which is always met by the traveler on the crest of either Cordillera, there is a greater accumulation of ashes, and less snow on the west slope. Cotopaxi is a fine example of this. In Pichincha, Altar, and Rumiñagua, however, the western wall is lowest, apparently broken down.‡ There is no synchronism in the eruptions of Cotopaxi and Pichincha. These volcanoes must have independent reservoirs, for the former is 3000 feet higher than the latter, and only thirty miles distant. The reputed eruptions of Pichincha are dated 1534, 1539, 1566, 1575, 1588, and 1660; that of 1534 resting on the assertions of Checa,

* It is a singular fact that true trachyte, pumice, and obsidian are wanting in the volcanic Galápagos Islands, only 700 miles west of Pichincha.

† As many of the crystals are partly fused, or have round angles, the porphyries were probably formed by the melting of a crystalline rock, the base becoming fused into a homogeneous material, while the less fusible crystals remain imbedded.—*Dr. Hunt.*

‡ In the Galápagos volcanoes the south wall is lowest, while the craters in Mexico and Sandwich Islands are lowest on the northeast.

Garcilazo, and Herrera, indorsed by Humboldt. Excepting the traditional eruption in 1534, which probably is confounded with that of Pichincha, Cotopaxi did not open till 1742; then followed the eruptions of 1743, 1744, 1746, 1766, 1768, 1803, 1851, and 1855. We must mention, however, that, since the recent awakening of Pichincha, Cotopaxi has been unusually silent. There is also a remarkable coincidence (which may not be wholly accidental) in the renewed activity of Pichincha, and the great eruption of Mauna Loa, both occurring in March, 1868. It is generally believed by the natives that Cotopaxi and Tunguragua are sympathetic.

There are fifty-one volcanoes in the Andean chain. Of these, twenty girdle the Valley of Quito, three active, five dormant, and twelve extinct.* Besides these are numerous mountain peaks not properly volcanic. Nowhere on the face of the earth is there such a grand assemblage of mountains. Twenty-two summits are covered with perpetual snow, and fifty are over ten thousand feet high.† All

* The altitudes of the most important Ecuadorian volcanoes are:

WESTERN CHAIN.	EASTERN CHAIN.
Chimborazo, 21,420 feet (Humboldt).	*Cayambi*, 19,648 feet (Humboldt); 19,358 (Wisse).
Caraguairazo, 19,183 feet (Humboldt). It is variously estimated from 15,673 feet to 19,720 feet; 18,000 feet is not far from the truth.	*Antisana*, 19,148 feet (Humboldt): 19,279 (Wisse).
Iliniza, 17,370 feet (Wisse); 16,300 (Hall).	*Cotopaxi*, 18,880 feet (Humboldt); 18,862 (Wisse).
Cotocachi, 16,440 feet (Humboldt); 16,409 (Wisse).	*Altar*, 17,400 feet.
Pichincha, 15,922 feet (Humboldt); 15,827 (Orton).	*Sangai*, 17,120 feet (Wisse).
	Tunguragua, 16,579 feet (Humboldt).
	Sincholagua, 16,434 feet (Humboldt).

† The snow-limit at the equator is 15,800 feet. No living creature, save the condor, passes this limit; naked rocks, fogs, and eternal snows mark the reign of uninterrupted solitude. The following is the approximate limit of perpetual snow in different latitudes:

0°	15,800 feet.	40°	8,300 feet.
27°	13,800 "	54°	3,700 "
33°	12,780 "	70°	3,300 "

of these would be visible from a single stand-point—the summit of Cotopaxi. The lofty peaks shoot up with so much method as almost to provoke the theory that the Incas, in the zenith of their power, planted them as signal monuments along the royal road to Cuzco. The eastern series is called the *Cordillera real*, because along its flank are the remnants of the splendid highway which once connected Quito and the Peruvian capital.* It can also boast of such tremendous volcanoes as Cotopaxi and Sangai. The Western Cordillera contains but one active volcano; but then it can point to peerless Chimborazo and the deep crater of Pichincha. These twenty volcanic mountains rise within a space only two hundred miles long and thirty miles wide. It makes one tremble to think of the awful crevice over which they are placed.†

The limit appears to descend more rapidly going south of the equator than in going north.

* We traveled over a portion of this ancient road in going from Riobamba to Cajabamba. It is well paved with cut blocks of dark porphyry. It is not graded, but partakes of the irregularity of the country. Designed, not for carriages, but for troops and llamas, there are steps when the ascent is steep.

† Grand as the Andes are, how insignificant in a general view! How slightly they cause our globe to differ from a perfect sphere! Cotopaxi constitutes only $\frac{1}{1100}$ of the earth's radius; and on a globe six feet in diameter, Chimborazo would be represented by a grain of sand less than $\frac{1}{20}$ of an inch in thickness.

CHAPTER VIII.

The Volcanoes of Ecuador.—Western Cordillera.—Chimborazo.—Iliniza.—Corazon.—Pichincha.—Descent into its Crater.

COMING up from Peru through the cinchona forests of Loja, and over the barren hills of Assuay, the traveler reaches Riobamba, seated on the threshold of magnificence—like Damascus, an oasis in a sandy plain, but, unlike the Queen of the East, surrounded with a splendid retinue of snowy peaks that look like icebergs floating in a sea of clouds.

On our left is the most sublime spectacle in the New World. It is a majestic pile of snow, its clear outline on the deep blue sky describing the profile of a lion in repose. At noon the vertical sun, and the profusion of light reflected from the glittering surface, will not allow a shadow to be cast on any part, so that you can easily fancy the figure is cut out of a mountain of spotless marble. This is Chimborazo—yet not the whole of it—you see but a third of the great giant. His feet are as eternally green as his head is everlastingly white; but they are far away beneath the bananas and cocoa-palms of the Pacific coast.

Rousseau was disappointed when he first saw the sea; and the first glimpse of Niagara often fails to meet one's expectations. But Chimborazo is sure of a worshiper the moment its overwhelming grandeur breaks upon the traveler. You feel that you are in the presence-chamber of the monarch of the Andes. There is sublimity in his kingly look, of which the ocean might be proud.

"All that expands the spirit, yet appals,
Gathers around this summit, as if to show
How earth may pierce to heaven, yet leave vain man below."

Well do we remember our disappointment as we stood before that wonder of the world—St. Peter's. We mounted the pyramid of steps and looked up, but were not overcome by the magnificence. We read in our guide-book that the edifice covers eight acres, and to the tip-top of the cross is almost five hundred feet; that it took three hundred and fifty years and twelve successive artists to finish it, and an expenditure of $50,000,000, and now costs $30,000 per annum to keep it in repair; still we did not appreciate its greatness. We pushed aside the curtain and walked in —walked a day's journey across the transept and up and down the everlasting nave, and yet continued heterodox. We tried hard to believe it was very vast and sublime, and knew we ought to feel its grandeur, but somehow we did not. Then we sat down by the Holy of Holies, and there we were startled into a better judgment by the astounding fact that the Cathedral of St. Paul—the largest edifice in Great Britain—could stand upright, spire, dome, body, and all, inside of St. Peter's! that the letters of the inscription which run around the *base* of the dome, though apparently but an inch, are in reality six feet high! Then, for the first time, the scales fell from our eyes; the giant building began to grow; higher and higher still it rose, longer and deeper it expanded, yet in perfect proportions; the colossal structure, now a living temple, put on its beautiful garments and the robe of majesty. And that dome! the longer we looked at it the vaster it grew, till finally it seemed to be a temple not made with hands; the spacious canopy became the firmament; the mosaic figures of cherubim and seraphim were endowed with life; and as we fixed our eyes on the zenith where the Almighty is represented in glory, we thought we had the vision of Stephen. Long we gazed upward into this heaven of man's creation, and gazed again till we were lost in wonder.

But the traveler needs no such steps to lift him up to the grand conception of the divine Architect as he beholds the great white dome of Chimborazo. It looks lofty from the very first. Now and then an expanse of thin, sky-like vapor would cut the mountain in twain, and the dome, islanded in the deep blue of the upper regions, seemed to belong more to heaven than to earth. We knew that Chimborazo was more than twice the altitude of Etna. We could almost see the great Humboldt struggling up the mountain's side till he looked like a black speck moving over the mighty white, but giving up in despair four thousand feet below the summit. We see the intrepid Bolivar mounting still higher; but the hero of Spanish-American independence returns a defeated man. Last of all comes the philosophic Boussingault, and attains the prodigious elevation of nineteen thousand six hundred feet—the highest point reached by man without the aid of a balloon; but the dome remains unsullied by his foot. Yet none of these facts increase our admiration. The mountain has a tongue which speaks louder than all mathematical calculations.

There must be something singularly sublime about Chimborazo, for the spectator at Riobamba is already nine thousand feet high, and the mountain is not so elevated above him as Mont Blanc above the vale of Chamounî, when, in reality, that culminating point of Europe would not reach up even to the snow-limit of Chimborazo by two thousand feet.* It is only while sailing on the Pacific that one sees Chimborazo in its complete proportions. Its very magni-

* But Chimborazo is steeper than the Alp-king; and steepness is a quality more quickly appreciated than mere massiveness. "Mont Blanc (says a writer in *Frazer's Magazine*) is scarcely admired, because he is built with a certain regard to stability; but the apparently reckless architecture of the Matterhorn brings the traveler fairly on his knees, with a respect akin to that felt for the leaning tower of Pisa, or the soaring pinnacles of Antwerp."

tude diminishes the impression of awe and wonder, for the Andes on which it rests are heaved to such a vast altitude above the sea, that the relative elevation of its summit becomes reduced by comparison with the surrounding mountains. Its altitude is 21,420 feet, or forty-five times the height of Strasburg Cathedral; or, to state it otherwise, the fall of one pound from the top of Chimborazo would raise the temperature of water 30°. One fourth of this is perpetually covered with snow, so that its ancient name, Chimpurazu—the mountain of snow—is very appropriate.* It is a stirring thought that this mountain, now mantled with snow, once gleamed with volcanic fires. There is a hot spring on the north side, and an immense amount of débris covers the slope below the snow-limit, consisting chiefly of fine-grained, iron-stained trachyte and coarse porphyroid gray trachyte; very rarely a dark vitreous trachyte. Chimborazo is very likely not a solid mountain: trachytic volcanoes are supposed to be full of cavities. Bouguer found it made the plumb-line deviate 7″ or 8″.

The valleys which furrow the flank of Chimborazo are in keeping with its colossal size. Narrower, but deeper than those of the Alps, the mind swoons and sinks in the effort to comprehend their grim majesty. The mountain appears to have been broken to pieces like so much thin crust, and the strata thrown on their vertical edges, revealing deep, dark chasms, that seem to lead to the confines of the lower world. The deepest valley in Europe, that of the Ordesa in the Pyrenees, is 3200 feet deep; but here are rents in the side of Chimborazo in which Vesuvius could be put away out of sight. As you look down into the fathomless fissure, you see a white fleck rising out of the gulf,

* "White Mountain" is the natural and almost uniform name of the highest mountains in all countries; thus Himalaya, Mont Blanc, Hoemus, Sierra Nevada, Ben Nevis, Snowdon, Lebanon, White Mountains of United States, Chimborazo, and Illimani.

and expanding as it mounts, till the wings of the condor, fifteen feet in spread, glitter in the sun as the proud bird fearlessly wheels over the dizzy chasm, and then, ascending above your head, sails over the dome of Chimborazo.* Could the condor speak, what a glowing description could he give of the landscape beneath him when his horizon is a thousand miles in diameter. If

> "Twelve fair counties saw the blaze from Malvern's lonely height,"

what must be the panorama from a height fifteen times higher!

Chimborazo was long supposed to be the tallest mountain on the globe, but its supremacy has been supplanted by Mount Everest in Asia, and Aconcagua in Chile.† In mountain gloom and glory, however, it still stands unrivaled. The Alps have the avalanche, "the thunderbolt of snow," and the glaciers, those icy Niagaras so beautiful and grand. Here they are wanting.‡ The monarch of the Andes sits motionless in calm serenity and unbroken silence. The silence is absolute and actually oppressive. The road from Guayaquil to Quito crosses Chimborazo at the elevation of fourteen thousand feet. Save the rush

* Humboldt's statement that the condor flies higher than Chimborazo has been questioned; but we have seen numbers hovering at least a thousand feet above the summit of Pichincha. Baron Müller, in his ascent of Orizaba, saw two falcons flying at the height of full 18,000 feet; Dr. Hooker found crows and ravens on the Himalayas at 16,500 feet; and flocks of wild geese are said to fly over the peak of Kintschinghow, 22,756 feet.

† Mount Everest is 29,000 feet, and Aconcagua 23,200. Schlagintweit enumerates thirteen Himalayan summits over 25,000 feet, and forty-six above 20,000. We have little confidence in the estimates of the Bolivian mountains. Chimborazo has nearly the same latitude and altitude as the loftiest peak in Africa, Kilima Njaro.

‡ Humboldt ascribes the absence of glaciers in the Andes to the extreme steepness of the sides, and the excessive dryness of the air. Dr. Loomis, above quoted, mentions indications of glacial action—moraines, and polished and striated rocks—on the crest of the Cordillera, between Peru and Bolivia, lat. 21° S.

of the trade wind in the afternoon, as it sweeps over the Andes, not a sound is audible; not the hum of an insect, nor the chirp of a bird, nor the roar of the puma, nor the music of running waters. Mid-ocean is never so silent. You can almost hear the globe turning on its axis. There was a time when the monarch deigned to speak, and spoke with a voice of thunder, for the lava on its sides is an evidence of volcanic activity. But ever since the morning stars sang together over man's creation, Chimbo has sat in sullen silence, satisfied to look "from his throne of clouds o'er half the world." There is something very suggestive in this silence of Chimborazo. It was once full of noise and fury; it is now a *completed* mountain, and thunders no more. How silent was Jesus, a completed character! The reason we are so noisy is that we are so full of wants; we are *unfinished* characters. Had we perfect fullness of all things, the beatitude of being without a want, we should lapse into the eternal silence of God.

Chimborazo is a leader of a long train of ambitious crags and peaks; but as he who comes after the king must not expect to be noticed, we will only take a glimpse of these lesser lights as we pass up the Western Cordillera, and then down the Eastern.

The first after leaving the monarch is Caraguairazo. The Indians call it "the wife of Chimborazo." They are separated only by a very narrow valley. One hundred and seventy years ago the top of this mountain fell in, and torrents of mud flowed out containing multitudes of fishes. It is now over seventeen thousand feet high, and is one of the most Alpine of the Quitonian volcanoes, having sharp pinnacles instead of the smooth trachytic domes — usually double domes — so characteristic of the Andean summits. And now we pass in rapid succession numerous picturesque mountains, some of them extinct volcanoes, as Iliniza, presenting two pyramidal peaks, the highest seventeen thousand feet above the sea, and Corazon, so named from its heart-shaped summit, till we reach Pichincha, whose smoking crater is only five miles distant in a straight line from the city of Quito, or eleven by the traveled route.

The crown of this mountain presents three groups of rocky peaks. The most westerly one is called Rucu-Pichincha, and alone manifests activity. To the northeast of Rucu is Guagua-Pichincha, a ruined flue of the same fiery furnace; and between the two is Cundur-guachana.* Pichincha is the only volcano in Ecuador which has not a true cone-crater. Some violent eruption beyond the reach of history or tradition has formed an enormous funnel-shaped basin 2500 feet deep,† 1500 in diameter at the bottom, and expanding upward to a width of three fourths of a mile. It is the *deepest* crater on the globe. That of Kilauea is 600 feet; Orizaba, 500; Etna, 300; Hecla, 100. Vesuvius is a portable furnace in comparison. The abyss is girt with a ragged wall of dark trachyte, which rises on the inside at various angles between 45° and perpendicularity. As we know of but one American besides the members of our expedition (Mr. Farrand, a photographer) who has succeeded in entering the crater of this interesting volcano, we will give a brief sketch of our visit.

Leaving Quito in the afternoon by the old arched gateway at the foot of Panecillo, and crossing a spur of the mountain, we stopped for the night at the Jesuit hacienda, situated in the beautiful valley of Lloa, but nearly ruined by the earthquake of 1859. On the damp walls of this monastery, perched 10,268 feet above the ocean, we found several old paintings, among them a copy of the *Visitation*

* Pichincha, in the Inca language, signifies "the boiling mountain;" Rucu means old; Guagua, young; and Cundur-guachana, the condor's nest.

† More accurately, 2527 feet; Wisse and Moreno made it 2460.

by Rubens. The sunset views in this heart of the Andes were surpassingly beautiful. Mounting our horses at break of day, and taking an Indian guide, we ascended rapidly, by a narrow and difficult path, through the forest that belts the volcano, up to the height of 12,000 feet, emerging gradually into a thicket of stunted bushes, and then entered the dreary paramo. Splendid was the view of the Eastern Cordillera. At least six dazzling white volcanoes were in sight just across the Valley of Quito, among them table-topped Cayambi, majestic Antisana, and princely Cotopaxi, whose tapering summit is a mile above the clouds. Toiling upward, we reached the base of the cone, where vegetation ceased entirely; and, tying our horses to some huge rocks that had fallen from the mural cliff above, started off on hands and feet for the crater. The cone is deeply covered with sand and cinders for about two hundred feet, and the sides are inclined at an angle of about 35°. At ten o'clock we reached the brim of the crater, and the great gulf burst suddenly into view. We can never forget the impression made upon us by the sight. We speak of many things here below as awful, but that word has its full meaning when carried to the top of Pichincha. There you see a frightful opening in the earth's crust nearly a mile in width and half a mile deep, and from the dark abyss comes rolling up a cloud of sulphurous vapors. Monte Somma in the time of Strabo was a miniature; but this crater is on the top of a mountain four times the height of the Italian volcano. Imagination finds it difficult to conceive a spectacle of more fearful grandeur or such solemn magnificence. It well accords with Milton's picture of the bottomless pit. The united effect of the silence and solitude of the place, the great depth of the cavity, the dark precipitous sides, and the column of smoke standing over an unseen crevice, was to us more impressive than thundering Cotopaxi or fiery

Crater of Pichincha.

Vesuvius. Humboldt, after standing on this same brink, exclaimed, "I have never beheld a grander or more remarkable picture than that presented by this volcano;" and La Condamine compared it to "the Chaos of the poets." Below us are the smouldering fires which may any moment spring forth into a conflagration; around us are black, ragged cliffs—fit boundary for this gateway to the infernal regions. They look as if they had just been dragged up from the central furnace of the earth. Life seems to have fled in terror from the vicinity; even lichens, the children of the bare rocks, refuse to clothe the scathed and beetling crags. For some moments, made mute by the dreadful sight, we stood like statues on the rim of the mighty caldron, with our eyes riveted on the abyss below, lost in contemplating that which can not be described. The panorama from this lofty summit is more pleasing, but equally sublime. Toward the rising sun is the long range of the Eastern Cordillera, hiding from our view the great valley of the Amazon. To right and left are the peaks of another procession of august mountains from Cotocachi to Chimborazo. We are surrounded by the great patriarchs of the Andes, and their speaker, Cotopaxi, ever and anon sends his muttering voice over the land. The view westward is like looking down from a balloon. Those parallel ridges of the mountain chain, dropping one behind the other, are the gigantic staircase by which the ice-crowned Chimborazo steps down to the sea. A white sea of clouds covers the peaceful Pacific and the lower parts of the coast. But the vapory ocean, curling into the ravines, beautifully represents little coves and bays, leaving islands and promontories like a true ocean on a broken shore. We seem raised above the earth, which lies like an opened map below us; we can look down on the upper surface of the clouds, and, were it night, down too upon the lightnings.

The crater of Pichincha has a sharp, serrated edge, which, happily for Quito, is broken down on the west side, so that in the next eruption the volcano will doubtless pour its contents into the wilds of Esmeraldas. The highest pinnacle is 15,827 feet; so that the mountain just enters the region of perpetual winter. Water boils at 185°. The summit is generally bare, though snow is always found in the clefts of the rocks. It is not compact or crystalline, but resembles a conglomerate of little hailstones.* Out of the mingled snow and pumice-dust rise a few delicate flowers, particularly the violet *Sida Pichinchensis*, the same which we had observed on the side of Chimborazo. Think of gay flowers a thousand feet higher than the top of Mont Blanc!

The first to reach the brink of the crater were the French Academicians in 1742. Sixty years after, Humboldt stood on the summit. But it was not till 1844 that any one dared to enter the crater. This was accomplished by Garcia Moreno, now President of Ecuador, and Sebastian Wisse, a French engineer. Humboldt pronounced the bottom of the crater "inaccessible, from its great depth and precipitous descent." We found it accessible, but exceedingly perilous. The moment we prepared to descend

* The snow on the top of Mont Blanc is like dry dust; in Lapland, in open places, it consists of hexagonal crystals, and is called by the inhabitants "sand-snow." The French and Spanish mathematicians, Bouguer, La Condamine, and Ulloa, in their story of ascending Pichincha, give a long and dreadful account of their sufferings from cold and rarefied air: "whilst eating, every one was obliged to keep his plate over a chafing-dish of coals, to prevent his food from freezing." The traveler nowadays finds only a chilling wind. This rise of temperature, coupled with the fact that La Condamine (1745), Humboldt (1802), Boussingault (1831), and Wisse (1863) give to Quito a decreasing altitude, inclines us to believe, with Boussingault, that the Andes are sinking. Since the activity of the volcano in 1868, the summit has been so warm that the snow has totally disappeared. Ice-cream has in consequence risen in price in Quito, as snow must be brought from Sincholagua, four days' journey.

our guide ran away. We went on without him, but when halfway down were stopped by a precipice.

On the 22d of October, 1867, we returned to Pichincha with another guide, and entered the crater by a different route. Manuel, our Indian, led us to the south side, and over the brink we went. We were not long in realizing the danger of the undertaking. Here the snow concealed an ugly fissure or covered a treacherous rock (for nearly all the rocks are crumbling); there we must cross a mass of loose sand moving like a glacier down the almost vertical side of the crater; and on every hand rocks were giving way, and, gathering momentum at each revolution, went thundering down, leaping over precipices, and jostling other rocks, which joined in the race, till they all struck the bottom with a deep rumbling sound, shivered like so many bombshells into a thousand pieces, and telling us what would be our fate if we made a single misstep. We followed our Indian in single file, keeping close together, that the stones set free by those in the rear might not dash those below from their feet; feeling our way with the greatest caution, clinging with our hands to snow, sand, rock, tufts of grass, or any thing that would hold for a moment; now leaping over a chasm, now letting ourselves down from rock to rock; at times paralyzed with fear, and always with death staring us in the face; thus we scrambled for two hours and a half, till we reached the bottom of the crater.

Here we found a deeply-furrowed plain, strewn with ragged rocks, and containing a few patches of vegetation, with half a dozen species of flowers. In the centre is an irregular heap of stones, two hundred and sixty feet high by eight hundred in diameter. This is the cone of eruption—its sides and summit covered with an imposing group of vents, seventy in number, all lined with sulphur and exhaling steam, black smoke, and sulphurous gas. The temperature of the vapor just within the fumarole is 184°, water boiling beside it at 189°. The central vent, or chimney, gives forth a sound like the violent bubbling of boiling water. As we sat on this fiery mount, surrounded by a circular rampart of rocks, and looked up at the immense towers of dark dolerite which ran up almost vertically to the height of twenty-five hundred feet above us, musing over the tremendous force which fashioned this awful amphitheatre—spacious enough for all the gods of Tartarus to hold high carnival—the clouds which hung in the thin air around the crest of the crater pealed forth thunder after thunder, which, reverberating from precipice to precipice, were answered by the crash of rocks let loose by the storm, till the whole mountain seemed to tremble like a leaf. Such acoustics, mingled with the flash of lightning and the smell of brimstone, made us believe that we had fairly got into the realm of Pluto. It is the spot where Dante's *Inferno* ought to be read.

Finishing our observations, and warming our dinner over the steaming crevices, we prepared to ascend. The escape from this horrid hole was more perilous than the entrance, and on reaching the top we sang, with grateful hearts, to the tune of "Old Hundred,"

> "Praise God, from whom all blessings flow."

We doubt whether that famous tune and glorious doxology were ever sung so near to heaven.

The second line,

> "Praise him all creatures here below,"

had a strange meaning fifteen thousand feet high.

There have been five eruptions of Pichincha since the Conquest. The last was in 1660; that of 1566 covered

Quito three feet deep with ashes and stones, while boiling water and bitumen descended in torrents. In 1867 the column of smoke did not rise above the crest of the crater, but the volcano has lately been showing signs of activity, such as it has not exhibited since the last grand eruption two centuries ago. On the 19th of March, 1868, detonations were audible at Quito, and three days after there were more thunderings, with a great column of vapor visible from Chillo, twelve miles to the east. These phenomena were accompanied by an unusual fall of rain. Since the great earthquake of August 16th, Pichincha has continued to send forth dense columns of black smoke, and so much fine sand that it is not possible to reach the crater. The solid products of Pichincha since the Conquest have been chiefly pumice, coarse-grained and granular trachyte, and reddish porphyroid trachyte. The roads leading to Quito cut through hills of pumice-dust. On the plain of Iñaquito and in the valley of Esmeraldas are vast erratic blocks of trachyte, some containing twenty-five cubic yards, having sharp angles, and in some cases a polished, unstriated surface. M. Wisse does not consider them to have been thrown out of Pichincha, as La Condamine and others have judged. It is true, as he says, that they could not have come out of the present cone at a less angle than 45°, for they would have hit the sides of the high rocky rampart and rolled back again; and at a higher angle they would not have reached their present location. But we see no reason why they could not be the upper portion of the solid trachyte cone blown into the air at the great eruption which cleared out this enormous crater. There is a *rumipamba*, or "field of stones," around each of the Quitonian volcanoes.

Leaving Pichincha, we travel northward along the battlemented Andes, passing by the conical mountains of

Yana-urcu and Cotocachí. Yana-urcu, or "black mountain," is a mass of calcined rocks. Cotocachí (from *cota?* and *cachí*, salt) is always snow-clad. On its side is Cuy-cocha, one of the highest lakes in the world (10,200 feet), and formed by the subsidence of a part of the volcano.

CHAPTER IX.

The Volcanoes of Ecuador.—Eastern Cordillera.—Imbabura.—Cayambi.—Antisana.—Cotopaxi.—Llanganati.—Tunguragua.—Altar.—Sangai.

NEAR the once busy city of Otovalo, utterly destroyed in the late earthquake, the two Cordilleras join, and, turning to the right, we go down the eastern range. The first in order is Imbabura,* which poured forth a large quantity of mud, with thousands of fishes, seven years before the similar eruption of Caraguairazo. At its feet is the beautiful lake of San Pablo, five miles in circumference, and very deep. It contains the little black fish (*Pimelodes cyclopum*) already referred to as the only species in the valley, and the same that was cast out by Imbabura and Caraguairazo. Next comes the square-topped Cayambi—the loftiest mountain in this Cordillera, being nineteen thousand five hundred feet. It stands exactly on the equator, a colossal monument placed by the hand of Nature to mark the grand division of the globe. It is the only snowy spot, says Humboldt, which is crossed by the equator. Beautiful is the view of Cayambi from Quito, as its enormous mass of snow and ice glows with crimson splendor in the farewell rays of the setting sun. No painter's brush could do justice to the prismatic tints which hover around the higher peaks. But this flood of glory is soon followed by the pure whiteness of death. "Like a gigantic ghost shrouded in sepulchral sheets, the mountain now hovers in the background of the landscape, towering ghastly through the twilight until darkness closes upon the scene."

* From *imba* (fish), and *bura*, to produce. Its name can not be older than 1691, unless the mountain made similar eruptions before. It has frequently ejected water.

Ten miles farther south is the bare-headed Guamani range, over which passes the road to the wild Napo country.* The view from the crest is magnificent; but, like every grand panorama, eludes description. As we look eastward over the beginnings of the mighty forest which stretches unbroken to the Atlantic, the vast ridges, trending north and south, and decreasing in height as they increase in distance, seem like the waves of a great ocean rolling toward the mountains.

Near by stands Antisana in his snowy robe. This volcano ranks next to Chimborazo in dignity. It has a double dome, and an elevation of 19,000 feet. Snow of Dian purity covers it for over 3000 feet; but, judging from the enormous streams of lava on its sides, it must have been a fierce volcano in ages past. The lava streams are worthy of the great mountain from which they flowed. One of them (called "Volcan d'Ansango") is ten miles long and five hundred feet deep, with an average slope of 15°. It is a magnificent sight, as seen from the surrounding paramo —a stream of dark, ragged rocks coming down out of the clouds and snows which cover the summit. The representative products of Antisana are a black, cellular, vitreous trachyte, a fine-grained, tough porphyroid trachyte, and a coarse reddish porphyroid trachyte. An eruption, as late as 1590, is recorded in *Johnston's Phys. Atlas.* Humboldt saw smoke issuing from several openings in March, 1802.

We ascended this volcano to the height of sixteen thousand feet. On its side is the celebrated hacienda of Antisana, which, more than sixty years ago, sheltered the great Humboldt from the sleet and rain and blast of this lofty region. It was a welcome refuge to us, for we had well nigh perished with cold on the dreary paramo. It is one of

* The culminating point of Guamani is *Sara-urcu*, a volcano which threw out a vast quantity of ashes in 1843 and 1856.

the highest human habitations in the world, being thirteen thousand three hundred feet above the sea, or a thousand feet higher than the Peak of Teneriffe.* The mean temperature is the same as that of Quebec, so that thirteen thousand feet in elevation at the equator is equal to 47° in latitude.† Here is an extensive corral, inclosing thousands of cattle, owned by a rheumatic old gentleman, Señor Valdevieso, who supplies the beef-market of Quito.‡ A desire for beef has alone brought man and his beast to this chilly altitude. It is difficult to get a quart of milk, and impossible to find a pound of butter at this hacienda. The predominant colors of the cattle are red and black. They feed on the wild paramo grass, and the beef is not only remarkably cheap, but superior in quality. The lasso is used in catching the animals, but not so skillfully as by the Gauchos of Rio Plata. It is a singular fact that cattle have followed men over the whole earth, from the coast of Africa to the highlands of Antisana. The same species is attacked by crocodiles and condors.

The atmospheric pressure is here so small that they frequently bleed at the nose and mouth when hunted. We have already given our experience in ascending high altitudes. We may add that while the pulse of Boussingault beat 106 pulsations at the height of 18,600 feet on Chimborazo, ours was 87 at 16,000 feet on Antisana. De Saussure says that a draught of liquor which would inebriate

* M. d'Abbadie professes to have visited a village in Abyssinia (Arquiage) which is 12,450 feet above the sea. Potosi stands 13,500 feet.

† This agrees with Humboldt's calculation that a difference of elevation of 278 feet produces the same effect on the annual temperature as a change of one degree of latitude. According to the experiments of Captain Pullen, the minimum temperature of the great depths of the ocean is 35°, and it commences soon after passing 12,000 feet.

‡ The great dépôts of cattle in Ecuador are at the two extremes of elevation, the lowlands of St. Elena and the highlands of Antisana. On the slope of Cayambi is another extensive cattle estate.

in the lowlands no longer has that effect on Mont Blanc. This appears to be true on the Andes; indeed, there is very little drunkenness in Quito. So the higher we perch our inebriate asylums, the better for the patients.

Near the hacienda is a little lake called Mica, on which we found a species of grebe, with wings so short it could not fly. Its legs, also, seem fitted only for paddling, and it goes ashore only to lay its eggs. It peeps like a gosling. Associated with them were penguins (in appearance); they were so shy we could not secure one. The query is, How came they there? Was this a centre of creation, or were the fowls upheaved with the Andes? They could not have flown or walked to this lofty lake, and there are no water-courses leading to it; it is surrounded with a dry, rolling waste, where only the condor lives. We turn to Darwin for an answer.*

The ragged Sincholagua† and romantic Rumiñagui follow Antisana, and then we find ourselves looking up at the most beautiful and most terrible of volcanoes. This is the far-famed Cotopaxi, or more properly Cutu-pacsi, meaning "a brilliant mass." Humboldt calls it the most regular and most picturesque of volcanic cones. It looks like a huge truncated cone rising out of the Valley of Quito, its sides deeply furrowed by the rivers of mud and water which have so often flowed out. The cone itself is about

* The grebe is considered by Messrs. Cassin and Lawrence to be the *Podiceps occipitalis*, Lisson (*P. calipareus et Chilensis* of Garnot), which occurs in large flocks on the coast of Chile and in the Straits of Magellan. It is quite different from the *P. micropterus* of Lake Titicaca. At Morococha, Peru, 15,600 feet above the sea, Herndon found snipes and ducks.

† In Brigham's *Notes on the Volcanic Phenomena of the Hawaiian Islands*, this volcano is put down as active, but there has been no eruption in the memory of man. Its lithology is represented in our collection by porous, gray, granular trachyte, fine-grained, compact trachyte, and dark porphyroid trachyte. The derivation of Sincholagua is unknown. Rumiñagui means the face of a rock. Cotopaxi, Sincholagua, and Rumiñagui, and Cotopaxi, Pichincha, and Guamani, form equilateral triangles.

six thousand feet high. The east side is covered with snow, but the west is nearly bare, owing to the trade winds, which, sweeping across the continent, carry the ashes westward. Cotopaxi is the loftiest of active volcanoes, though its grand eruptions are a century apart, according to the general rule that the higher a volcano the less frequent its eruptions, but all the more terrible when they do occur. Imagine Vesuvius on the summit of Mont Blanc, and you have the altitude of Cotopaxi.

The top just reaches the middle point of density in the atmosphere, for at the height of three miles and a half the air below will balance that above. The crater has never been seen by man; the steepness of the sides and the depth of the ashes covering them render it inaccessible. The valiant Col. Hall tried it with scaling ladders, only to fail. The telescope reveals a parapet of scoria on the brim, as on Teneriffe. Humboldt's sketch of the volcano, so universally copied, is overdrawn. It makes the slope about 50°, while in truth it is nearer 30°. The apical angle is 122° 30′.*

Cotopaxi is slumbering now; or, as Mr. Coan says of Hilo, it is "in a state of solemn and thoughtful suspense." The only signs of life are the deep rumbling thunders and a cloud of smoke lazily issuing from the crater.† Sometimes at night the smoke looks like a pillar of fire, and fine ashes and sand often fall around the base, to the great annoyance of the farmers. On the south side is a huge rock of porphyry, called the Inca's Head. Tradition has it that this was the original summit of the volcano, torn off and

* MM. Zurcher and Margalli make the slope 55° ! and Guzman, 69° 30′ ! ! The slope of Mauna Loa is 6° 30′; of Etna, 9°; of Teneriffe, 12° 30′; of Vesuvius, 35°. While cinder-cones may have an angle of 40°, lava-cones seldom exceed 10°.

† Even this has now (August, 1869) ceased, save an occasional grumble, and the Tacungans are trembling with fear of another eruption.

hurled down by an eruption on the very day Atahuallpa was murdered by Pizarro. The last great eruption occurred in 1803, though so late as 1855 it tossed out stones, water, and sand. Heaps of ruins, piled up during the lapse of ages, are scattered for miles around the mountain, among them great boulders twenty feet square. In one place (Quinchevar) the accumulation is 600 feet deep. Between Cotopaxi and Sincholagua are numerous conical hills covering the paramo, reminding one of the mud volcanoes of Jorullo.

Pumice and trachyte are the most common rocks around this mountain, and these are augitic or porphyroid. Obsidian also occurs, though not on the immediate flank, but farther down near Chillo. In plowing, thousands of pieces as large as "flints" are turned up. The natives know nothing about their origin or use; the large specimens were anciently polished and used for mirrors. But Cotopaxi is the great pumice-producing volcano. The new road up the valley cuts through a lofty hill formed by the successive eruptions; the section, presenting alternate layers of mud, ashes, and pumice, is a written history of the volcano.* The cone itself is evidently composed of similar beds superimposed, and holding fragments of porphyry and trachyte. What is Vesuvius, four thousand feet high, to Cotopaxi, belching forth fire from a crater fifteen thousand feet higher, and shooting its contents three thousand feet

* Compare the following sections:

COTOPAXI (near Tiupullo).		VESUVIUS (at Pompeii).	
Soil	1 ft. 0 in.	Soil	3 ft. 0 in.
Fine yellow pumice	5 " 0 "	Brown incoherent tuff	1 " 6 "
Compact black ashes, with seams of pumice	10 " 0 "	Small scoriæ and white lapilli	0 " 3 "
Fine yellow pumice	1 " 6 "	Brown earthy tuff	4 " 9 "
Compact black ashes	12 " 0 "	Whitish lapilli	0 " 1 "
Fine yellow pumice	2 " 0 "	Gray solid tuff	0 " 3 "
Compact black ashes, with seams of pumice.		Pumice and white lapilli	0 " 3 "

above its snow-bound summit, with a voice of thunder heard six hundred miles!

Leaving this terrible "safety-valve" to the imprisoned fires under our feet, we travel along the wooded flanks and savage valleys of the Llanganati Mountains, whose lofty blue ridge is here and there pointed with snow.* It is universally believed that the Incas buried an immense quantity of gold in an artificial lake on the sides of this mountain during the Spanish invasion, and many an adventurous expedition has been made for it. The inhabitants will tell you of one Valverde, a Spaniard, who, from being very poor, had suddenly become very rich, which was attributed to his having married an Indian girl whose father showed him where the treasure was hidden, and accompanied him on various occasions to bring away portions of it; and that Valverde returned to Spain, and on his death-bed bequeathed the secret of his riches to the king. But since Padre Longo suddenly disappeared while leading an expedition, the timid Ecuadorians have been content with their poverty.†

And now we have reached the perfect cone of Tunguragua, the rival of Cotopaxi in symmetry and beauty.‡ It stands 16,500 feet above the Pacific, its upper part covered with a splendid robe of snow, while the sugar-cane grows in the romantic town of Baños, 10,000 feet below the summit. A cataract, 1500 feet high, comes down at three bounds from the edge of the snow to the warm valley beneath; and at Baños a hot ferruginous spring and a stream

* Immediately south of Cotopaxi, the Cordillera consists of paramos sown with lakes and morasses, and is rarely covered with snow. Llanganati is probably from *llánga*, to touch: they touch the sources of nearly all the Ecuadorian rivers.

† The story is doubtless due to the fact that the eastern streams, which issue from the foot of this cordillera, are auriferous.

‡ From Tungúri, the ankle-joint, alluding to its apical angle. It is a little steeper than Cotopaxi, having a slope of 38°.

of ice-water flow out of the volcano side by side. Here, too, the fierce youth of the Pastassa, born on the pumice slopes of Cotopaxi, dashes through a deep tortuous chasm and down a precipice in hot haste, as if conscious of the long distance before it ere it reaches the Amazon and the ocean. Tunguragua was once a formidable mountain, for we discovered a great stream of lava reaching from the clouds around the summit to the orange-groves in the valley, and blocking up the rivers which tumble over it in beautiful cascades. It has been silent since 1780; but it can afford to rest, for then its activity lasted seven years.*

Close by rises beautiful Altar, a thousand feet higher. The Indians call it Capac-urcu, or the "Chief." They say it once overtopped Chimborazo; but, after a violent eruption, which continued eight years, the walls fell in. Its craggy crest is still more Alpine than Caraguairazo; eight snowy peaks shoot up like needles into the sky, and surround an altar to whose elevated purity no mortal offering will ever attain. The trachyte which once formed the summit of this mountain is now spread in fragments over the plain of Riobamba.

Leaving this broken-down volcano, but still the most picturesque in the Andes, we travel over the rough and rugged range of Cubillin, till our attention is arrested by terrific explosions like a naval broadside, and a column of smoke that seems to come from the furnace of the Cyclops. It is Sangai, the most active volcano on the globe. From its unapproachable crater, three miles high, it sends forth a constant stream of fire, water, mud, and ashes.†

* Spruce asserts that he saw smoke issuing from the western edge in 1857; and Dr. Terry says that in 1832 smoke ascended almost always from the summit. Dr. Taylor, of Riobamba, informs the writer that smoke is now almost constantly visible. The characteristic rock is a black vitreous trachyte resembling pitchstone, but anhydrous.

† La Condamine (1742) adds "sulphur and bitumen."

No intermission has been noticed since the Spaniards first saw it three hundred years ago. Stromboli is the only volcano that will compare with it. Its ashes are almost always falling on the city of Guayaquil, one hundred miles distant, and its explosions, generally occurring every hour or two, are sometimes heard in that city. Wisse, in 1849, counted 267 explosions in one hour.

We have now completed the series. What an array of snow-clad peaks wall in the narrow Valley of Quito—Nature's Gothic spires to this her glorious temple! If ever there was a time when all these volcanoes were active in concert, this secluded vale must have witnessed the most splendid pyrotechnics conceivable. Imagine fifty mountains as high as Etna, three of them with smoking craters, standing along the road between New York and Washington, and you will have some idea of the ride down this gigantic colonnade from Quito to Riobamba. If, as Ruskin says, the elements of beauty are in proportion to the increase of mountainous character, Ecuador is artistically beautiful to a high degree.

Here, amid these Plutonic peaks, are the energies of volcanic action best studied. The constancy of the volcanic fires is a striking fact. First we have the deluges of submarine lavas, which were poured out long before the Andes lifted their heads above the waters; then alternate porphyritic strata, feldspathic streams, and gypseous exhalations; then, at a later day, floods of basaltic lava; next the old tertiary eruptions; and, lastly, the vast accumulations of boulders, gravel, ashes, pumice, and mud of the present day, spread over the Valley of Quito and the west slope of the Cordilleras to an unknown depth beneath the sea. The incessant eruptions of Sangai, and the frequent earthquakes, show that the subterranean energy which heaved the Andes is not yet expended.

CHAPTER X.

The Valley of Quito.—Riobamba.—A Bed of "Fossil Giants."—Chillo Hacienda.—Otovalo and Ibarra.—The Great Earthquake of 1868.

THE Valley of Quito has about the same size and shape as the basin of Salt Lake, but it is five thousand feet higher.* The two cordilleras inclosing it are tied by the mountain-knots of Assuay and Chisinchi, so that the valley is subdivided into three basins, those of Cuenca, Ambato, and Quito proper, which increase in beauty and altitude as we travel north. There are several subordinate transversal dikes and some longitudinal ridges, but all the basins lie parallel to the axes of the cordilleras—a characteristic feature of the Andes. The deep valleys on the outside flanks are evidently valleys of erosion, but the basins between the cordilleras were created with them.

The first is fifty miles long. It contains the cities of Loja and Cuenca,† the former distinguished for its cinchona forests, the latter for Inca graves and mines of precious metals. The middle basin (130 miles in length) is covered with vast quantities of volcanic débris, the outpourings of Cotopaxi, Tunguragua, and Altar, on one side, and of Chimborazo and Caraguairazo on the other. Nothing relieves

* Compare the table-lands in the Old World:

Thibet	11,500 feet.
South Africa	6,000 "
Mysore (India)	2,880 "
Spain	2,240 "
Bavaria	1,770 "

† The altitude of Loja is 6768 feet; of Cuenca, 8640 feet.

the barrenness of the landscape but hedges of century plant, cactus, and wild heliotrope, which border the roads. Whirlwinds of sand are often seen moving over the plain. The mean temperature is 61°.5. Here exist, we can not say thrive, the cities of Riobamba, Ambato, and Tacunga, already noticed. Riobamba,* properly Rayobamba, the plain of lightning, was founded at the beginning of this century, or shortly after the destruction of the old city. Excepting the ecclesiastical buildings, the houses are of one story, built of stone plastered with mud, sometimes of adobe or bamboo, and the windows are grated like those of a prison. As in all Spanish-American towns, the main church fronts the great Plaza where the weekly fairs are held. Save on fair-day, the city is lifeless. Nothing is exported to the coast except a few eggs and fowls, lard and potatoes. Such is the power of habit, an Indian will take a hen to Bodegas and sell it for four reals (50 cents) when he could get three for it in Riobamba, and six on the road. Another instance of this dogged adherence to custom was related to us by Dr. Taylor: The Indians were accustomed to bring the curate of a certain village a bundle of alfalfa every day. A new curate, having no use for so much, ordered them not to bring any more. He was besieged by five hundred of his wild parishioners, and had he not been a powerful man, they would have killed him. They told him they were accustomed to bring the curate that much of alfalfa, and should continue.

Old Riobamba (Cajabamba) is situated twelve miles to the west. This has been the scene of some of the most terrible paroxysms that ever shook the Andes. In 1797 a part of Mount Cicalfa was thrown down, crushing the city at its foot; hills arose where valleys existed; rivers disap-

* According to Villavicencio, *Rio* (or *Ric*) is Quichua for road; *bamba* is plain.

peared, and others took their places; and the very site of the city was rent asunder. The surviving inhabitants could not tell where their houses had stood, and property was so mingled that litigation followed the earthquake. Judging from the numerous sculptured columns lying broken and prostrate throughout the valley, the city must have had a magnificence now unknown in Ecuador. Around a coat of arms (evidently Spanish) we read these words: *Malo mori quam fedari*, "I would rather die than be disgraced." In the spring of 1868 another convulsion caused a lake to disappear and a mountain to take its place.

Near Punín, seven miles southwest of Riobamba, we discovered in a deep ravine numerous fossil bones, belonging chiefly to the mastodon, and extinct species of the horse, deer, and llama. They were imbedded in the middle of an unstratified cliff, four hundred feet high, of very compact silt or trachytic clay, free from stones, and resting on a hard quartzoze sandstone. In the bed of the stream which runs through the ravine (charged with nitrate of soda) are some igneous rocks. The bones were drifted to this spot and deposited (many of them in a broken state) in horizontal layers along with recent shells. We have, then, this remarkable fact, that this high valley was tenanted by elephantine quadrupeds, all of which passed away before the arrival of the human species, and yet while the land, and probably the sea also, were peopled with their present molluscan inhabitants. This confirms the statement of Mr. Lyell, that the longevity of mammalian species is much inferior to that of the testacea. It is interesting to speculate on the probable climate and the character of the vegetation in this high valley when these extinct mammifers lived. The great pachyderm would have no difficulty in thriving at the present day at Quito, on the score of temperature or altitude. The mammoth once flourished in Siberia; and Gibbon met an elephant on the high table-lands of Bolivia that had walked over the Cordillera at the pass of Antarangua, sixteen thousand feet above the sea. Darwin thinks that the climate of the Cordilleras has changed since the pleistocene period. "It is a marvelous fact in the history of mammalia (says this naturalist) that in South America a native horse should have lived and disappeared, to be succeeded in after ages by the countless herds descended from the few introduced with the Spanish colonists."

The high ridge of Chisinchi, stretching across the great plateau from Cotopaxi to Iliniza, separates the ever-green Valley of Quito from the arid and melancholy valleys of Cuenca and Ambato. It rolls out like a rich carpet of emerald verdure between the towering mountains of Pichincha and Antisana, Cotacachi and Cayambi. This was the centre of the most ancient native civilization after that of Titicaca. Here, while the darkness of the Middle Ages was settling over Europe, dwelt the Quitus, whose origin is lost in the mists of fable. Then, while Peter the Hermit was leading his fanatic host against the Saracens, the Cara nation waged a more successful crusade, and supplanted the Quitus. Here, too, in the bloody days of Pizarro, reigned, and was buried, the last of the Incas, ill-fated Atahuallpa. To him, indeed, it was a more delightful spot than the vale of Vilcamayu—the paradise of Peru.

The Puengasi Hills, running through the valley from north to south, partially divide the capital and its vicinity from the charming Valley of Chillo, spread out at the foot of Antisana. Here is the venerable hacienda of Chillo, where Humboldt and Bonpland resided for some time. It is owned by the Aguirres, who are grand-nephews of Don Carlos Montufar, the companion of the famous travelers. The hacienda contains two valuable paintings—an original

"Crucifixion" by Titian, and a portrait of the great German from life, as he appeared in 1803. This latter relic interested us exceedingly, and, through the kindness of Sr.

Humboldt in 1802.

Aguirre, we were allowed to photograph it. It represents Humboldt in his prime, a traveler on the Andes, dressed after the court-fashion of Berlin; very different from the usual portrait—an old man in his library, his head, thinly covered with gray hair, resting on his bosom.

Thirty miles north of Quito, near the volcanic Imbabura, is the ruined city of Otovalo, a thousand feet lower than the capital. It was well built, and contained 7000 inhabitants. Quichua was the prevailing language. Its chief trade was in saddles, ponchos, straw hats, and fruit. Here was the cotton factory, or *quinta*, of Sr. Pareja. Three miles from Otovalo was the enterprising Indian village of Cotocachí, at the mountain of the same name. It was noted for its hand-loom products. A heap of ruins now marks the locality. It is a doomed spot, suffering more than any other town in 1859.

Four miles northwest of Otovalo was the city of Ibarra, picturesquely seated on a plain 2000 feet lower than Quito, and surrounded with orchards and gardens. It numbered nearly 10,000 souls. It was not a commercial place, but the residence of landed proprietors. The neighborhood produced cotton, sugar, and fruit. A league distant was Carranqui, the birthplace of Atahuallpa. And, finally, the great valley fitly terminates in the plain of Atuntaqui,* where the decisive battle was fought which ushered in the reign of the Incas.

This northern province of Imbabura was the focus of the late terrible earthquake. At half past one on Sunday morning, August 16, 1868, with scarcely a premonitory sign (save a slight trembling at 3 P.M. the previous day), there was an upheaving of the ground, and then one tremendous shock and rocking of the earth, lasting one minute. In that brief moment the rich and flourishing province became a wilderness, and "Misericordia!" went up, like the sound of many waters, from ten villages and cities. Otovalo, Ibarra,

* Atuntaqui received its name from the big drum which was kept here in the days of Huayna-Capac, to give the war-signal.

Cotocachí, and Atantaqui are heaps of ruins. At Otovalo 6000 perished. After the first shock, not a wall a yard high remained. Houses, in some instances, seemed to have been cut from their foundation, and thrown ten feet distant.

Ibarra.

The large stone fountain in the Plaza was thrown many yards. The cotton factory, which was built on the edge of a ravine, was by one stroke reduced to fragments. Such was the force of the concussion, the looms smashed each other, the carding-machines were thrown on their sides, and the roof, with part of the machinery, was found in the river below. The proprietor was killed. Throughout this whole region roads were broken up, and vast chasms created crossing the country in all directions. One is 2000 yards long, 500 yards broad, and 80 yards deep. Large fissures were opened on the sides of Cotocachí and Imbabura, from which issued immense torrents of water, mud, and bituminous substances, carrying away and drowning hundreds of cattle. A caravan of mules going to Chillo with cotton bales was found four days after grazing on a narrow strip of land, on each side of which was a fearful chasm, while the muleteers were killed.

At Quito comparatively little damage was done. Fifteen lives were lost, and the churches, convents, and many private houses are in a state of dilapidation. Domes and arches, which are much used because of the scarcity of timber, were first to fall.

In the fierceness of the shock, and the extent of the territory shaken, the earthquake of August, 1868, is without a parallel in the New World. The destruction of life (50,000 officially reported in Ecuador alone) has not been equaled in any other earthquake during this century. The tremor was felt over four republics, and from the Andes to the Sandwich Islands. The water-wave was felt on the coast of New Zealand sixteen hours after it had set a United States gunboat on the sand-hills of Arica. In some respects it is surpassed only by the Lisbon earthquake, which reached from Sweden to the West Indies, and from Barbary to Scotland. The loss of property seems to have been greatest in Peru, and the loss of life greatest in Ecuador. The commotion seemed to be most violent along the Western Cordillera, though it was felt even on the Napo.

There are few places where the crust of our planet is

long at rest. Brazil, Egypt, Russia, and Greenland are comparatively free from earthquakes. But had we delicate instruments scattered throughout the world, upheaval and subsidence would doubtless be detected in every part of the so-called *terra firma*. The sea, and not the land, is the true image of stability.

> "Time writes no wrinkle on thy azure brow:
> Such as creation's dawn beheld, thou rollest now."

Earthquakes have occurred in every period of geological history, and are independent of latitude. The first well-known earthquake came in the year 63, and shattered Pompeii and Herculaneum sixteen years before they were overwhelmed by the first recorded eruption of Vesuvius. The most celebrated earthquake, and perhaps the most terrible manifestation of force during the human period, was in 1755. The shock, which seemed to originate in the bed of the Atlantic, pervaded one twelfth of the earth's surface. Unhappy Lisbon stood in its path.

An earthquake is a vertical vibration, having an undulatory progression. An example of the simple bounding movement occurred in 1797, when the city of Riobamba, in the Quito Valley, was buried under part of a mountain shaken down by the violent concussion, and men were tossed several hundred feet. We saw one massive structure which had nearly turned a somersault. The ordinary vibrations seldom exceed two feet in height. The wave-movement has a rate of from twenty to thirty miles a minute, depending on the elasticity of the rock and the elevations on the surface. When two undulations cross each other, a rotatory or twisting motion is produced. The waves are generally transmitted along the lines of primary mountain chains, which are doubtless seated on a fracture. The Lisbon waves moved from southwest to northeast, or parallel to the mountain system of the Old World; those of the United States, in 1843, ran parallel to the volcanic chain in Mexico. In South America they roll along the Andes. That of 1797 left its tracks along a westerly line from Tunguragua through Peliléo and Guáno. It is a little singular, that while the late trembling at Quito seemed to come from the north, the great shock in Peru preceded that in Ecuador by three days. Though the origin of earthquakes is deep-seated, the oscillation is mostly superficial, as deep mines are little disturbed. The most damage is done where the sedimentary plains abut against the hard, upturned strata of the mountains. The shock is usually brief. That of Caracas lasted fifty seconds, that of Lisbon six minutes; but Humboldt witnessed one in South America which continued a quarter of an hour.

Several hypotheses have been advanced to account for earthquakes. Rogers ascribes them to billowy pulsations in the molten matter upon which the flexible crust of the earth floats. Mallet thinks they may be viewed as an uncompleted effort to establish a volcano. Dana holds that they are occasioned by the folding up of the rocks in the slow process of cooling and consequent contraction of the earth's crust. In this process there would occur enormous fractures to relieve the tension; tilted strata would slip, and caverns give way. All this no doubt takes place; but the sudden, paroxysmal heavings incline us to refer the cause to the same eruptive impulse which makes Vesuvius and Cotopaxi discharge pent-up subterranean vapor and gas. The most destructive earthquakes occur when the overlying rocks do not break and give vent to the imprisoned gas. There is some connection between volcanoes and earthquakes; the former are, to a certain extent, "safety-valves." The column of smoke from the volcano of Pasto suddenly disappeared just before the great earthquake at Riobamba. In the spring of 1868 Pichincha and Cotopaxi showed signs of increasing activity, but in the summer became quiet again. Cotocachí and Sangai, 200 miles apart, were awaked simultaneously; the former, silent for centuries, sent forth dense masses of earth and volcanic matter to a distance of many miles, covering thousands of acres; the latter thundered every half hour instead of hourly, as before. Still, the greatest earthquakes do not occur in the vicinity of active volcanoes. Lisbon and Lima (where, on an average, forty-five shocks occur annually, and two fearful ones in a century) are far distant from any volcanic vent; likewise Northern India, South Africa, Scotland, and the United States.

An earthquake is beyond the reach of calculation. Professor Perrey, of Dijon, France, is endeavoring to prove that there is a periodicity in earthquakes, synchronous with that in the tides of the ocean, the greatest number occurring at the time of new and full moon.* If this theory be sustained, we must admit the existence of a vast subterranean sea of lava. But all this is problematical. Earthquakes appear independently of the geology of a country, though the rate of undulation is modified by the mineral structure. Earthquake waves seem to move more rapidly through the comparatively undisturbed beds of the Mississippi Valley than through the contorted strata of Europe. Meteorology is unable to indicate a coming earthquake, for there is no sure prophecy in sultry weather, sirocco wind,

* Professor Quinby, of the University of Rochester, has, at our request, calculated the position of the moon at the late earthquake: "August 16th, 1868, 1 A.M., the moon was on meridian 137° 21′ east of that of Quito, or 42° 39′ past the lower meridian of Quito, assuming the longitude of Quito west of Greenwich to be 79°, which it is very nearly. This is but little after the vertex of the tidal wave should have passed the meridian of Quito, on the supposition that the interior of the earth is a liquid mass. The age of the moon at that time was 27.36 days, *i. e.*, it was only about two days before new moon." At the time of the earthquake, 8 A.M., March 22, 1859, the moon was on meridian 25° 48′ east of that of Quito, and was 17.6 days old. Shocks have since occurred, March 20th at 3 A.M., and April 10th at 8 A.M., 1869.

and leaden sky. The Lisbon shock came without a warning. Sudden changes of the weather, however, often occur after an earthquake. Since the great convulsion of 1797 the climate of the Valley of Quito is said to be much colder. A heavy rain often follows a violent earthquake in Peru.

No amount of familiarity with earthquakes enables one to laugh during the shock, or even at the subterranean thunders which sound like the clanking of chains in the realm of Pluto. All animated nature is terror-stricken. The horse trembles in his stall; the cow moans a low, melancholy tune; the dog sends forth an unearthly yell; sparrows drop from the trees as if dead; crocodiles leave the trembling bed of the river and run with loud cries into the forest; and man himself becomes bewildered and loses all capacity. When the earth rocks beneath our feet (the motion resembling, in the words of Darwin, "that felt by a person skating over thin ice which bends under the weight of his body"), something besides giddiness is produced. We feel our utter insignificance in the presence of a mysterious power that shakes the Andes like a reed. But more: there is an awful sensation of insecurity. "A moment (says Humboldt) destroys the illusion of a whole life: our deceptive faith in the repose of nature vanishes, and we feel transported, as it were, into a region of unknown destructive forces." A judgment day seems impending, and each moment is an age when one stands on a world convulsed.

CHAPTER XI.

"The Province of the Orient," or the Wild Napo Country.—The Napos, Zaparos, and Jívaros Indians.—Preparations to cross the Continent.

On the eastern slope of the Ecuadorian Andes, between the Marañon and its tributary the Putumayo, lies the Napo country. This almost unknown region has the area of New York and New England together. The government of Quito, by a sonorous decree in 1854, baptized it "La Provincia del Oriente." Peru likewise claims it, but neither republic has done any thing to colonize it. A dense primeval forest, broken only by the rivers, covers the whole territory, and is the home of wild races untouched by civilization.* There is not a road in the whole province. A footpath, open only in the dry season, and barely passable then, connects Quito and the Rio Napo. Congress lately promised to put Canélos in communication with the capital; but the largest villages in this vast and fertile region—Archidona, Canélos, and Macás—still remain isolated from the outer world.† Ecuador once appointed a functionary under the high-sounding title of "Governor of the Orient," with a salary of $700; but now the Indians are not troubled with any higher official than an alcalde.

* The boundary-line between Ecuador and Peru is about as indefinite as the eastern limit of Bolivia, Brazilians claiming "as far west as the cattle of the empire roam."

† Quito might be made more accessible on the Atlantic than on the Pacific side. But Ecuadorians dote on Guayaquil, and refuse to connect themselves directly with the great nations of the East. We believe there is a glorious future for Quito, when it will once more become a city of palaces. But it will not come until a road through the wilderness and a steamer on the Napo open a short communication with the wealth of Amazonia and the enterprise of Europe.

The country is very thinly inhabited. The chief tribes are the semi-Christianized Napos (sometimes called Quijos), dwelling on the north bank of the Napo; the peaceful but uncivilized Záparos, living between the Napo and Pastassa, and the warlike Jívaros, spread over the unexplored region between the Pastassa and Santiago.

These oriental tribes would probably be assigned by D'Orbigny to the Antisian branch of the Alpine races of South America. Dwelling amid the darkness of primeval forests, and on the gloomy banks of mountain torrents, they have acquired modifications of character, physical and moral, which distinguish them from the natives of the high and open regions, or the steaming lowlands of the Amazon. In color, however, they do not appear to us to be entitled to the name of "white men;" they approach nearer to the bronze complexion of the Quichuans than the yellow cast of the Brazilians. We see no evidence of that "bleaching process" resulting from a life under the dense canopy of foliage of which the learned French naturalist speaks, neither did we perceive the force of his statement that the color of the South American bears a very decided relation to the humidity of the atmosphere.

The features of the Napo Indians are Quichuan, especially the low forehead, squarely-built face, and dull expression; but in stature they exceed the mountaineers. From a skull in our possession we take the following measurements, adding for comparison the dimensions of an ancient Peruvian cranium in Dr. Morton's collection:

	Napo.	Peruvian.
Longitudinal diameter	6½ in.	6.1 in.
Parietal "	5⅝ "	6. "
Frontal "	4 "	4.7 "
Vertical "	4½ "	5.5 "
Capacity	83$\frac{1}{64}$ cub. in.	83 cub. in.
Facial angle	70°	81°

From this it will be seen that the capacity of this individual Napo is 8 cubic inches greater than the average bulk (75 cubic inches) of the old Peruvians; a trifle less than the average North American (84); 10 cubic inches less than the European (94); and the same as the average Polynesian and native African. He has a rounded head, somewhat prominent vertex, not an excessive protuberance of brain behind—a line through the meatus dividing it into very nearly equal parts; but a narrow front as viewed from above, small vertical diameter, quadrangular orbits, vertical teeth, and low facial angle. These characters place him between the Toltecan and the more barbarous tribes of the New World.

The Napos are nominally subject to the Ecuadorian government, which is represented by three or four petty alcaldes; but the Jesuit missionaries, who have established a bishopric and three curacies, generally control affairs—spiritual, political, and commercial. The Indians of each village annually elect one of their number governor, who serves without salary, and whose only show of authority is a silver-headed cane about four feet long. He is attended by half a dozen "justices," whose duty it is to supply the curate, alcalde, and any traveling *blanco* who may happen to be in town with daily food at a reasonable rate.

The religion of the Napos is a mixture of Paganism and Christianity. In common with all the other orient tribes, they believe in good and evil principles, and in metempsychosis. They swear in the name of the devil. They bury their dead horizontally, in a coffin made of a part of a canoe, with a lid of bamboo. They are very kind to the aged. Monogamy is the rule: the usual age of wedlock is sixteen or seventeen. The parents negotiate the marriage, and the curate's fee is one castellano ($3 50). When a person dies they hold an Irish "wake" over the body, and then take the widow to the river and wash her. They have seven semi-religious feasts in a year. To us they appeared to be nothing more than meaningless drunken frolics. Attired in their best, with head-dresses consisting of a circlet of short, richly-colored feathers from the breast of the toucan, surmounted with the long tail-feathers of the macaw, and with necklaces of beads, seeds, and monkeys' teeth, they keep up a constant monotonous tapping on little drums, and trot around a circle like dogs on a tread-mill, stopping only to drink chicha. This is kept up for three weeks, when they all start off, with wives and children, for the forest to hunt monkeys for meat.

Chicha, the favorite drink of all the Andean Indians, is here brewed from yuca, not from corn and barley as in the Quito Valley. So true is it, as Humboldt remarks, that almost every where man finds means of preparing some kind of beverage from the vegetable kingdom. The Chilotans, Darwin informs us, make chicha from a species of *Bromelia*. In every zone, too, we find nations in a low degree of civilization living almost exclusively upon a single animal or plant. Thus the Laplander has his reindeer, the Esquimaux his seal, the Sandwich Islander his tara-root, the Malay his sago-palm, the Napo Indian his yuca.

Yuca is the staple food in this region. It is more commonly roasted, but is sometimes ground into flour. The manufacture of chicha is primitive, and not a little disgusting. A "bee," usually old women, sit around a wooden trough; each one takes a mouthful of yuca root, and, masticating it, throws it into the trough. The mass is then transferred to large earthen jars containing water, and left to ferment. The liquor is slightly acid, but not intoxicating unless taken in excess. This is done on feast-days, when the poor Indian keeps his stomach so constantly distended for weeks that the abdominal protrusion is not only unsightly, but alarming to a stranger. Chicha-drinking is a part of the worship of these simple aborigines. They seem to think that the more happy they make themselves while paying their devotions to the Creator, the better he is satisfied. The Jesuits have found it impossible to change this method of praise. Here, as among all rude nations, an ancient custom is one half the religion. In eating meat (usually monkey, sea-cow, and peccari), we observed that they did not tear or bite it, but, putting one end of a long piece in the mouth, cut off what they could not get in, as Darwin noticed among the Fuegians. They keep no domestic animals except fowls.

As to dress, they make use of a coarse cotton cloth, called *lienzo*, woven by the more enlightened Indians of Quito, dyeing it a dull brown by means of achote juice. The men wear a strip of this around the loins, and the women a short skirt. On feast-days, or when musquitoes are thick, the men add a little poncho and pantaloons. They do not properly tattoo, but color the skin with achote or anatto. This substance, which serves so many purposes in this part of the world, is the red powder which covers the seeds contained in the prickly bur of the *Bixa orellana*. The pigment is an article of commerce on the Amazon, and is exported to Europe, where it is used for coloring butter, cheese, and varnish. They have no fixed pattern; each paints to suit his fancy. Usually, however, they draw horizontal bands from the mouth to the ears, and across the forehead; we never saw curved lines in which higher savages, like the Tahitians, tattoo.

The Napos have the provoking apathy of all the New World aborigines. As Humboldt observed of another tribe, "their poverty, stoicism, and uncultivated state render them so rich and so free from wants of every kind, that neither money nor other presents will induce them to turn three steps out of their ways." They maintain a passive dignity in their bearing not seen in the proudest pope or emperor. They seldom laugh or smile, even under the inspiration of chicha, and months of intercourse with them did not discover to us the power of song, though Villavicencio says they do sometimes intone fragments of prose in their festival orgies. They manifest little curiosity, and little power of mimicry, in which wild men generally excel the civilized.* The old Spartans were never so laconic. In conversation each says all he has to say in three or four words till his companion speaks, when he replies in the same curt, ejaculatory style. A long sentence, or a number of sentences at one time, we do not remember of hearing from the lips of a Napo Indian.†

The women do most of the work, while their lazy lords drink up the chicha and swing in their hammocks, or possibly do a little hunting.‡ They catch fish with bone hooks, seines, spears, and by poisoning the water with *barbasco*.§ This last method is quite common throughout equatorial America. Mashing the root, they throw it into the quiet coves of the river, when almost immediately the fish rise to the surface, first the little fry and then the larger specimens. The poison seems to stupefy rather than kill,

* All savages appear to possess to an uncommon degree the power of mimicry.—*Darwin.*

† Gibbon observes of his Indian paddlers on the Marmoré: "They talk very little; they silently pull along as though they were sleeping, but their eyes are wandering all the time in every direction."

‡ Some of these feminines, however, have a method of retaliation which happily does not exist farther north. They render their husbands idiotic by giving them an infusion of *floripondio*, and then choose another consort. We saw a sad example of this near Riobamba, and heard of one husband who, after being thus treated, unconsciously served his wife and her new man like a slave. *Floripondio* is the seed of the *Datura sanguinea*, which is allied to the poisonous *stramonium* used by the priests of Apollo at Delphi to produce their frantic ravings.

§ *Jacquinia armillaris*, an evergreen bush. The Indians on the Tapajos use a poisonous liana called *timbó* (*Paullinia pinnata*).

for we observed that some individuals behaved in a most lively manner shortly after they were caught. The Indians drink the water with impunity.

The Napos are not brave; their chief weapons for hunting are spears of chonta wood, and blowpipes (*bodaqueras*) made of a small palm having a pith, which, when removed, leaves a polished bore, or of two separate lengths of wood, each scooped out with patient labor and considerable skill by means of the incisor teeth of a rodent. The whole is smeared with black wax, a mouth-piece fitted to the larger end, and a sight made of bone imbedded in the wax. Through this tube, about ten feet long, they blow slender arrows cut from the leaf-stalks of a palm. These are winged with a tuft of silk-cotton (common cotton would be too heavy), and poisoned with *urarí*, of which we shall speak hereafter. This noiseless gun is universally used on the Upper Amazon.*

The Zaparos in physiognomy somewhat resemble the Chinese, having a middle stature, round face, small eyes set angularly, and a broad, flat nose. Their language is of simple construction, but nasal and guttural. They have no words for numbers above three, but show their fingers; above ten they know nothing. They take to themselves single names, not double. They reckon time by moons and the ripening of certain fruits. Their name for God is Piátzo, but we could not learn that it conveyed any distinct idea. They believe the evil spirit, "Mungia," is a black spectre dwelling in the woods. They think the souls of the good and brave enter beautiful birds and feed on delicious fruits, while cowardly souls become dirty reptiles. Polygamy is common. They bury in the sitting posture,

* It is there called *zarabatana* or *gravatana;* by the Peruvians *pucuna*. It corresponds to the *sumpitan* of Borneo. It is difficult to recognize the use of the blow-gun, but the natives will kill at the distance of 150 feet. One which we brought home sent the slender arrow through the panel of a door.

with the hammock of the deceased wrapped around him. The very old men are buried with the mouth downward. They make use of a narcotic drink called *Ayahuasca*, which produces effects similar to those of opium. The Zaparos are pacific and hospitable, but there is little social life among them; they never cluster into large villages, but inhabit isolated ranchos. Nomadic in their habits, they wander along the banks of the Napo, between the Andes and the Marañon. They manufacture, from the twisted fibre of the chambiri-palm,* most of the twine and hammocks seen in Eastern Ecuador. Their government is patriarchal.

The Jívaros, or "Red Indians" *par excellence*, are the most numerous and the most spirited of the oriental tribes. They are brave and resentful, yet hospitable and industrious. While the Napos and Zaparos live in rude, often temporary huts of split bamboo, the warlike Jívaros erect houses of hard wood with strong doors. Blood relations live together on the communal principle, the women keeping the rear half of the house, which is divided by a partition. Many Jívaros approach the Caucasian type, the beard and lighter skin hinting a percentage of Spanish blood; for this tribe was never conquered by the Incas, nor did it brook Spanish avarice and cruelty, but in one terrible conflict (1599) the intruder was swept out of existence. The wives of the El Dorado adventurers spent the rest of their days in the harems of the Jívaros. These Indians have the singular custom and art of compressing the heads of their notable captives; taking off the skin entire and drying it over a small mould, they have a hideous mummy which preserves all the features of the original face, but on a re-

* This thorny palm is called *tucum* in Brazil. The fibres of the budding top are used. A woman will twist a hundred yards of twine a day, and make a living by selling hammocks for twenty-five cents a piece.

duced scale.* They also braid the long black hair of their foes into girdles, which they wear as mementoes of their prowess. They use chonta-lances with triangular points, notched and poisoned, and shields of wood or hide. They have a telegraphic system which enables them to concentrate their forces quickly in time of war; large drums are placed on the tops of the hills, and a certain number of strokes, repeated along the line, rapidly convey intelligence to the most distant habitation.

An odd custom prevails among these wild Indians when an addition is made to the family circle. The woman goes into the woods alone, and on her return washes herself and new-born babe in the river; then the husband immediately takes to his bed for eight days, during which time the wife serves him on the choicest dainties she can procure.† They have also the unique practice of exchanging wives. The Jívaro speech is sonorous and energetic. They do not use salt; so that they distinguish the Napo tribes as the "Indians who eat salt." The chief articles manufactured by them are cotton goods and blowpipes. They trade mostly at Canélos and Macás, generally purchasing iron implements, such as hatchets and knives.

Canélos consists of about seventy families of Quichua-speaking Indians, and lies on the south bank of the Bobonaza. A trail connects it with Baños, at the foot of Tunguragua. Canélos was founded in 1536, and derives its name from its situation in the Canéla, or American cinnamon forest. The bark of the tree has the flavor of the

* Bates (ii., 132) speaks of a similar custom among the ancient Mundurucus: "They used to sever the head with knives made of broad bamboo, and then, after taking out the brain and fleshy parts, soak it in bitter vegetable oils, and expose it several days over the smoke of a fire, or in the sun."

† A like custom existed among some Brazilian and Guiana tribes. It also prevailed to some extent among the ancient Cantabrians and Corsicans, the Congos and Tartars, and in the Southern French provinces.

Ceylon aromatic; but, according to Dr. Taylor, it is cassia. Macás, in the days of Spanish adventure a prosperous city under the name of "Sevilla de Oro," is now a cluster of huts on the banks of the Upano. Its trade is in tobacco, vanilla, canela, wax, and copal. The Spaniards took the trouble to transplant some genuine cinnamon-trees from Ceylon to this locality, and they flourished for a time.

On the 30th of October we left Quito on our march across the continent, by the way of the Napo wilderness. The preparations for our departure, however, commenced long before that date. To leave Quito in any direction is the work of time. But to plunge into that *terra incognita* "el Oriente," where for weeks, perhaps months, we should be lost to the civilized world and cut off from all resources, east or west, demanded more calculation and providence than a voyage round the world.

We were as long preparing for our journey to the Amazon as in making it. In the first place, not a man in Quito could give us a single item of information on the most important and dangerous part of our route. Quitonians are not guilty of knowing any thing about trans-Andine affairs or "oriental" geography. From a few petty traders who had, to the amazement of their fellow-citizens, traversed the forest and reached the banks of the Napo, we gleaned some information which was of service. But on the passage down the Napo from Santa Rosa to the Marañon, a distance of over five hundred miles, nobody had any thing to say except the delightful intelligence that in all probability, if we escaped the fever, we would be murdered by the savages. The information we received was about as definite and reliable as Herndon obtained respecting any tributary to the Lower Amazon: "It runs a long way up; it has rapids; savages live upon its banks; every thing grows there." From M. Gillette, a Swiss gentleman trading at Pará in Moyabamba hats, we learned about the movements of the Peruvian steamer on the Marañon; but how long it would take us to cross the mountains and the forest, and descend the river, we must find out by trial.

The commissary department was of primal importance. As, from all we could learn, we could not depend upon obtaining supplies from the Indians or with our guns,* it was necessary to take provisions to last till we should reach the Marañon. But how long we should be in the forest and on the river, or what allowance to make for probable delays, it was impossible to prophesy. The utmost caution and forethought were therefore needed, for to die of starvation in the wilderness was, for all practical purposes, equivalent to falling into the hands of cannibals. As it turned out, however, we made a most fortunate hit, for on arriving at Pebas—the first village on the Marañon—we found we had just enough solid food left to have one grand jubilee dinner.

For the benefit of future travelers, and for the curiosity of others, we give the bill of fare we provided for this journey—stomachs, five; time, forty-two days:

Flour	100 lbs.	Sugar	90 lbs.	Soda	1 lbs.
Corn meal	27 "	Chocolate	25 "	Tea	2 "
Pea flour	30 "	Dried meat†	47 "	Ham	10 "
Mashka	47 "	Salt	10 "	Tamarinds	9 "
Crackers	100 "	Lard	10 "	Eggs	170.
Rice	50 "	Cream tartar.	1½ "	Anisado ...pts.	5.

To this we added by purchase from the Indians a few chickens and eggs, five gallons of sirup, and a peck of rice;

* The scarcity of game is well illustrated by the fate of Pizarro and his comrades. In returning from their expedition to the Napo country, they nearly perished with hunger, living on lizards, dogs, horses, saddles, sword-belts, etc., and reached Quito looking more like spectres than men.

† "Jerked beef," as it is called in South America, consists of thin strips cut off the carcass after skinning and dried in the sun. The butchers do not distinguish between sirloin and round.

and on the river we helped ourselves to a little wild game, as fish, peccari, deer, and turtles' eggs. But these made only a drop in the commissary bucket; had we depended upon finding provisions on the road, we must have perished from sheer hunger. Game, in the dry season, is exceedingly scarce. Our provisions were packed in kerosene cans, a part of which were soldered up to keep out moisture (for the Valley of the Napo is a steaming vapor-bath) and to keep out the hands of Indians. More than once have these treacherous yet indispensable guides robbed the white man of his food, and then left him to his fate; we lost not a pound by theft. A four-gallon keg of aguardiente,* from which we dealt out half a gill daily to each man, kept our Indians in good humor.

As we must ascend to the cold altitude of fifteen thousand feet, and then descend to the hot Valley of the Amazon, we were obliged to carry both woolen and cotton garments, besides rubber ponchos to shield them from the rain by day, and to form the first substratum of our bed at night. Two suits were needed in our long travel afoot through the forest; one kept dry for the nightly bivouac, the other for day service. At the close of each day's journey we doffed every thread of our wearing apparel, and donned the reserved suit, for we were daily drenched either from the heavens above or by crossing swollen rivers and seas of mud. Then, too, as boots would not answer for such kind of travel, we must take *alpargates*, a native sandal made of the aloe fibre, and of these not a few, for a pair would hardly hold together two days. Two bales of *lienzo*, besides knives, fish-hooks, thread, beads, looking-glasses, and other trinkets, were also needed; for the Napo

* This is the rum of the Andes, corresponding to the *cashaça* of Brazil. It is distilled from sugar-cane. When double-distilled and flavored with anise, it is called *anisado*.

Indians must be paid in such currency. There *lienzo*, not gold and silver, is the cry. On this we made a small but lawful profit, paying in Quito eighteen cents per yard, and charging on the river twenty-five.

An extensive culinary apparatus, guns and ammunition, taxidermal and medicinal chests, physical instruments, including a photographic establishment, rope, macheta, axe,. saw, nails, candles, matches, and a thousand *et cætera*, completed our outfit. Among the essential *et cætera* were generous passports and mandatory letters from the President of Ecuador and the Peruvian Chargé d'Affaires, addressed to all authorities on the Napo and the Marañon. They were obligingly procured for us by Señor Hurtado, the Chilian minister (then acting for the United States), through the influence of a communication from our own government, and were of great value to the expedition.*

* The following is a copy of the President's order:

REPUBLICA DEL ECUADOR.

Ministeria de Estado en el Despacho del Interior. — Quito á 18 de Octubre, de 1867.

APERTORIA.

A las autoridades del transito hasta el Napo, i á los demas empleados civiles i militares de la provincia del Oriente:

El Sor. James Orton, ciudadano de los EE.UU. de América, profesor de la Universidad de Rochester en Nueva-York, i jefe de una comision cientifica del Instituto de Smithsonian de Washington, vá á la provincia de Oriente con el objeto de esplorarla en cumplimiento de su encargo. S.E. el Presidenta de la República ordena á U.U. presten al espresado Sor. Orton i su comitiva cuantas consideraciones merecen sus personas, i los ausilios i co-operacion que necesiten para verificar su viaje i hacer sus estudios i observaciones.

Dios gue. á U.U.

R. CARVAJAL.

CHAPTER XII.

Departure from Quito.—Itulcachi.—A Night in a Bread-tray.—Crossing the Cordillera.—Guamani.—Papallacta.—Domiciled at the Governor's.—An Indian Aristides.—Our Peon Train.—In the Wilderness.

FORTY miles east-southeast of Quito, on the eastern slope of the Eastern Cordillera, and on the western edge of the great forest, is the Indian village of Papallacta. From the capital to this point there is a path just passable for horses; but thence to the Napo travelers must take to their feet. Through the intervention of the curate of Papallacta, who has great influence over his wild people, but who has wit enough to reside in Quito instead of his parish, we engaged the Indian governor to send over thirteen beasts and three peons to carry our party and baggage to Papallacta. Wednesday morning the quadrupeds were at the door of our hotel, five of them *bestias de silla.* These horses, judging by size, color, shape, and bony prominences, were of five different species. The saddles, likewise, differed from one another, and from any thing we had ever seen or desired to see. One of them was so narrow and deep none of us could get into it; so, filling up the cavity with blankets, we took turns in riding on the summit. By noon, October 30th, we had seen our Andean collections in the hands of arrieros bound for Guayaquil, whence they were to be shipped by way of Panama to Washington, and our baggage train for Napo headed toward the rising sun. So, mounting our jades, we defiled across the Grand Plaza and through the street of St. Augustine, and down the Carniceria to the Alameda, amid the *vivas* and *adeos* of our Quitonian friends, who turned out to see the largest expedition that ever left the city for the wild Napo country since the days of Pizarro. Few there were who expected to hear of our safe arrival on the shores of the Atlantic.

Crossing the magnificent plain of Iñaquito, we reached in an hour the romantic village of Guápulo. Here is an elegant stone church dedicated to the Virgin of Guadaloupe, to which the faithful make an annual pilgrimage. Thence the road led us through the valley of the Guaillabamba (a tributary to the Esmeraldas), here and there blessed with signs of intelligent life—a mud hut, and little green fields of cane and alfalfa, and dotted with trees of wild cherry and myrtle, but having that air of sadness and death-like repose so inseparable from a Quitonian landscape. The greater part of this day's ride was over a rolling country so barren and dreary it was almost repulsive. What a pity the sun shines on so much useless territory!

Just before sunset we arrived at Itulcachi, a great cattle estate at the foot of the eastern chain of mountains. The hacienda had seen better days, and was poorly fitted to entertain man or beast. The major-domo, however, managed to make some small potato soup, and find us shelter for the night. In the room allotted us there were three immense kneading-troughs and two bread-boards to match, for a grist-mill and bakery were connected with the establishment. In default of beds, we made use of this furniture. Five wiser men have slept in better berths, but few have slept more soundly than we did in the bread-trays of Itulcachi.

The following day we advanced five miles to Tablon, an Indian hamlet on the mountain side. Here we waited over night for our cargo train, which had loitered on the road. This was the only spot in South America where we found milk to our stomachs' content; Itulcachi, with its herds of cattle, did not yield a drop. Our dormitory was a mud hovel, without an aperture for light or ventilation, and in this dark hole we all slept on a heap of barley. Splendid was the view westward from Tablon. Below us were the beautiful valleys of Chillo and Puembo, separated by the isolated mountain of Ilaló; around them, in an imposing semicircle, stood Cayambi, Imbabura, Pichincha, Corazon, Iliniza, Rumiñagui, Cotopaxi, Sincholagua, and Antisana. As the sun went down in his glory behind the western range, the rocky head of Pichincha stood out in bold relief, and cast a long shadow over the plain. At this halting-place we made the mortifying discovery that the barelegged Indian who had trotted by our side as a guide and body-servant, and whom we had ordered about with all the indifference of a surly slaveholder, was none other than his Excellency Eugenio Mancheno, governor of Papallacta! After this we were more respectful.

The next morning, our baggage having come up, we pushed up the mountain through a grand ravine, and over metamorphic rocks standing on their edges with a wavy strike, till we reached a polylepis grove, 12,000 feet above the sea. We lunched under the wide-spreading branches of these gnarled and twisted trees, which reminded us of the patriarchal olives in the Garden of Gethsemane, and then, ascending over the monotonous paramo, we stood at the elevation of 15,000 feet on the narrow summit of the Guamani ridge. Some priest had been before us and planted a cross by the roadside, to guide and bless the traveler on his way.

Of the magnificent prospect eastward, over the beginning of the Amazonian Valley, which this lofty point commands, we have already spoken. There was a wild grandeur in the scene—mountain behind mountain, with deep intervening valleys, all covered with one thick, unbroken mass of foliage. A tiny brook, the child of everlasting snows still higher up, murmured at our feet, as if to tell us that we were on the Atlantic slope, and then dashed into the great forest, to lose itself in the mighty Amazon, and be buried with it in the same ocean grave. The trade-wind, too, came rushing by us fresh from that sea of commerce which laves the shores of two worlds. Guamani gave us also our finest view of Antisana, its snow-white dome rising out of a wilderness of mountains, and presenting on the north side a profile of the human face divine.

And now we rapidly descended by a steep, narrow path, and over paramo and bog, to a little tambo, where we had the luxury of sleeping on a bed of straw. Here we made the acquaintance of two Indians from the Napo, who were on the way to Quito with the mail—probably half a dozen letters. A strip of cloth around the loins, and a short cape just covering the shoulders, were all their habiliments. We noticed that they never sat down, though a bench was close by them; they would squat for an hour at a time. The day following we took our last horseback ride in South America. It was short, but horrible. Through quagmire and swamp, and down a flight of rocky stairs, in striking imitation of General Putnam's famous ride—over rocks, too, made wondrously slippery by a pitiless rain, but which our unshod Indian horses descended with great dexterity, only one beast and his rider taking a somerset—thus we traveled two hours, reaching Papallacta at 11 A.M.

We put up at the governor's. This edifice, the best in town, had sides of upright poles stuccoed with mud, a thatched roof, and ground floor, on which, between three stones, a fire was built for cookery and comfort. Three or four earthen kettles, and as many calabashes and wooden spoons, were the sum total of kitchen utensils. A large flat stone, with another smaller one to rub over it, was the mill for grinding corn; and we were astonished to see how quickly our hostess reduced the grains to an impalpable meal. The only thing that looked like a bed was a stiff rawhide thrown over a series of round poles running lengthwise. This primitive couch, and likewise the whole house, the obsequious governor gave up to us, insisting upon sleeping with his wife and little ones outside, though the nights were cold and uncomfortable. Parents and children were of the earth, earthy—unwashed, uncombed, and disgustingly filthy. We found the governor one day taking lice for his lunch. Sitting behind his little boy, he picked out the little parasites with his nails, and crushed them between his teeth with a look of satisfaction. Eating lice is an old Indian custom, and universal in the Andes. In Inca times it was considered an infallible remedy against sore eyes. We have seen half a dozen women sitting on the ground in a row, picking out vermin from each other's heads. We thought the arrangement was a little unfair, for the first in the series had no lice to eat, and the animals were left to roam undisturbed in the capillary forest of the last.

Papallacta is a village of thirty dwellings, situated in a deep valley on the north slope of Antisana, nearly surrounded by an amphitheatre of sandstone and basaltic precipices. Here, too, is the terminus of the fourth great lava stream from the volcano; it is not mentioned by Humboldt. Papallacta is a thousand feet higher than Quito, yet vegetation is more tropical. Its name signifies "the potato country," but not a potato could we find here. Though Mancheno was governor, he was not really the greatest man in Papallacta. This was Carlos Caguatijo; he was the ruling man, for he could read, write, and speak Spanish, while the governor knew nothing but Quichua. Carlos, moreover, was a good man; he had an honest, Quaker-like air about him, and his face reminded us of George Washington's. In all his transactions we noticed no attempt to prevaricate or deceive; what he promised he performed to the letter. It was refreshing to meet one such upright soul in Ecuador, though we found him not of Caucasian blood, nor dwelling under the tiled roofs of the proud capital. The old man was the spiritual father of Papallacta, and, in the absence of the curate, officiated in the little church. With him, therefore, and not with our host the governor, we negotiated for peons to take us through the wilderness.

The journey from Papallacta to the Napo occupied us thirteen days, including four days of rest. It was performed on foot, for the "road" is a trail. But the untraveled reader can have little idea of a trail in a tropical forest: fording bridgeless rivers, wading through interminable bogs, fens, marshes, quagmires, and swamps, and cutting one's way through dense vegetation, must be done to be understood. Half the year there is no intercourse between Quito and its Oriental province, for the incessant heavy rains of summer swell every rivulet into a furious torrent, and the path is overgrown and rendered impassable even by an Indian. The only time for travel is between November and April, for then, though it rains nearly every day, the clouds drop down in showers, not floods. But even then the traveler must sometimes wait two or three weeks beside a swollen river in imminent danger of starving, and throughout the journey entertain the comforting prospect that his Indians may eat up his provisions to lighten their load, or suddenly desert him as they did Dr. Jameson. There are other routes across South America much more feasible than the one we chose; these will be described in Chapter XXIII. But they all yield in interest to this passage along the equatorial line, and especially in the line of history. Who has not heard of Gonzalo Pizarro and his fatal yet famous expedition into "the land of cinnamon?" How he was led farther and farther into the wilderness by the glittering illusions of an El Dorado,* till the faithless Orellana, deserting him, floated down the Napo and made the magnificent discovery of the mighty Amazon. Gonzalo, "who was held to be the best lancer that ever went to these countries—and all confess that he never showed his back to the enemy"—returned to Quito with a few survivors to tell a tale of almost unparalleled suffering. A century elapsed (1539–1637) before any one ascended from Pará to Quito by way of the Rio Napo; this was accomplished by Pedro Teixeira.

An Indian will carry three arrobas (seventy-five pounds) besides his own provisions, his provisions for the journey consisting of about twenty-five pounds of roasted corn and barley-meal. The trunk or bundle is bound to his back by withes, which pass across the forehead and chest; a poncho or a handful of leaves protects the bare back from chafing. All our luggage (amounting to nearly fifteen hundred pounds) was divided and packed to suit this method of transportation, so that we required twenty Indians. So many, however, of the right kind—for they must be athletic young men to endure the fatigues of such a journey—could not be furnished by the little village of Papallacta, so we were obliged to wait a few days till more Indians could be summoned from a neighboring town. When these arrived, the little world of Papallacta, men, women, and children, assembled in front of the governor's house, while Don Carlos sat by our side on a raised seat by

* The king of this fabulous land was said to wear a magnificent attire fragrant with a costly gum, and sprinkled with gold dust. His palace was of porphyry and alabaster, and his throne of ivory.

Napo Peon.

the doorway. A long parley ensued, resulting in this: that we should pay one hundred Ecuadorian dollars for the transfer of our baggage to Archidona; while Carlos solemnly promised for the young men that they should start the next morning, that they should arrive at Archidona within a stipulated time, and that they should not depend upon us for an ounce of food. The powerful influence of the curate, which we had secured, and the proclamation from the president, which Carlos read aloud in the ears of all the people, together with the authoritative charge of Carlos himself, had the desired effect; not a transportation company in the United States ever kept its engagement more faithfully than did these twenty peons—and this, too, though we paid them in advance, according to the custom of the country. Upon a blanket spread at our feet the money was counted out, and Carlos slowly distributed it with a grave and reverend air, to every Indian five dollars.*

Tuesday morning, November 5th, the peons promptly shouldered their burdens, and we, shod with *alpargates*, and with Alpine staff in hand (more needed here than in Switzerland), followed after, leaving the governor to sleep inside his mansion, and to eat his lice unmolested. On a little grassy knoll just outside the town our train halted for a moment—the Indians to take their fill of chicha, and bid their friends good-by, and we to call the roll and take an inventory. Our leader was Isiro, a bright, intelligent, finely-featured, stalwart Indian. He could speak Spanish, and his comrades acknowledged his superiority with marked deference. Ten women and children followed us for two days, to relieve the men of their burdens. Their assistance was not needed in the latter part of the journey, for our keen appetites rapidly lightened the provision cans. Starting again, we plunged at once into the forest, taking a northeasterly course along the left bank of a tributary

* We give below the autograph of this wisest man in all the Oriente:

"Recibio del Señor James Orton la suma de centos (100) pesos por vente (20) peones hasta Archidona.

Carlos Caspualiso

"Papallacta, 4 Nov., 1867."

to the Coca. The ups and downs of this day's travel of twelve miles were foreshadowings of what might come in our "views afoot" in South America. We encamped at a spot the Indians called Maspa. Herndon says: "The (Peruvian) Indians take no account of time or distance; they stop when they get tired, and arrive when God pleases."* But our Napo companions measured distance by hours quite accurately, and they always traveled as far as we were willing to follow. In ten minutes they built us a booth for the night; driving two crotchets into the ground, they joined them with a ridge-pole, against which they inclined a number of sticks for rafters. These they covered with palm-leaves, so adroitly put together that our roof was generally rain-proof. After ablution and an entire change of garments, we built a fire, using for fuel a green tree called *sindicaspi* (meaning the wood that burns), a special provision in these damp forests where every thing is dripping with moisture. The fall of a full-grown tree under the strokes of a Yankee axe was a marvel in the eyes of our Indians. Our second day's journey was far more difficult than the first, the path winding up steep mountains and down into grand ravines, for we were crossing the outlying spurs of the Eastern Cordillera. Every where the track was slippery with mud, and often we sank two feet into the mire. How devoutly we did wish that the Ecuadorian Congress was compelled to travel this horrid road once a year! At 10 o'clock we reached a lone habitation called Guila, where wooden bowls are made for the Quito market. Here we procured a fresh Indian to take the place of one of our peons who had given out under his burden. We advanced this day sixteen miles in ten hours, sleeping under an old bamboo hut beside a babbling brook bearing the euphonious name of Pachamama.

* "Distance is frequently estimated by the time that a man will occupy in taking a chew of coca," or 37½ minutes.—*Herndon.*

CHAPTER XIII.

Baeza.—The Forest.—Crossing the Cosanga.—Curi-urcu.—Archidona.—Appearance, Customs, and Belief of the Natives.—Napo and Napo River.

EIGHT hours' hard travel from Pachamama brought us to Baeza. This "Antigua Ciudad," as Villavicencio calls it, was founded in 1552 by Don Egilio Ramirez Dávalos, and named after the quite different spot where Scipio the Younger routed Asdrubal a thousand years before. It consists of two habitations, the residence of two families of Tumbaco Indians, situated in a clearing of the forest on the summit of a high ridge running along the right bank of the Coca. This point, about one hundred miles east of Quito, is important in the little traffic of the Oriente. All Indian trains from the capital to the province pass through Baeza, where the trail divides; one branch passing on easterly to San José, and thence down through Abila and Loreto to Santa Rosa; the other leading to the Napo through Archidona. Here we rested one day, taking possession of one half of the larger hut—a mere stockade with a palm-leaf roof, without chairs, chimney, or fire-place, except any place on the floor. We swung our hammocks, while our Indians stretched themselves on the ground beneath us. The island of Juan Fernandez is not a more isolated spot than Baeza. A dense forest, impenetrable save by the trails, stretches away on every side to the Andes and to the Atlantic, and northerly and southerly along the slope of the entire mountain chain. The forest is such an entangled mass of the living and the fallen, it is difficult to say which is the predominant spirit—life or death. It is the cemetery, as well as the birthplace, of a world of vegetation. The trees are more lofty than on the

Lower Amazon, and straight as an arrow, but we saw none of remarkable size. A perpetual mist seems to hang on the branches, and the dense foliage forms dark, lofty vaults, which the sunlight never enters. The soil and air are always cool, and never dry. Every thing is penetrated with dampness. All our watches stopped, and remained immovable till we reached Pará. It is this constant and excessive humidity which renders it so difficult to transport provisions or prepare an herbarium. The pending branches of moss are so saturated with moisture that sometimes the branches are broken off to the peril of the passing traveler. Yet the climate is healthy. The stillness and gloom are almost painful; the firing of a gun wakes a dull echo, and any unlooked-for noise is startling. Scarce a bird or a flower is to be seen in these sombre shades. Nearly the only signs of animal life visible thus far were insects, mostly butterflies, fireflies, and beetles. The only quadruped seen on our journey to the Napo was a long-tailed marten caught by the Indians. The silence is almost perfect; its chief interruption is the crashing fall of some old patriarch of the forest, overcome by the embrace of loving parasites that twine themselves about the trunk or sit upon the branches. The most striking singularity in these tropical woods is the host of lianas or air-roots of epiphytous plants, which hang down from the lofty boughs, straight as plumb-lines, some singly, others in clusters; some reaching half way to the ground, others touching it and striking their rootlets into the earth. We found lianas over one hundred feet long. Sometimes a toppling tree is caught in the graceful arms of looping *sipôs*, and held for years by this natural cable. It is these dead trunks, standing like skeletons, which give a character of solemnity to these primeval woods. The wildest disorder is seen along the mountain torrents, where the trees, prostrated by the undermining current, lie mingled with huge stones brought down by the force of the water. In many places the crowns of stately monarchs standing on the bank interlock and form a sylvan arch over the river.

We left Baeza by the southerly trail for Archidona. From Papallacta we had traveled east, or parallel to the streams which flow down from the mountains. We were now to cross them (and their name is legion), as also the intervening ridges; so that our previous journey was nothing to that which followed. Sometimes we were climbing up an almost vertical ascent, then descending into a deep, dark ravine, to ford a furious river; while on the lowlands the path seemed lost in a jungle of bamboos, till our Indian "bushwhackers" opened a passage with their machetas, and we crept under a low arcade of foliage. This day we enjoyed something unusual in our forest trail—a distant view. The path brought us to the verge of a mountain, whence we could look down on the savage valley of the Cosanga and upward to the dazzling dome of Antisana; it was our farewell view of that glorious volcano. At the distance of twelve miles from Baeza we reached the banks of the Rio Cosanga, camping at a spot called Chiniplaya. This is the river so much dreaded by Indians and whites traversing the Napo wilderness. It is fearfully rapid—a very Tigris from its source to its junction with the Coca. The large, smooth boulders strewn along its bed show its power. Here, sixty miles from its origin in the glaciers of Antisana, it is seventy-five feet wide, but in the wet season it is one hundred yards. The day following we threaded our difficult way, a *via dolorosa*, fifteen miles up the left bank of the Cosanga, where we crossed and camped on the opposite side. The Indians had thrown a log over the deepest part of the river, and the rest we forded without much danger; but that very night the rain raised the river to such a magnitude that the little bridge was carried off. Had we been one day later, we might have waited a week on the other side of the impassable gulf. Between this point where we forded and Chiniplaya, fifteen miles below, the barometer indicated a fall of five hundred feet. The roar of the rushing waters is like that of the sea. In the beautiful language of Darwin (*Journal*, p. 316): "The sound spoke eloquently to the geologist; the thousands and thousands of stones, which, striking against each other, made the one dull, uniform sound, were all hurrying in one direction. It was like thinking on time, when the minute that now glides past is irrecoverable. So was it with these stones. The ocean is their eternity, and each note of that wild music told of one more step toward their destiny."

On account of the heavy rain and the sickness of a peon, whom finally we were obliged to leave behind, we rested one day; but on the morrow we traveled fourteen miles, crossing the lofty Guacamayo ridge,* fording at much risk the deep Cochachimbamba, and camping at a spot (the Indians have a name for almost any locality in the forest) called Guayusapugaru. The next day we must have advanced twenty miles, besides crossing the furious Hondachi. This river was very much swollen by the rains, and it was only by the aid of a rope that we made the passage. One stout Indian was carried down stream, but soon recovered himself.

As we had lowered our altitude since leaving Papallacta seven thousand feet, the climate was much warmer, and vegetation more prolific. Nowhere else between the Andes and the Atlantic did we notice such a majestic forest. The tree-ferns, ennobled by the tropical sun and soil, have a

* Humboldt speaks of this as an active volcano, "from which detonations are heard almost daily." We heard nothing. It is possible that he meant Guamani.

palm-like appearance, but with rougher stems and a usual height of fifty feet. Plants akin to our "scouring rush" rise twenty-five feet. We saw to-day the "water tree," or *huadhuas* of the natives, a kind of bamboo, which sometimes yields between the joints two quarts of clear, tasteless water. Late in the evening we reached an old rancho called *Curi-urcu* ("the mountain of gold"); but we had traveled so far ahead of our cargo-train we did not see it again till the next morning. We were obliged, therefore, to sleep on the ground in our wet clothes, and put up with hard commons—half parched corn, which our Indian guides gave us, and unleavened cakes or flour-paste baked on the coals. Thence, after a short day's journey of ten miles, we arrived at Archidona, by a path, however, that was slippery with a soft yellow clay. We were a sorry-looking company, soaked by incessant rains, exhausted by perspiration, plastered with mud, tattered, and torn; but we were kindly met by the Jesuit bishop, who took us to his own habitation, where one Indian washed our feet, and another prepared a most refreshing drink of *guayusa* tea. We then took up our quarters at the Government House, opposite the bishop's, sojourning several days on account of our swollen feet, and also on account of a swollen river which ran between us and the Napo. Here we made a valuable collection of birds, lizards, fishes, and butterflies.

Archidona is situated in a beautiful plain on the high northern bank of the Misagualli, two thousand feet above the Atlantic. The site is a cleared spot in the heart of an almost boundless forest; and it was a relief, not easily conceived, to emerge from beneath the dense leafy canopy into this open space and look up to the sky and to the snowy Andes. The climate is uniform and delightful, the mean annual temperature being seventy-seven degrees. Sand-flies, however, resembling our "punkies," abound; and the natives are constantly slapping their naked sides, eating the little pests as the Papallactans do their lice.* Archidona is the largest village in the Napo country, containing about five hundred souls. The houses are of split bamboo and palm-thatch, often hid in a plantation of yuca and plantain. The central and most important structure is the little church; its rude belfry, portico, chancel, images, and other attempts at ornament remind us of the fitting words of Mrs. Agassiz, that "there is something touching in the idea that these poor, uneducated people of the forest have cared to build themselves a temple with their own hands, lavishing upon it such ideas of beauty and taste as they have, and bringing at least their best to their humble altar." Founded by Dávalos in 1560, Archidona has been a missionary station for two hundred years. The people are child-like and docile, but the bishop confessed there was no intellectual advance. Every morning and evening, at the tinkling of a little bell, all Archidona assembled in the open porch, where the bishop taught them to sing and pray. It was a novel sight to see these children of the forest coming out of the woods on all sides and running up to the temple—for these natives, whenever they move, almost invariably go on a run. The men are tall and slim and of a dark red color, and their legs are bent backward at the knees. The governor was the only portly individual we saw. The women are short, with high shoulders, and are very timid; they seldom stand erect, and with the knees bent forward they run sneakingly to church. Their eyes have a characteristic, soft, drooping look. They carry their babes generally on the hip; not on the back, as in Quito. The men are hatless, shirtless, and shoeless; their only gar-

* The Chasuta Indians, Herndon says, eat musquitoes that they catch on their bodies with the idea of restoring the blood which the insect has abstracted.

ments are short drawers, about six inches long, and little ponchos, both of lienzo, dyed a dark purple with achote—the red seeds of the bixa, which the cooks of Quito use to color their soups. All paint their bodies with the same pigment. The women wear a frock reaching from the waist to the knees; it is nothing more than a yard or two of lienzo wound around the body. The Archidonians are the most Christianized of all the Napo Indians, but they can not be called religious. Their rites (they can hardly be said to have a creed) are the *a*, *b*, *c*, of Romanism, mingled with some strange notions—the relics of a lost paganism. They are very superstitious, and believe, as before remarked, in the transmigration of souls. Maniacs they think are possessed by an evil demon, and therefore are treated with great cruelty. Negroes (of whom a few specimens have come up the Napo from Brazil) are held to be under the ban of the Almighty, and their color is ascribed to the singeing which they got in the flames of hell. They do not believe in disease; but, like the Mundurucus on the Tapajos, say that death is always caused by the sorceries of an enemy. They usually bury in the church or in the tambo of the deceased. Celibacy and polygamy, homicide and suicide, are rare.

The only sign of industry in Archidona is the manufacture of pita thread from the aloe. It is exported to Quito on human backs. The inhabitants also collect copal at the headwaters of the Hondachi, and use it for illumination. It can be bought in Archidona for three or four cents a pound. The gum exudes from a lofty leguminous tree having an oak-like bark. It resembles the animé of Madagascar rather than the copal of India, which flows from an entirely different tree. Guayusa, or "Napo tea," is another and celebrated production of Archidona. It is the large leaf of a tall shrub growing wild. An infusion of guayusa, like the *maté* of Paraguay (which belongs to the same genus *Ilex*), is so refreshing it supplies for a long time the place of food. The Indians will go to Quito on this beverage alone, its virtues being similar to those of *coca*, on the strength of which the posts of the Incas used to travel incredible distances. It is by no means, however, such a stimulant. It is a singular fact, observes Dr. Jameson, that tea, coffee, cacao, maté, and guayusa contain the same alkaloid caffeine. The last, however, contains only one fifteenth as much of the active principle as tea, and no volatile oil. Herndon found guayusa on the Ucayali.

At Archidona we took a new set of peons for Napo, as the Papallactans do not travel farther. The distance is sixteen miles, and the path is comparatively good, though it crosses two rivers, the Misagualli and Tena. On this journey we found the only serpent seen since leaving Quito. This solitary specimen was sluggish and harmless, but exceedingly beautiful. It was the *Amphisbœna fuliginosa*, or "slow-worm." It lives in the chambers of the Saüba ants. We met a procession of these ants, each carrying a circular piece of a leaf vertically over its head. These insects are peculiar to tropical America, and are much dreaded in Brazil, where they soon despoil valuable trees of their foliage. They cut the leaves with their scissor-like jaws, and use them to thatch the domes at the entrance of their subterranean dwellings.

At Napo we took possession of the governor's house. Each village in the Napo province was obliged to build an edifice of split bamboo for that dignitary; and, as he no longer exists, they are left unoccupied. They generally stand on the highest and best site in the town, and are a god-send to travelers. Immediately on our arrival, the Indian governor and his staff of justices called to see what we wanted, and during our stay supplied us with chickens, eggs, plantains, yucas, and fuel. His excellency would always come, silver-headed cane in hand, though the justices had only six eggs or a single fowl to bring us. The alcalde also paid us his respects. He is an old blanco (as the whites are called), doing a little traffic in gold dust, lienzo, and pita, but is the highest representative of Ecuador in the Napo country. Here, too, we met, to our great delight, Mr. George Edwards, a native of Connecticut, who has settled himself, probably for life, in the depths of this wilderness. He was equally rejoiced to see the face and hear the speech of a countryman. His industry and upright character have won for him the respect and good-will of the Indians, and he is favorably known in Quito. The government has given him a tract of land on the Yusupino, two miles west of Napo village. Here he is cultivating vanilla, of which he has now three thousand plants, and also his patience, for six years elapse after transplanting before a pod appears. He has been so long in the country (thirteen years) his English would now and then run off into Spanish or Quichua.

Napo is prettily situated on the left bank of the Rio Napo, a dense forest inclosing it on every side. The maximum number of inhabitants is eighty families; but many of these are in town only in festival seasons. It was well for us that we reached the Napo during the feasts; otherwise we might not have found men enough to man our canoes down the river. There are three or four blancos, petty merchants, who follow the old Spanish practice of compulsory sales, forcing the Indians to take lienzo, knives, beads, etc., at exorbitant prices, and making them pay in gold dust and pita. This kind of commerce is known under the name of *repartos*. It is hard to find an Indian whose gold or whose labor is not claimed by the blancos. The present and possible productions of this region are:

bananas, plantains, yucas,* yams, sweet potatoes, rice, beans, corn, lemons, oranges, chirimoyas, anonas (a similar fruit to the preceding), pine-apples, palm cabbages, guavas, guayavas, castor-oil beans, coffee, cacao, cinnamon, India-rubber, vanilla (two kinds),† chonta-palm nuts, sarsaparilla, contrayerva (a mint), tobacco (of superior quality), and guayusa; of woods, balsam, red wood, Brazil wood, palo de cruz, palo de sangre, ramo caspi, quilla caspi, guayacan (or "holy wood," being much used for images), ivory palm, a kind of ebony, cedar, and aguana (the last two used for making canoes); of dyewoods, sarne (dark red), tinta (blue), terriri, and quito (black); of gums, estoraque (a balsam) and copal, besides a black beeswax, the production of a small (Trigona) bee, that builds its comb in the ground; of manufactures, pita, hammocks, twine, calabashes, aguardiente (from the plantain), chicha (from the yuca),‡ sugar and molasses (from the cane, which grows luxuriantly), and manati-lard; of minerals, gold dust. The gold, in minute spangles, is washed down by the rivers at flood time, chiefly from the Llanganati Mountains. The articles desired in exchange are lienzo, thread, needles, axes, hoes, knives, fish-hooks, rings, medals, crosses, beads, mirrors, salt, and poison. Quito nearly monopolizes the trade; though a few canoes go down the Napo to the Marañon after salt and poison. The salt comes from near Chasuta, on the Huallaga;§ the *urari* from the Ticuna Indians. It takes about twenty

* Sometimes called *yuca dulce*, or sweet yuca, to distinguish it from the *yuca brava*, or wild yuca, the mandioca of the Amazon, from which farina is made. The yuca is the beet-like root of a little tree about ten feet high. It is a good substitute for potatoes and bread.

† Vanilla belongs to the orchid family, and is the only member which possesses any economical value. It is a graceful climber and has a pretty star-like flower.

‡ In Peru, the liquor made from yuca is called *masato.*

§ Rock-salt is found on both sides of the Andes. "The general character of the geology of these countries would rather lead to the opinion that its origin is in some way connected with volcanic heat at the bottom of the sea." —Darwin's *Observations*, pt. iii., p. 235.

days to paddle down to the Marañon, and three months to pole up. The Napo is navigable for a flat-bottomed steamer as far as Santa Rosa,* and it is a wonder that Anglo-Saxon enterprise has not put one upon these waters. The profits would be great, as soon as commercial relations with the various tribes were established.† Four yards of coarse cotton cloth, for example, will exchange for one hundred pounds of sarsaparilla. *Urari* is sold at Napo for its weight in silver. By a decree of the Ecuadorian Congress, there will be no duty on foreign goods entering the Napo for twenty years. The Napo region, under proper cultivation, would yield the most valuable productions of either hemisphere in profusion. But agriculture is unknown; there is no word for plow. The natives spend most of their time in idleness, or feasting and hunting. Their weapons are blow-guns and wooden spears; our guns they call by a word which signifies "thunder and lightning." Laying up for the future or for commerce is foreign to their ideas. The houses are all built of bamboo tied together with lianas, and shingled with leaves of the sunipanga palm. The Indians are peaceful, good-natured, and idle. They seldom steal any thing but food. Their only stimulants are chicha, guayusa, and tobacco. This last they roll up in plantain leaves and smoke, or snuff an infusion of it through the nose from the upper bill of a toucan. "The Peruvians (says Prescott, quoting Garcilasso) differ from every other Indian nation to whom tobacco was known by using it only for medicinal purposes in the form of snuff." There is no bread on the Napo; the nearest ap-

* "The Napo (Herndon was told) is very full of sand-banks, and twenty days from its mouth (or near the confluence of the Curaray) the men have to get overboard and drag the canoes!"—*Report*, p. 229.

† The chief difficulty throughout the Upper Amazon is in getting the Indians to concentrate along the bank. But honorable dealing would accomplish this in time.

proach to flour is yuca starch. There are no clocks or watches; time is measured by the position of the sun. The mean temperature at Napo village is about one degree warmer than that of Archidona. Its altitude above the sea is 1450 feet. The nights are cool, and there are no musquitoes; but sand-flies are innumerable. Jiggers also have been seen. There are no well-defined wet and dry seasons; but the most rain falls in May, June, and July. The lightning, Edwards informed us, seldom strikes. Dysentery, fevers, and rheumatism are the prevailing diseases; and we saw one case of goître. But the climate is considered salubrious. Few twins are born; and there are fewer children than in Archidona—a difference ascribed by some to the exposure of the Napo people in gold washing; by others to the greater quantity of guayusa drunk by the Archidonians.

The Napo is the largest river in the republic. From its source in the oriental defiles of Cotopaxi and Sincholagua to its embouchure at the Marañon, its length is not far from eight hundred miles, or about twice that of the Susquehanna.* From Napo village to the mouth of the river our barometer showed a fall of a thousand feet. At Napo the current is six miles an hour; between Napo and Santa Rosa there are rapids; and between Santa Rosa and the Marañon the rate is not less than four miles an hour. At Napo the breadth is about forty yards; at Coca the main channel is fifteen hundred feet wide; and at Camindo it

* Its actual source is the Rio del Valle, which runs northward through the Valle Vicioso. Its longest tributary, the Curaray, rises only a few miles to the south in the Cordillera de los Mulatos. The two rivers run side by side 4° of longitude before meeting. Coca, the northern branch, originates in the flanks of Cayambi. The Napo and its branches are represented incorrectly in every map we have examined. The Aguarico is confounded with the Santa Maria and made too long, and the Curaray is represented too far above the mouth of the Napo. There are no settlements between Coca and Camindo.

is a full Spanish mile. Below Coca the river throws out numerous canals, which, isolating portions of the forest-clad lowlands, create numerous picturesque islands. Around and between them the river winds, usually making one bend in every league. The tall trees covering them are bound together by creeping plants into a thick jungle, the home of capybaras and the lair of the jaguar. The islands, entirely alluvial, are periodically flooded, and undergo a constant round of decay and renovation. Indeed, the whole river annually changes its channel, so that navigation is somewhat difficult. The Indians, on coming to a fork, were frequently at a loss to know which was the main channel. Then, too, the river is full of snags and *plaias*, or low, shelving sand-banks, rising just above the water-level—the resort of turtles during the egg season. It was interesting to trace the bed of the river as we floated down; on the rapid slope of the Cordilleras rushing over or rolling along huge boulders, which farther on were rapidly reduced in size, till, in time, boulders were broken into pebbles, pebbles turned into sand, and sand reduced to impalpable mud.* The *plaias* are not auriferous. Below Coca there is a wilderness of lagunes, all connected with the river, the undisturbed retreat of innumerable water-fowl. The only spot on the Napo where the underlying rocks are exposed is near Napo village. There it is a dark slate, gently dipping east. Farther west, in fact, throughout this side of the Andes, the prevailing rock is mica-schist. But the entire Napo country is covered with an alluvial bed, on the average ten feet thick.

* From specimens of sand which we obtained at different points in descending the river, we find that at Coca it contains 17.5 per cent. of pure quartz grains, the rest being colored dark with augite; at the mouth of the Napo there is 50 per cent. of pure quartz, the other half being light-colored and feldspathic.

CHAPTER XIV.

Afloat on the Napo.—Down the Rapids.—Santa Rosa and its mulish Alcalde.—Pratt on Discipline.—Forest Music.—Coca.—Our Craft and Crew.—Storm on the Napo.

WE embarked November 20th on our voyage down the river. It is no easy matter to hire or cajole the Indians for any service. Out of feast-time they are out of town, and during the festival they are loth to leave, or are so full of chicha they do not know what they want. We first woke up the indolent alcalde by showing him the President's order, and then used him to entice or to compel (we know not his motive power) eight Indians, including the governor, to take us to Santa Rosa. We paid them about twenty-four yards of lienzo, the usual currency here. They furnished three canoes, two for baggage and one covered with a palm-leaf awning for ourselves. The canoes were of red cedar, and flat-bottomed; the paddles had oval blades, to which short, quick strokes were given perpendicularly to the water entering and leaving. But there was little need of paddling on this trip.

The Napo starts off in furious haste, for the fall between Napo village and Santa Rosa, a distance of eighty miles, is three hundred and fifty feet. We were about seven hours in the voyage down, and it takes seven days to pole back. The passage of the rapids is dangerous to all but an Indian. As Wallace says of a spot on the Rio Negro, you are bewildered by the conflicting motions of the water. Whirling and boiling eddies burst as if from some subaqueous explosion; down currents are on one side of the canoe, and an up current on the other; now a cross stream at the bows and a diagonal one at the stern, with a foaming Scylla on your right and a whirling Charybdis on the left. But our nervousness gave way to admiration as our popero, or pilot, the sedate governor, gave the canoe a sheer with the swoop of his long paddle, turning it gracefully around the corner of a rock against which it seemed we must be dashed, and we felt like joining in the wild scream of the Indians as our little craft shot like an arrow past the danger and down the rapids, and danced on the waters below.

In four hours we were abreast the little village of Aguano; on the opposite bank we could see the tambos of the gold washers. At 5 P.M. we reached the deserted site of Old Santa Rosa, the village having been removed a few years ago on account of its unhealthy location. It is now overgrown with sour orange and calabash trees, the latter bearing large fruit shells so useful to the Indians in making pilches or cups. In pitch darkness and in a drizzling rain we arrived at New Santa Rosa, and swung our hammocks in the Government House.

Santa Rosa, once the prosperous capital of the Provincia del Oriente, now contains about two hundred men, women, and children. The town is pleasantly situated on the left bank of the river, about fifteen feet above the water level. A little bamboo church, open only when the missionary from Archidona makes his annual visit, stood near our quarters. The Indians were keeping one of their seven feasts in a hut near by, and their drumming was the last thing we heard as we turned into our hammocks, and the first in the morning. The alcalde, Pablo Sandoval, is the only white inhabitant, and he is an Indian in every respect save speech and color. His habitation is one of the largest structures on the Napo; the posts are of chonta-palm, the sides and roof of the usual material—split bamboo and

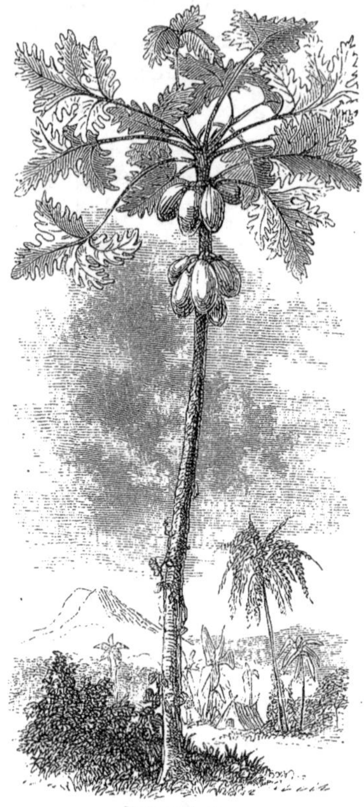
Papaya-tree.

palm leaves. It is embowered in a magnificent grove of plantains and papayas. In the spacious vestibule is a bench, on which the Indian governor and his staff seat themselves every morning to confer with the alcalde. In one corner stands a table (the only one we remember seeing on the Napo); on the opposite side are heaped up jars, pots, kettles, hunting and fishing implements, paddles, bows and arrows. Between the posts swing two chambiri hammocks. From Santa Rosa to Pará the hammock answers for chair, sofa, *tête-à-tête*, and bed. When a stranger enters, he is invited to sit in a hammock; and at Santa Rosa we were always presented with a cup of guayusa; in Brazil with a cup of coffee. Sandoval wore nothing but shirt and pantaloons; the dignity of the barefooted functionary was confined to his Spanish blood. He had lived long among the Zaparos; and from him, his daughter, and a Zaparo servant, we obtained much valuable information respecting that wild and little-known tribe.

At Santa Rosa we procured Indians and canoes for the Marañon. This was not easily done. The Indians seemed reluctant to quit their feasts and go on such a long voyage, and the alcalde was unwilling they should go, and manufactured a host of lies and excuses. He declared there was but one large canoe in town, and that we must send to Suno for another, and for men to man it. There were indeed few Indians in Santa Rosa, for while we were disputing a large number went off with shoutings down the river, to spend weeks in the forest hunting monkeys.* It was a stirring sight to see these untamed red men in the depths of the Napo wilderness starting on a monkey crusade; but it was still more stirring to think of paddling our own canoe down to Brazil. After some time lost in word-fighting, we tried the virtues of authority. We presented the president's order, which commanded all civil and military powers on the Napo to aid, and not to hinder, the expedition; then we put into his hand an official letter from the alcalde of Napo (to whom Pablo was subordinate), which, with a flourish of dignified Spanish, threatened Santa Rosa with the doom of Sodom and Gomorrah if any impediment was placed in our way.

To all this Edwards, who had kindly accompanied us down the river thus far, added, with frightful gestures, that he purposed to report him to the Quito government. After this bombardment Sandoval was another man, and the two canoes and four Indians we wanted were forthcoming. We had to wait, however, two days for the Indians to prepare their chicha for the journey and to cover the canoes with palm awnings. The price of a canoe for the Marañon is twenty-five varas of lienzo, and the same for each Indian. Unfortunately we had only fifty varas left; but, through the influence of the now good-natured alcalde, we induced the Indians to take the balance in coin. After many de-

* Monkeys form an article of food throughout tropical America. The meat is tough, but keeps longer than any other in that climate. The Indians told Gibbon that "the tail is the most delicate part when the hair is properly singed."

lays, we put our baggage into one canoe, and ourselves into the other, and pushed off into the rapid current of the Napo. We had three styles of valediction on leaving. Our Indian quartet, after several last drinks of chicha, bade their friends farewell by clasping hands, one kissing the joined hands, and then the other. Sandoval muttered *adios* in reply to ours, meaning, no doubt, good riddance, while we shouted a hearty good-bye to Edwards as he pushed his way up stream to continue his lonely but chosen Indian life on the banks of the Yusupino.

The Napo at Santa Rosa runs at least five miles an hour, and we were soon picking our way—now drifting, now paddling—through a labyrinth of islands and snags. The Indians, so accustomed to brutal violence from the hands of the whites, had begged of us, before our departure, that we would not beat them. But shortly after we left, one of them, who was literally filled with chicha, dropped his paddle and tumbled into a heap at the bottom of the canoe, dead drunk. Pratt, our gigantic Mississippi boatman, whom we had engaged at Quito as captain and cook down the river, and who was an awful Goliath in the eyes of the red-skins, seized the fellow and gave him a terrible shaking, the like of which was never seen or heard of in all Napo. At once the liquor left the muddled brain of the astonished culprit, and, taking his paddle, he became from that hour the best of the crew. This was the only case of discipline on the voyage. Always obsequious, they obeyed us with fear and trembling. None of them could speak Spanish, so we had provided ourselves with a vocabulary of Quichua. But some English words, like the imperative *paddle!* were more effective than the tongue of the Incas. Indeed, when we mixed up our Quichua with a little Anglo-Saxon, they evidently thought the latter was a terrible anathema, for they sprang to their places without delay.

In seven hours we arrived at Suno, a collection of half a dozen palm booths, five feet high, the miserable owners of which do a little fishing and gold-washing. They gave us possession of their largest hut, in which they had been roasting a sea-cow, and the stench was intolerable. Nevertheless, one of our number bravely threw down his blanket within, and went to sleep; two swung their hammocks between the trees, and the rest slept in the canoe. Here, for the first time since leaving Guayaquil, we were tormented by musquitoes. Bats were also quite numerous, but none of them were blood-thirsty; and we may add that nowhere in South America were we troubled by those diabolical imps of imaginative travelers, the leaf-nosed species. So far as our experience goes, we can say, with Bates, that the vampire, so common on the Amazon, is the most harmless of all bats. It has, however, a most hideous physiognomy. A full-grown specimen will measure twenty-eight inches in expanse of wing. Bates found two species on the Amazon—one black, the other of a ruddy hue, and both fruit-eaters.

The nocturnal music of these forests is made by crickets and tree-toads. The voice of the latter sounds like the cracking of wood. Occasionally frogs, owls, and goat-suckers croak, hoot, and wail. Between midnight and 3 A.M. almost perfect silence reigns. At early dawn the animal creation awakes with a scream. Pre-eminent are the discordant cries of monkeys and macaws. As the sun rises higher, one musician after another seeks the forest shade, and the morning concert ends at noon. In the heat of the day there is an all-pervading rustling sound, caused by the fluttering of myriad insects and the gliding of lizards and snakes. At sunset parrots and monkeys resume their chatter for a season, and then give way to the noiseless flight of innumerable bats chasing the hawk-moth and beetle. There is scarcely a sound in a tropical forest which is joyous and cheering. The birds are usually silent; those that have voices utter a plaintive song, or hoarse, shrill cry. Our door-yards are far more melodious on a May morning. The most common birds on the Napo are macaws, parrots, toucans, and ciganas. The parrots, like the majority in South America, are of the green type. The toucan, peculiar to the New World, and distinguished by its enormous bill, is a quarrelsome, imperious bird. It is clumsy in flight, but nimble in leaping from limb to limb. It hops on the ground like a robin, and makes a shrill yelping—*pia-po-o-co*. Ecuadorians call it the *predicador*, or preacher, because it wags its head like a priest, and seems to say, "God gave it you." The feathers of the breast are of most brilliant yellow, orange, and rose colors, and the robes of the royal dames of Europe in the sixteenth century were trimmed with them. The cigana or "gypsy" (in Peru called "chansu") resembles a pheasant. The flesh has a musky odor, and it is for this reason, perhaps, that they exist in such numbers throughout the country. The Indians never eat them. In no country as in the Amazonian Valley is there such a variety of insects; nowhere do we find species of larger size or greater beauty. It is the richest locality for butterflies; Bates found twelve hundred species in Brazil alone, or three times as many as in all Europe. The splendid metallic-blue, and the yellow and transparent-winged, are very abundant on the Napo; some rise high in the air; others, living in societies, look like fluttering clouds. Moths are comparatively rare. The most conspicuous beetle on the river is a magnificent green species (*Chrysophora chrysochlora*), always found arboreal, like the majority of tropical coleopters; they look like emerald gems clinging to the branches. There are two kinds of bees, the black and yellow, which the Napos name respectively *cushillo mishke* (monkey honey) and *sara mishke* (corn honey). It is singular these Indians have no term for bees, but call them honey, and distinguish them by their color. The black species is said to make the most honey, and the yellow the best. The quadrupeds of the Oriente are few and far between in the dry season. Not a sloth nor armadillo did we see. But when the rains descend the wilderness is a menagerie of tigers and tapirs, pumas and bears, while a host of reptiles, led by the gigantic boa, creep forth from their hiding-places. The most ferocious carnivores are found in the mountains, and the most venomous serpents haunt the lowlands. Darwin says that we ought not to expect any closer similarity between the organic beings on the opposite sides of the Andes than on the opposite shores of the ocean. We will remark that we obtained a peccari, a number of birds not accustomed to high flights, and five reptilian species, on the Pacific slope, identical with species found on the Napo.

Breakfasting on fried yucas, roasted plantains, fish, and guayusa, we set sail, arriving at Coca at 2 P.M. This little village, the last we shall see till we come within sight of the Amazon, is beautifully located on the right bank, twenty-five feet above the river, and opposite the confluence of the Rio Coca. Though founded twenty years ago, it contains only five or six bamboo huts, a government-house, church, alcalde's residence, and a *trapiche* for the manufacture of aguardiente and sirup from the cane.* The alcalde was a worthless blanco, who spent most of his time swinging in a hammock slung between the posts of his veranda, and playing with a tame parrot when not drunk or asleep. This spot is memorable in history. Pizarro having reached it from Quito by way of Baeza and

* The *trapiche* or sugar-mill of the Andes is a rude affair. The cane is pressed between cogged wooden cylinders worked by bullocks, and the juice is received in troughs made of hollowed logs.

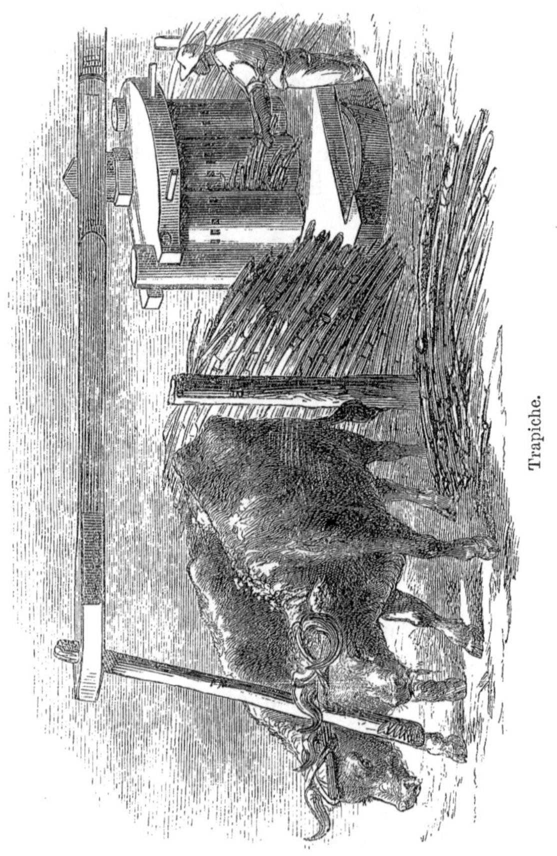

Trapiche.

the Coca, halted and built a raft or canoe (Prescott says a brig), in which Orellana was sent down the river to reconnoitre, but who never returned. Up to this point the Napo has an easterly course; but after receiving the Coca, it turns to the southeast. We remained here two days to construct a more comfortable craft for our voyage to the Amazon, a distance of at least five hundred miles. The canoe is the only means of navigation known to the Indians. But the idea of spending fifteen days cooped, cribbed, and cramped in a narrow canoe, exposed to a tropical sun and furious rains, was intolerable.

Our Santa Rosa canoes were about thirty feet long. These were placed about five feet apart and parallel, and then firmly secured by bamboo joists. Over these we spread a flooring of split bamboo, and planted four stout chonta sticks to support a palm-thatched roof. A rudder (a novel idea to our red-skinned companions), and a box of sand in the stern of one of the boats for a fire-place, completed our rig. The alcalde, with a hiccough, declared we would be forever going down the river in such a huge craft, and the Indians smiled ominously. But when our gallant ship left Coca obediently to the helm, and at the rate of six miles an hour when paddles and current worked together, they shouted "*bueno!*" Our trunks and provision-cans were arranged along the two sides of the platform, so that we had abundance of from for exercise by day and for sleeping under musquito-tents at night. A little canoe, which we bought of the alcalde, floated alongside for a tender, and was very serviceable in hunting, gathering fuel, etc. In the "forecastle"—the bows of the large canoes which projected beyond our cabin—sat three Indians to paddle. The fourth, who was the governor of Santa Rosa, we honored with the post of steersman; and he was always to be seen on the poop behind the kitchen, standing bolt upright, on the alert and on the lookout. On approaching any human habitation, the Indians blew horns to indicate that they came as friends. These horns must have come from Brazil, as there are no bovines on the Napo. Whenever they enter an unknown lagune they blow their horns also to charm the *yacu-mama*, or mother-of-waters, as they call the imaginary serpent.

At different points down the river they deposited pots

of chicha for use on their return. The mass breeds worms so rapidly, however, as Edwards informed us, that after the lapse of a month or two it is a jumble of yuca scraps and writhing articulates. But the owner of the heap coolly separates the animal from the vegetable, adds a little water, and drinks his chicha without ceremony. During leisure hours the Indians busied themselves plaiting palm leaves into ornaments for their arms and heads. Not a note did they whistle or sing. Yet they were always in good humor, and during the whole voyage we did not see the slightest approach to a quarrel. At no time did we have the least fear of treachery or violence.

The Napos are not savages. Their goodness, however, as Bates says of the Cucáma tribe, consists more in the absence of active bad qualities than in the possession of good ones. Of an apathetic temperament and dull imagination, we could not stir them into admiration or enthusiam by any scientific wonder; the utmost manifestation of surprise was a cluck with the tongue.* Upon presenting the governor with a vest, he immediately cut off the buttons, and, dividing the cloth into four parts, shared it with his fellows.† When it rained they invariably took off their ponchos, but in all our intercourse with these wild men we never noticed the slightest breach of modesty. They strictly maintained a decent arrangement of such apparel as they possessed. A canoe containing a young Indian, his bride, and our governor's wife and babe, accompanied us down to the Marañon. They were going after a load of salt for Sandoval. The girl was a graceful paddler, and

* Bates says the Mundurucus express surprise by making a clicking sound with their teeth, and Darwin observes that the Fuegians have the habit of making a chuckling noise when pleased.

† The like perfect equality exists among the Fuegian tribes. "A piece of cloth given to one is torn into shreds and distributed, and no one individual becomes richer than another."—*Darwin.*

Our Craft on the Napo.

had some well-founded pretensions to beauty. Her coarse, black hair was simply combed back, not braided into plaits as commonly done by the Andean women. All, both male and female, painted their faces with achote to keep off the sand-flies.

Pratt managed the helm (the governor could not work the Yankee notion) and the kitchen. At Santa Rosa we had added to our Quito stock of provisions some manati-lard (bottled up in a joint of a bamboo) and sirup, and at Coca we took in three fowls, a bag of rice, and a bunch of bananas. So we fared sumptuously every day. We left Coca on Thanksgiving Day, November 28th, and to imitate our distant friends, we sacrificed an extra meal—fricasseed chicken, jerked beef, boiled yucas, bananas, oranges, lemonade, and guayusa. Favored by a powerful current and the rhythmic paddling of our Santa Rosans, we made this day sixty miles; but our average daily run was fifty miles. The winds (doubtless the trades) were almost unchangeably from the east; but an occasional puff would come from the northwest, when we relieved our paddlers by hoisting a blanket for a sail. Six o'clock was our usual hour of departure, and ten or twelve hours our traveling time, always tying up at a plaia or island, of which there are hosts in the Napo, but never to the main land, for fear of unfriendly Indians and the still more unwelcome tiger. Our crew encamped at a respectful though hailing distance.

On the second day from Coca we were caught in a squall, and to save our roof we ran ashore. Nearly every afternoon we were treated to a shower, accompanied by a strong wind, but seldom by thunder and lightning, though at Coca we had a brilliant thunder-storm at night. They always came after a uniform fashion and at a regular hour, so that we learned when to expect them. About noon the eastern horizon would become suddenly black, and when this had spread to the zenith we heard the rush of a mighty wind sweeping through the forest, and the crash of falling trees, and then down fell the deluge. The Indians have a saying that "the path of the sun is the path of the storm." These storm-clouds moved rapidly, for in half an hour all was quiet on the Napo. At Quito, two hundred miles west, the usual afternoon shower occurs two hours later. To-day we enjoyed our last glimpse of the Andes. Far away across the great forest we had traversed we could see the beautiful cone of Cotopaxi and the flat top of Cayambi standing out in proud pre-eminence. Long will it be ere we forget this farewell view of the magnificent Cordillera.

CHAPTER XV.

Sea-Cows and Turtles' Eggs.—The Forest.—Peccaries.—Indian Tribes on the Lower Napo.—Anacondas and Howling Monkeys.—Insect Pests.—Battle with Ants.—Barometric Anomaly.—First View of the Amazon.—Pebas.

THE thirtieth of November was an exciting day on the monotonous Napo. We fell in with numerous sea-cows sporting in the middle of the stream. They were greatly disturbed by the sight of our huge craft, and, lifting their ugly heads high out of the water, gave a peculiar snort, as if in defiance, but always dived out of sight when fired upon. The sea-cow is called *vaca marina* by the Spaniards, *peixe boy* by the Brazilians, and *manati* in the West Indies. It has no bovine feature except in its upper lip. The head and skin remind one of a large seal. In many respects it may be likened to a hippopotamus without tusks or legs. It has a semicircular flat tail, and behind the head are two oval fins, beneath which are the breasts, which yield a white milk. The flesh resembles pork, with a disagreeable, fishy flavor.

To-day we anchored at several plaias to hunt turtles' eggs. Our Indians were very expert in finding the nests. Guided approximately by the tracks of the *tortugas*, as the turtles are called, they thrust a stick into the sand, and wherever it went down easily they immediately commenced digging with their hands, and invariably "struck" eggs. In four nests, whose contents we counted, there were one hundred and thirty-two, one hundred and fourteen, one hundred and twelve, and ninety-seven; but we have heard of one hundred and sixty eggs in a single nest. The turtles lay in the night, and in pits about two feet deep, which they excavate with their broad, webbed paws. The eggs are about an inch and a half in diameter, having a thin, leathery shell, a very oily yolk, and a white which does not coagulate. The Indians ate them uncooked. We used them chiefly in making corn griddles.

Here, as throughout its whole course, the Napo runs between two walls of evergreen verdure. On either hand are low clay banks (no rocks are visible), and from these the forest rises to a uniform height of seventy or eighty feet. It has a more cheerful aspect than the sombre, silent wilderness of Baeza. Old aristocrats of the woods are overrun by a gay democracy of creepers and climbers, which interlace the entire forest, and, descending to take root again, appear like the shrouds and stays of a line-of-battle ship. Monkeys gambol on this wild rigging, and mingle their chatter with the screams of the parrot. Trees as lofty as our oaks are covered with flowers as beautiful as our lilies. Here are orchids of softest tints;* flowering ferns, fifty feet high; the graceful bamboo and wild banana; while high over all countless species of palm wave their nodding plumes. Art could not arrange these beautiful forms so harmoniously as nature has done.

The tropics, moreover, are strangers to the uniformity of association seen in temperate climes. We have so many social plants that we speak of a forest of oaks, and pines, and birches; but there variety is the law. Individuals of the same species are seldom seen growing together. Every

* Some orchid is in flower all the year round. The finest species is the *odontoglossum*, having long, chocolate-colored petals, margined with yellow. "Such is their number and variety (wrote Humboldt) that the entire life of a painter would be too short to delineate all the magnificent Orchideæ which adorn the recesses of the deep valleys of the Peruvian Andes." For many curious facts respecting the structure of these flowers, see Darwin's *Fertilization of Orchids.*

Hunting Turtles' Eggs.

tree is surrounded by strangers that seemingly prefer its room to its company; and, such is the struggle for possession of the soil, it is difficult to tell to which stem the different leaves and flowers belong. The peculiar charm of a tropical forest is increased by the mystery of its impenetrable thicket. Within that dense, matted shrubbery, and behind that phalanx of trees, the imagination of the traveler sees all manner of four-footed beasts and creeping things. Tropical vegetation is of fresher verdure, more luxuriant and succulent, and adorned with larger and more shining leaves than the vegetation of the north. The leaves are not shed periodically—a character common, not only to the equator, but also to the whole southern hemisphere. Yet there is a variety of tints, though not autumnal. The leaves put on their best attire while budding instead of falling—passing, as they come to maturity, through different shades of red, brown, and green. The majority of tropical trees bear small flowers. The most conspicuous trees are the palms, to which the prize of beauty has been given by the concurrent voice of all ages. The earliest civilization of mankind belonged to countries bordering on the region of palms. South America, the continent of mingled heat and moisture, excels the rest of the world in the number and perfection of her palms. They are mostly of the feathery and fan-like species; the latter are inferior in rank to the former. The peculiarly majestic character of the palm is given not only by their lofty stems, but also in a very high degree by the form and arrangement of their leaves. How diverse, yet equally graceful, are the aspiring branches of the jagua and the drooping foliage of the cocoa, the shuttlecock-shaped crowns of the ubussú and the plumes of the jupati, forty feet in length. The inflorescence always springs from the top of the trunk, and the male flowers are generally yellowish. Unlike the oak, all species of which have similar fruit, there is a vast difference in the fruits of the palm: compare the triangular cocoa-nut, the peach-like date, and grape-like assaï. The silk-cotton tree is the rival of the palm in dignity; it has a white bark and a lofty flat crown. Among the loveliest children of Flora we must include the mimosa, with its delicately pinnated foliage, so endowed with sensibility that it seems to have stepped out of the bounds of vegetable life. The bamboo, the king of grasses, forms a distinctive feature in the landscape of the Napo, frequently rising eighty feet in length, though not in height, for the fronds curve downward. Fancy the airy grace of our meadow grasses united with the lordly growth of the poplar, and you have a faint idea of bamboo beauty.

The first day of winter (how strangely that sounds under a vertical sun!) was Sunday; but it was folly to attempt to rest where punkies were as thick as atoms, so we floated on. It was only by keeping in mid-river and moving rapidly enough to create a breeze through our cabin, that life was made tolerable. A little after noon we were again obliged to tie up for a storm. Not a human being nor a habitation have we seen since leaving Coca; and to-day nothing is visible but the river, with its islands, and plaias, and the green palisades—the edges of the boundless forest. Not a hill over one hundred feet high are we destined to see till we reach Obidos, fifteen hundred miles eastward. Were it not for the wealth of vegetation—all new to trans-tropical eyes—and the concerts of monkeys and macaws, oppressively lonely would be the sail down the Napo between its uninhabited shores. But we believe the day, though distant, will come when its banks will be busy with life. Toward evening three or four canoes pulled out from the shore and came alongside. They were filled with the lowest class of Indians we have seen in South America.

The women were nearly nude; the man (there was only one) had on a sleeveless frock reaching to the knees, made from the bark of a tree called *llanchama*. All were destitute of eyebrows; their hair was parted in the middle, and their teeth and lips were dyed black. They had rude pottery, peccari meat, and wooden lances to sell. Like all the Napo Indians, they had a weakness for beads, and they wore necklaces of tiger and monkey teeth. They were stupid rather than brutal, and probably belonged to a degraded tribe of the great Zaparo family. With Darwin, "one's mind hurries back over past centuries, and then asks, could our progenitors have been men like these?—men whose very signs and expressions are less intelligible to us than those of the domesticated animals; men who do not possess the instinct of those animals, nor yet appear to boast of human reason, or, at least, of arts consequent on that reason. I do not believe it is possible to describe or paint the difference between savage and civilized man. It is the difference between a wild and tame animal; and part of the interest in beholding a savage is the same which would lead every one to desire to see the lion in his desert, the tiger tearing his prey in the jungle, or the rhinoceros wandering over the wild plains of Africa."

On the morrow our falcon-eyed Indians whispered "*cuche*" long before we saw any thing.* Williams went ashore and came upon a herd of peccaries, killing two. The peccari is a pugnacious, fearless animal. It is not frightened by the noise of fire-arms, and when wounded is a dangerous foe; but captured when young, it is easily tamed. It has a higher back than the domestic hog, and cleanlier habits; an odoriferous gland on the loins, and three-toed hind feet. We preserved the skins for science and a ham for the table; the rest we gave to our crew and fellow-voyagers,

* In the Quichua of Quito the peccari is called *saino*.

who devoured every thing, even the viscera. They sat up late that night, around their camp-fire, cooking peccari meat: part they parboiled in a pot, and some they roasted, skewered on sticks which slanted over the flames; the rest they cured with smoke, for lack of salt. The meat, though rank, is palatable, but not equal to macaw, which we served up the next day.*

We had now passed the mouth of the Aguarico, leaving behind us the Christian Quitus and the peaceful Zaparos. Henceforth the right bank of the Napo is inhabited by the Mazanes and Iquitos; while on the left are the wilder Santa Marias, Anguteros, Oritos, and Orejones. The Orejones, or "Big Ears," enlarge those appendages to such an extent that they are said to lie down on one ear and cover themselves with the other. This practice is now going out of fashion. These Indians received their name, Orejones, or Oregones, from the Spaniards, on account of this singular custom of inserting disks of wood in the ears to enlarge them; the like practice prevailed among the tribes on the Columbia River, Oregon. They trade in hammocks, poisons, and provisions. The Anguteros, or Putumayos, have a bad reputation. They are reported to have killed and robbed sarsaparilla traders coming up stream. Nevertheless, we kept watch only one night during the voyage, though we always anchored to an island, and between Coca and the Amazon we did not see twenty-five men. Equally rare were the savage brutes—not a jaguar showed himself, and only one anaconda. The anaconda, or water-boa (*Eunectes murinus*†), is larger and more formidable

* The Uaupes on the Napo, according to Wallace, will not eat peccari meat. "Meat putrifies in this climate (of the Tapajos) in less than twenty-four hours, and salting is of no use unless the pieces are cut in thin slices and dried immediately in the sun."—*Bates.*

† The specific name was strangely given for its habit, when young, of darting upon mice. Anaconda is a Ceylonese word.

than the boa-constrictor which lives on the land. It has a hideous appearance, broad in the middle, and tapering abruptly at both ends. We did not learn from the natives that anacondas over twenty feet long had been seen on the Napo, but specimens twice that size are found on the Amazon. Land boas do not often exceed fifteen feet in length.

Gangs of the large howling monkeys often entertained us with their terrific, unearthly yells, which, in the truthful language of Bates, "increased tenfold the feeling of inhospitable wildness which the forest is calculated to inspire." They are of a maroon color (the males wear a long red beard), and have under the jaw a bony goître—an expansion of the os hyoides—by means of which they produce their loud, rolling noise. They set up an unusual

A Howler.

chorus whenever they saw us, scampering to the tops of the highest trees, the dams carrying the young upon their backs. They are the only monkeys which the natives have not been able to tame. Vast numbers of screaming parrots and macaws flew over our heads, always going in pairs and at a great height. Groups of "gypsy-birds" were perched on the trees overhanging the river, and black ducks, cormorants, and white cranes floated on the water or stalked along the plaias.

But one form of life superabounded. From the rising of the sun to the going down thereof clouds of ubiquitous sand-flies filled our cabin, save when the wind was high. As soon as the sand-flies ceased, myriads of musquitoes began their work of torture, without much preparatory piping, and kept it up all night.* These pests were occasionally relieved or assisted by piums—minute flies that alight unnoticed, and squatting close to the skin, suck their fill of blood, leaving dark spots and a disagreeable irritation. Our hands were nearly black with their punctures. We also made the acquaintance of the montúca, a large black fly whose horny lancets make a gash in the flesh, painless but blood-letting. All these insects are most abundant in the latter part of the rainy season, when the Marañon is almost uninhabitable. The apostrophe of Midshipman Wilberforce was prompted by sufferings which we can fully appreciate: "Ye greedy animals! I am ashamed of you. Can not you once forego your dinner, and feast your mind with the poetry of the landscape?" Right welcome was the usual afternoon squall, which sent these pests "kiting" over the stern.

On Wednesday we fell in with a petty sarsaparilla trader, with two canoes, bound for the Marañon. He was sick with fever. Sarsaparilla (written *salsaparrilha* in Brazil, and meaning "bramble vine") is the root of a prickly, climbing plant found throughout the whole Amazonian forest, but chiefly on dry, rocky ground. On the morning of the seventh day from Coca we passed the mouth of the Curaray, the largest tributary of the Napo. It rises on the slopes of the Llanganati mountains, and is considered au-

* Sand-flies are called by the natives *musquitoes*, and what we call musquitoes they call *sancudos*.

riferous. It is probably derived from *curi*, gold. Seeing a hut on the banks, we sent an Indian to purchase provisions; he returned with a few yucas and eggs. The day following we were attacked from a new quarter. Stopping to escape a storm, a party went ashore to cut down a tree of which we desired a section. It fell with its top in the river, just above our craft; when lo! to our consternation, down came countless hosts of ants (*Ecitons*). Myriads were, of course, swept down stream, but myriads more crawled up the sides of our canoes, and in one minute after the tree fell our whole establishment, from hold to roof, was swarming with ants. We gave one look of despair at each other, our provisions and collections, and then commenced a war of extermination. It was a battle for life. The ants, whose nest we had so suddenly immersed in the Napo, refused to quit their new lodgings. As we were loosely dressed, the tenacious little creatures hid themselves under our clothing, and when plucked off would leave their heads and jaws sticking in the skin. At last the deck was cleared by means of boots, slippers, and towels; but, had the ants persevered, they might have taken possession of the boat.

To-day we saw a high bank (called in Quichua *puca-urcu*, or red hill) consisting of fine laminated clays of many colors—red, orange, yellow, gray, black, and white. This is the beginning of that vast deposit which covers the whole Amazonian Valley. It rests upon a bed of lignite, or bituminous shale, and a coarse, iron-cemented conglomerate. The latter is not visible on the Napo, but crops out particularly at Obidos and Pará. The Indians prepare their paints from these colored clays.

Our Santa Rosans seemed to have little tact in fishing; still their spears and our hooks gathered not a few representatives of ichthyic life in the Napo. The species most common belong to the genus *Pimelodus*, or cat-fish tribe. Below the Curaray the sand bars yielded turtles' eggs of a different kind from those found above, the *tracajá*. They were smaller and oval, and buried only six or eight inches deep, thirty in a nest.

December 9.—Passed early this morning the mouth of the Mazan; four huts at the junction. To-day we noticed the anomaly first observed by Herndon. From Papallacta to the Curaray the rise of the mercury was regular, but on the lower Napo there were great fluctuations. At one time both barometer and boiling apparatus, with which we made daily and simultaneous observations, unanimously declared that our canoes were gliding up stream, though we were descending at the rate of five miles an hour. The temperature is decidedly lower and the winds are stronger as we near the Amazon.

December 10.—Our last day on the Napo. In celebration of the event we killed a fine young doe as it was crossing the river. It closely resembled the Virginia deer. At 9 A.M. the Indians shouted in their quiet way—"*Marañon!*" It was as thrilling as *Thalatta* to Xenophon's soldiers. We were not expecting to reach it till night, being deceived by Villavicencio's map, which, in common with all others, locates the Curaray and Mazan too far to the north. We halted for an hour at Camindo, a little fishing hamlet claimed by Peru, and then hastened to get our first sight of the Amazon. With emotions we can not express, we gazed upon this ocean-stream. The march of the great river in its silent grandeur is sublime. In its untamed might it rolls through the wilderness with a stately, solemn air, showing its awful power in cutting away the banks, tearing down trees, and building up islands in a day. Down the river we can look till the sky and water meet as on the sea, while the forest on either hand dwindles in the perspective to a long black line. Between these even walls of ever-living green the resistless current hurries out of Peru, sweeps past the imperial guns of Tabatinga into Brazil, and plows its way visibly two hundred miles into the Atlantic.

At a small island standing where the Napo pays tribute to the monarch of rivers, mingling its waters with the Huallaga and Ucayali, which have already come down from the Peruvian Andes, we bade adieu to our captain and cook, who, in the little canoe, paddled his way westward to seek his fortune in Iquitus. At this point the Marañon (for so the natives call the Upper Amazon) does not appear very much broader than the Napo; but its depth is far greater, and there are few sand-bars.* The water is always of a turbid yellow; while the Napo, though muddy during our voyage, is usually clear. The forest, moreover, on the banks of the Marañon, is not so striking as on the tributary. The palms are not so numerous, and the uniform height of the trees gives a monotonous, sea-like horizon.

We arrived at Pebas December 12, ten hours after leaving the mouth of the Napo, and a month and a half from Quito. The first individual we met addressed us in good English, and proved to be Mr. Hauxwell, a well-known collector of birds and insects, who has resided thirty years on the Amazon. His house, the largest and best in town, though but a roofed stockade, was generously placed at our disposal, and the fatted calf—an immense turtle—was immediately killed. To us, after the transit of the Andes and the dangers and hardships of the wilderness and the river, it seemed as if we had reached the end of our jour-

* Herndon makes the mouth of the Napo 150 yards broad, and the soundings six or seven fathoms. This is not a fair representation; for the Napo, like all the other tributaries, empties its waters by several mouths. At Camindo, five miles above the confluence, the Napo is certainly a mile wide.

ney, though we were over two thousand miles from the Atlantic. Pebas is situated on a high clay bluff beside the Ambi-yacu, a mile above its entrance into the Marañon. Excepting Mr. Hauxwell, the Peruvian governor, and two or three other whites, the inhabitants are Indians of the Orejones and Yagua tribes. The exportations are hammocks, sarsaparilla, palo de cruz, and urarí. Palo de cruz is the very hard, dark-colored wood of a small leguminous tree bearing large pink flowers. Urarí is the poison used by all the Amazonian Indians; it is made by the Ticunas on the Putumayo, by boiling to a jelly the juices of certain roots and herbs, chiefly of the *Strychnos toxifera*, though it does not contain any trace of strychnine. Tipped with urarí, the needle-like arrow used in blow-guns will kill an ox in twenty minutes and a monkey in ten. "We have reason to congratulate ourselves (wrote the facetious Sidney Smith) that our method of terminating disputes is by sword and pistol, and not by these medicated pins." But the poison appears to be harmless to man and other salt-eating animals, salt being an antidote.* We were not troubled with sand-flies after leaving the plaias of the Napo, but the musquitoes at Pebas were supernumerary. Perhaps, however, it was a special gathering on our account, for the natives have a notion that just before the arrival of a foreigner the musquitoes come in great numbers.

Many of the Indians are disfigured by dark blotches on the skin, the effect of a cutaneous disease very prevalent in

* Urarí is mentioned by Raleigh. Humboldt was the first to take any considerable quantity to Europe. The experiments of Virchau and Münster make it probable that it does not belong to the class of tetanic poisons, but that its particular effect is to take away the power of voluntary muscular movement, while the involuntary functions of the heart and intestines still continue. See *Ann. de Chim. et de Phys.*, t. xxxix., 1828, p. 24; and Schömberg's *Reisen in Britisch Guiana*, th. i., s. 441. The frightful poison, *tieuté* of India, is prepared from a Java species of *strychnos.*

Central Amazonia. Here we first noticed the singular habit among the children of eating clay. This habit is not confined to the Otomacs on the Oronoco, nor to Indians altogether; for negroes and whites have the same propensity—Mr. Hauxwell found it impossible to restrain his own children. Bates ascribes the morbid craving to the meagre diet. This may be true to some extent, but it is certainly strange that the extraordinary desire to swallow earth (chiefly unctuous clays) is found only in the tropics, where vegetation is so rank and fruit so abundant.

CHAPTER XVI.

Down the Amazon.—Steam on the Great River.—Loreto.—San Antonio.—Tabatinga.—Brazilian Steamers.—Scenery on the Amazon.—Tocantíns.—Fonte Boa.—Ega.—Rio Negro.—Manáos.

WE left Pebas for Tabatinga in the Peruvian steamer "Morona," Captain Raygado. Going up to Jerusalem by railroad, or ascending the Nile by a screw whisking the sacred waters, is not so startling as the sight of a steamer in the heart of South America. There is such a contrast between the primeval wildness of the country and the people and this triumph of civilized life; and one looks forward to the dazzling future of this great valley, when the ships of all nations will crowd the network of rivers for the gold and perfumes, the gems and woods of this western Ophir. The natives call the steamer the "devil's boat," or "big canoe;" but they manifest little curiosity. Our Napo Indians were evidently afraid of it, and stood afar off. The first steamers that broke the deep solitude of the Marañon were the "Huallaga" and "Tirado," brought out in 1853 by Dr. Whittemore, for Peru. They were built in New York, of Georgia pine, costing Peru $75,000, and reflected no credit on the United States; they lie rotting near Nauta. Peru has now two iron steamers of London make—the "Morona" and "Pastassa"—besides two smaller craft for exploring the tributaries. These steamers are for government service, but three more are building in England with passenger accommodations. The "Morona" has a tonnage of five hundred, and an engine of one hundred and fifty horse-power. The engineers are English, and the cook is a Chinaman. She makes monthly trips between Yurimaguas, on the Huallaga River, and Tabatinga, on the Brazilian frontier. Her rate down stream is eighteen miles an hour, and from eleven to twelve against the current. These steamers do not pay expenses at present; but they preserve the authority of Peru on the Marañon, and supply with material the government works at Iquitos. They also do a little commerce, taking down sarsaparilla and Moyabamba hats, and bringing up English dry-goods. There were not half a dozen passengers on board.

The only towns of any consequence west of Pebas are Iquitos, Nauta, and Yurimaguas. Peru claims them—in fact, all the villages on the Marañon. Iquitos is the most thriving town on the Upper Amazon. It is situated on an elevated plain on the left bank of the river, sixty miles above the mouth of the Napo. In Herndon's time it was "a fishing village of 227 inhabitants;" it now contains 2000. Here are the government iron-works, carried on by English mechanics. In 1867 there were six engineers, two iron-molders, two brass-molders, two coppersmiths, three blacksmiths, three pattern-makers, two boiler-makers, five shipwrights, three sawyers, besides bricklayers, brick-makers, carpenters, coopers, etc.; in all forty-two. All the coal for the furnaces is brought from England—the lignite on the banks of the Marañon is unfit for the purpose. A floating dock for vessels of a thousand tons has just been built. Nauta lies on the north bank of the Marañon, opposite the entrance of the Ucayali. Its inhabitants, about 1000, trade in fish, sarsaparilla, and wax from Ucayali. Yurimaguas is the port of Moyabamba, a city of 10,000 souls, six days' travel southwest. This vast eastern slope, lying on the branches of the Marañon, is called the Montaña of Peru. It is a region of inexhaustible fertility, and would yield ample returns to energy and capital. The villages are open to foreign commerce, free of duty; but at present the voice of civilized man is seldom heard, save on the main fluvial highway between Moyabamba and the Brazilian frontier. The Portuguese are the most adventurous traders. The value of imports to Peru by the Amazonian steamers during 1867 was $324,533; of exports, $267,748.

In two hours and a half we arrive at Maucallacta, or "Old Town," an Indian village on the right bank of the river. Here our passports were viséd by the Peruvian governor, and the steamer wooded up. One of the hands on the "Morona" was Manuel Medina, a mameluco, who was employed by Bates and Agassiz in their explorations. We left at noon of the following day, and anchored for the night off Caballococha, for the Peruvian steamers run only in the daytime. Caballococha, or "Horse-lake," is a Ticuna town, situated on a level tract of light loam, closely surrounded by the dense forest, and beside a caño of clear water leading to a pretty lake. Ecuador claims this town, and likewise all the settlements on the Marañon; but her learned geographer, Villavicencio, with characteristic ignorance of the country, has located it on the *north* bank of the river!

We passed in the afternoon the little tug "Napo," having on board Admiral Tucker, the rebel, who, with some associates, is exploring the tributaries of the Upper Amazon for the Peruvian government. They had just returned from a voyage of two hundred and fifty miles up the Javarí. One of the party had a tame tiger-cat in his arms. We arrived at Loreto early the next morning. This village of twenty houses and a church is prettily situated on the left bank, with a green slope in front. It is the most easterly town of Peru on the Amazon. Here resides Mr.

Wilkens, the Brazilian consul, of German birth, but North American education. The inhabitants are Peruvians, Portuguese, Negroes, and Ticuna Indians. The musquitoes hold high carnival at this place. In two hours we were at San Antonio, a military post on the Peruvian frontier, commanded by a French engineer, Manuel Charon, who also studied in the United States. One large building, and a flag-staff on a high bluff of red clay, were all that was visible of San Antonio; but the "Morona" brought down a gang of Indians (impressed, no doubt) to build a fort for twenty guns. The site is in dispute, a Brazilian claiming it as private property. The white barracks of Tabatinga, the first fortress in Brazil, are in plain sight, the voyage consuming but twenty minutes. Between San Antonio and Tabatinga is a ravine, on either side of which is a white pole, marking the limits of the republic and the empire.

Tabatinga has long been a military post, but, excepting the government buildings, there are not a dozen houses. Numerous Indians, however, of the Ticuna tribe, dwell in the neighboring forest. The commandante was O Illustrissimo Señor Tenente Aristides Juste Mavignier, a tall, thin, stooping officer, dressed in brown linen. He received us with great civility, and tendered a house and servant during our stay in port. We preferred, however, to accept the hospitalities of the "Morona" till the arrival of the Brazilian steamer. Señor Mavignier was commandante of Manáos when visited by Agassiz, and presented the Professor with a hundred varieties of wood. With the like courtesy, he gave us a collection of reptiles, all of them rare, and many of them new species. He showed us also a live raposa, or wild dog, peculiar to the Amazon, but seldom seen. Tabatinga stands on an eminence of yellow clay, and is defended by twelve guns. The river in front is quite narrow, only about half a mile wide. Here our passports, which had been signed at Maucallacta and Loreto, were indorsed by the commandante. They were afterward examined at Ega, Manáos, and Pará. The mean temperature of Tabatinga we found to be 82°.* Some rubber and salt fish are exported, but nothing of consequence is cultivated. Grapes, the people say, grow well, but are destroyed by the ants. The only fruit-trees we noticed were the mamaï (in Spanish, papaya), aracá, and abío. The papaw-tree bears male and female flowers on different trees, and hence receives the name of *papaya* or *mamaï*, according to one's view of the pre-eminence of the sex. The juice of this tree is used by the ladies of the West Indies as a cosmetic, and by the butchers to render the toughest meat tender. The fruit is melon-shaped, and of an orange-yellow color. Vauquelin discovered in it *fibrine*, till lately supposed to be confined to the animal kingdom.

The Peruvian steamers connect at Tabatinga with the Brazilian line. There are eight imperial steamers on the Amazon: the "Icamiaba," running between Tabatinga and Manáos; the "Tapajos" and "Belem," plying between Manáos and Pará; the "Inca" and "Manáos," between Obidos and Pará; besides two steamers on the Tocantíns, one between Pará and Chares, and projected lines for the Negro, Tapajos, and Madeira. The captains get a small salary, but the perquisites are large, as they have a percentage on the freight. One captain pocketed in one year $9000.

We embarked, December 12, on the "Icamiaba," which promptly arrived at Tabatinga. The commander, formerly a lieutenant in the Imperial Navy, and for twelve years a popular officer on the Upper Amazon, was a polished gentleman, but rigid disciplinarian. As an example of

* According to Lieutenant Azevedo, the latitude of Tabatinga is 4° 14′ 30″; longitude, 70° 2′ 24″; magnetic variation, 6° 35′ 10″ N.E.

Brazilian etiquette, we give his full address from one of our letters of introduction:

"Ilmo. Sr. Capn. de Fragata
Nuno Alvez Pereira de Mello Cardozo,
Digno Commandante de Vapor
Icamiaba."

The "Icamiaba" was an iron boat of four hundred and fifty tons, with two engines of fifty horse-power each. The engineer was an Austrian, yet the captain gave his orders in English, though neither could speak the language. The saloon, with berths for twenty-five passengers, was above deck, and open at both ends for ventilation. The passengers, however, usually swung their hammocks on the upper deck, which was covered by an awning. This was a delightfully breezy and commanding position; and though every part of the steamer was in perfect order, this was scrupulously neat. Here the table was spread with every tropical luxury, and attentively served by young men in spotless attire. Happy the traveler who sits at the table of Commandante Cardozo. The refreshment hours were: Coffee as soon as the passengers turned out of their hammocks, and sometimes before; breakfast at ten, dinner at five, and tea at eight. Live bullocks, fowls, and turtles were kept on board, so that of fresh meat, particularly beef (the first we had tasted since leaving Quito), there was no lack. At breakfast we counted nine different courses of meat. The Peruvian steamers are limited to turtle and salt fish. Rice and farina are extensively used in Brazil, but we saw very little tapioca. Farina is the flour of the country, and is eaten in hard, dry grains; it will not keep in any other form. It can not be very nutritious, as it contains little gluten. All bread and butter are imported from the United States and England. The captains of Brazilian steamers are their own stewards; and in the midst of other business in port, they stop to negotiate for a chicken, or a dozen eggs, with an Indian or Negro. The "Icamiaba" left Tabatinga with only three first-class passengers, besides our own party. On no Amazon steamer did we meet with a lady passenger. Madame Godin, who came down the river from the Andes, and Mrs. Agassiz, who ascended to Tabatinga, were among the few ladies who have seen these upper waters. But how differently they traveled! one on a raft, the other on the beautiful "Icamiaba."

Between Tabatinga and Teffé, a distance of five hundred miles, is perhaps the most uncivilized part of the main river. Ascending, we find improvements multiply as we near the mountains of Peru; descending, we see the march of civilization in the budding cities and expanding commerce culminating at Grand Pará. The scenery from the deck of an Amazonian steamer, if described, appears monotonous. A vast volume of smooth, yellow water, floating trees and beds of aquatic grass, low, linear-shaped, wooded islets, a dark, even forest—the shores of a boundless sea of verdure, and a cloudless sky occasionally obscured by flocks of parrots: these are the general features. No busy towns are seen along the banks of the Middle Amazon; only here and there a palm hut or semi-Indian village half buried in the wilderness. We agree with Darwin (speaking of the Plata), that "a wide expanse of muddy water has neither grandeur nor beauty." The real grandeur, however, of a great river like this is derived from reflecting upon its prospective commercial importance and its immense drainage. A lover of nature, moreover, can never tire of gazing at the picturesque grouping and variety of trees, with their mantles of creeping plants; while a little imagination can see in the alligators, ganoid fishes, sea-cows, and tall gray herons, the ichthyosaurus, holoptychius, dinotherium, and brontozoum of ancient days. Here and there the river is bordered with low alluvial deposits covered with feathery-topped arrow-grass and amphibious vegetation; but generally the banks are about ten feet high and magnificently wooded; they are abrupt, and land-slides are frequent.

A few minutes after leaving Tabatinga we passed the mouth of the Javarí, which forms the natural boundary between Peru and Brazil. Henceforth the river loses the name of Marañon, and is called Solimoens, or, more commonly, simply Amazon. We were ten hours in reaching San Paulo, a wretched Ticuna village of five hundred souls, built on a grassy table-land nearly one hundred feet high. Steps have been cut in the slippery clay bluff to facilitate the ascent. Swamps lie back of the town, rendering it unhealthy. "On damp nights (says the Naturalist on the Amazon) the chorus of frogs and toads which swarm in weedy back-yards creates such a bewildering uproar that it is impossible to carry on a conversation in doors except by shouting."

In ten hours more we had passed the Putumayo and entered the Tunantíns, a sluggish, dark-colored tributary emptying into the Amazon about two hundred miles below the Javarí.* On the bank of white earth, which strongly contrasts with the tinted stream, is a dilapidated hamlet of twenty-five hovels, built of bamboo plastered with mud and whitewashed. We saw but one two-storied house; and all have ground-floors and double-thatched roofs. The inhabitants are semi-civilized Shumána and Passé Indians and half-breeds; but in the gloomy forest which hugs the town live the wild Caishanas. The atmosphere is close and steaming, but not hot, the mercury at noon standing at 83°. The place is alive with insects and birds. The nights on

* Herndon says (p. 241), "the Tunantíns is about fifty yards broad, and seems deep with a considerable current."

Kitchen on the Amazon.

the Amazon were invariably cool; on the Lower Amazon, cold, so that we required a heavy blanket.

Taking on board wood, beeves, turtles, salt fish, and water-melons, we left at half past 2 P.M. The Brazilian steamers run all night, and with no slackening of speed. At one o'clock we were awakened by a cry from the watch,

"Stop her!" And immediately after there was a crash; but it was only the breaking of crockery caused by the sudden stoppage. The night was fearfully dark, and for aught we knew the steamer was running headlong into the forest. Fortunately there was no collision, and in a few minutes we were again on our way, arriving at Fonte Boa at 4 A.M. This little village stands in a palm grove, on a high bank of ochre-colored sandy clay, beside a slue of sluggish black water, eight miles from the Amazon.* The inhabitants, about three hundred, are ignorant, lazy mamelucos. They dress like the majority of the semi-civilized people on the Amazon: the men content with shirt and pantaloons, the women wearing cotton or gauze chemises and calico petticoats. Fonte Boa is a museum for the naturalist, but the headquarters of musquitoes, small but persistent. Taking in a large quantity of turtle-oil, the "Icamiaba" turned down the caño, but almost immediately ran aground, and we were two hours getting off. These yearly shifting shoals in the Amazon can not be laid down in charts, and the most experienced pilots often run foul of them. In twelve hours we entered the Teffé, a tributary from the Bolivian mountains. Just before reaching the Great River it expands into a beautiful lake, with a white, sandy beach. On a grassy slope, stretching out into the lake, with a harbor on each side of it, lies the city of Ega. A hundred palm-thatched cottages of mud and tiled frame houses, each with an inclosed orchard of orange, lemon, banana, and guava trees, surround a rude church, marked by a huge wooden crucifix on the green before it, instead of a steeple. Cacao, assaï, and pupunha palms rise above the town, adding greatly to its beauty; while back of all, on the summit of the green slope, begins the pictur-

* Smyth says the town gets its name from the clearness of the water; but Herndon found it muddy, and, to our eyes, it was dark as the Negro.

esque forest, pathless, save here and there a faint hunter's track leading to the untrodden interior. The sheep and cattle grazing on the lawn, a rare sight in Alto Amazonas, gives a peaceful and inviting aspect to the scene. The inhabitants, numbering about twelve hundred, are made up of pure Indians, half-castes, negroes, mulattoes, and whites. Ega (also called Teffé) is the largest and most thriving town between Manáos and Iquitos, a distance of twelve hundred miles. It is also one of the oldest settlements on the river, having been founded during the English revolution, or nearly two centuries ago. Tupi is the common idiom. The productions of the country are cacao, sarsaparilla, Brazil nuts, bast for caulking vessels, copaiba balsam, India-rubber, salt fish, turtle-oil, manati, grass hammocks, and tiles. Bates calculates the value of the annual exports at nearly forty thousand dollars. The "Icamiaba" calls here twice a month; besides which there are small schooners which occupy about five months in the round trip between Ega and Pará. "The place is healthy (writes the charming Naturalist on the Amazon), and almost free from insect pests; perpetual verdure surrounds it; the soil is of marvelous fertility, even for Brazil; the endless rivers and labyrinths of channels teem with fish and turtle; a fleet of steamers might anchor at any season of the year in the lake, which has uninterrupted water communication straight to the Atlantic. What a future is in store for the sleepy little tropical village!" Here Bates pursued butterflies for four years and a half, and Agassiz fished for six months.

Ega is the half-way point across the continent, but its exact altitude above the sea is unknown. Herndon's boiling apparatus gave two thousand feet, and, what is worse, the lieutenant believed it. Our barometer made it one hundred feet; but as our instrument, though perfect in itself, behaved very strangely on the Middle Amazon, we do

Natives on the Middle Amazon.

not rely on the calculation. The true height is not far from one hundred and twenty-five feet, or one fifth the elevation of the middle point in the North American continent.* Taking on board salt fish, turtle-oil, and tiles, we

* For a discussion of the barometric perturbations on the Amazon, see *American Journal of Science* for Sept., 1868.

left Ega two hours after midnight, reaching Coary at noon. The Amazon began to look more like a lake than a river, having a width of four or five miles. Floating gulls and rolling porpoises remind one of the sea. Coary is a huddle of fifteen houses, six of them plastered without, whitewashed, and tiled. It is situated on a lake of the same name — the expanded outlet of a small river whose waters are dark brown, and whose banks are low and covered with bushes. Here we took in turtles and turtle-oil, Brazil nuts and cocoa-nuts, rubber, salt fish, and wood; and, six hours after leaving, more fish and rubber were received at Cudajá. Cudajá is a lonely spot on the edge of an extensive system of back-waters and lakes, running through a dense unexplored forest inhabited by Múra savages.

At three in the afternoon of Christmas, seventy-four hours' running time from Tabatinga, we entered the Rio Negro. Strong is the contrast between its black-dyed waters and the yellow Amazon. The line separating the two rivers is sharply drawn, the waters meeting, not mingling. Circular patches of the dark waters of the Negro are seen floating like oil amid the turbid waters of the Amazon. The sluggish tributary seems to be dammed up by the impetuous monarch. The banks of the latter are low, ragged, perpendicular beds of clay, covered with a bright green foliage; the Negro is fringed with sandy beaches, with hills in the background clothed with a sombre, monotonous forest containing few palms or leguminous trees. Musquitoes, piums, and montucas never trouble the traveler on the inky stream. When seen in a tumbler, the water of the Negro is clear, but of a light-red color; due, undoubtedly, to vegetable matter. The visible mouth of the river at this season of the year (December) is three miles wide, but from main-land to main-land it can not be less than twenty.

In forty minutes after leaving the Amazon we arrived at Manáos. This important city lies on the left bank of the Negro, ten miles from its mouth and twenty feet above high-water level. The site is very uneven, and consists of ferruginous sandstone. There was originally a fort here, erected by the Portuguese to protect their slave-hunting expeditions among the Indians on the river—hence the ancient name of Barra. On the old map of Father Fritz (1707) the spot is named *Taromas.* Since 1852 it has been called Manáos, after the most warlike tribe. Some of the houses are two-storied, but the majority are low adobe structures, white and yellow washed, floored and roofed with tiles, and having green doors and shutters. Every room is furnished with hooks for hanging hammocks. We did not see a bed between Quito and New York except on the steamers. The population, numbering two thousand,* is a mongrel set—Brazilians, Portuguese, Italians, Jews, Negroes, and Indians, with divers crosses between them. Laziness is the prominent characteristic. A gentleman offered an Indian passing his door twenty-five cents if he would bring him a pitcher of water from the river, only a few rods distant. He declined. "But I will give you fifty cents." Whereupon the half-clothed, penniless aboriginal replied: "I will give you a dollar to bring me some."† While every inch of the soil is of exuberant fertility, there is always a scarcity of food. It is the dearest spot on the Amazon. Most of the essentials and all of the luxuries come from Liverpool, Lisbon, and New York. Agriculture is at a discount on the Amazon. Brazilians will not work; European immigrants are traders; nothing can be done with Indians; and negroes are

* Official returns for 1848 give 3614; Bates (1850) reckons 3000.

† Darwin met a similar specimen in Banda Oriental: "I asked two men why they did not work. One gravely said the days were too long; the other that he was too poor."

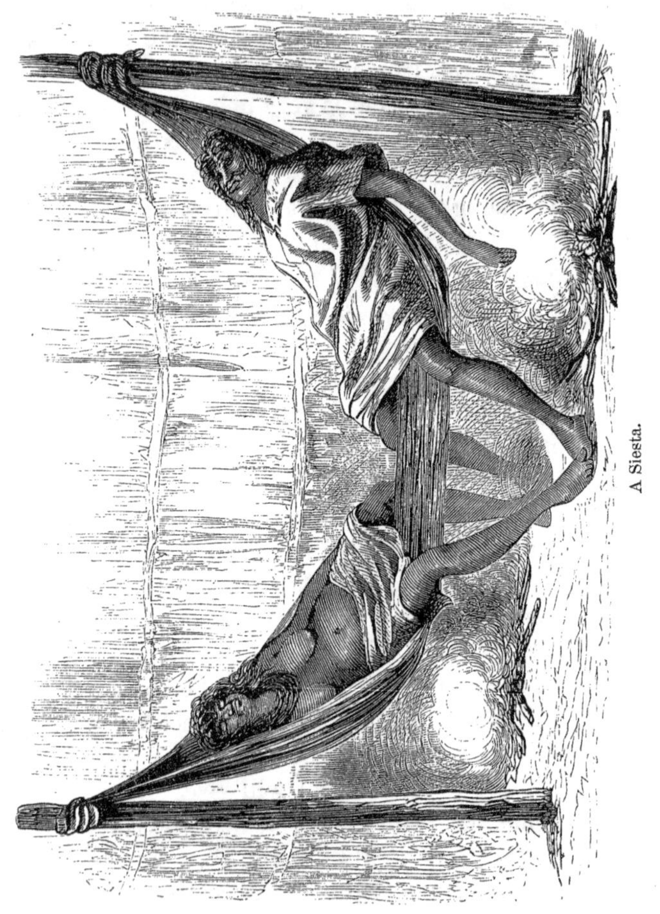

A Siesta.

few in number, the slave-trade being abolished, emancipation begun, and the Paraguayan war not ended. A laboring class will ever be a desideratum in this tropical country. With a healthy climate,* and a situation at the juncture of

* It is, however, one of the warmest spots on the river. The average temperature, according to Azevedo and Pinto, is only 79.7°; but the highest

two great navigable rivers, Manáos is destined to become the St. Louis of South America. In commercial advantages it is hardly to be surpassed by any other city in the world, having water communication with two thirds of the continent, and also with the Atlantic. It is now the principal station for the Brazilian line of steamers. Here all goods for a higher or lower point are reshipped. The chief articles of export are coffee (of superior quality), sarsaparilla, Brazil nuts, piassaba, and fish. The Negro at this point is really five or six miles wide, but the opposite shore is masked by low islands, so that it appears to be but a mile and a half.

The country around Manáos is quite romantic for the Amazonian Valley. The land is undulating and furrowed by ravines, and the vegetation covering it is marvelously rich and diversified. In the forest, two miles from the city, there is a natural curiosity celebrated by all travelers from Spix and Martius down. A rivulet coming out of the wilderness falls over a ledge of red sandstone ten feet high and fifty feet broad, forming a beautiful cascade. The water is cool, and of a deep orange color. The foundation of a fine stone cathedral was laid in Manáos fourteen years ago, but this generation is not likely to witness the dedication. Life in this Amazonian city is dull enough: commerce is not brisk, and society is stiff; balls are about the only amusements. On Sunday (the holiday) every body who can afford it comes out in Paris fashions. There are carts, but no coaches. We called upon the President at his "Palace"—an odd term for a two-storied, whitewashed edifice. His excellency received us with less formality and more cordiality than we expected to find in the solemn officials of the empire. The first glance at the

point reached on the Amazon in 1862 (87.3°) was at Manáos, and the extraordinary height of 95° has been noted there.

reception-room, with the four chairs for visitors set in two lines at right angles to the chair of state, promised cold etiquette; but he addressed us with considerable familiarity and evident good-will. We found, however, that his authority was quite limited, for a written order which he gave us for a subordinate did not receive the slightest consideration. At the house of a Jew named Levy we met a party of Southerners, Captains Mallory, Jones, Sandedge, and Winn, commanded by Dr. Dowsing, who, since "the late onpleasantness," as Nasby calls it, have determined to settle in this country. The government grants them twenty square leagues of land on any tributary, on condition that they will colonize it. They were about to start for the Rio Branco on an exploring tour.

CHAPTER XVII.

Down the Amazon.—Serpa.—Villa Nova.—Obidos.—Santarem.—A Colony of Southerners.—Monte Alégre.—Porto do Moz.—Leaving the Amazon. —Breves.—Pará River.—The City of Pará.—Legislation and Currency. —Religion and Education.—Nonpareil Climate.

AT 10 P.M. we left Manáos in the "Tapajos," an iron steamer of seven hundred tons. We missed the snow-white cleanliness and rigid regularity of the "Icamiaba," and Captain José Antunes Rodrigues de Oliveira Catramby was quite a contrast to Lieutenant Nuno. There were only five first-class passengers besides ourselves (and four of these were "dead-heads"), though there were accommodations for sixty-four. Between Manáos and Pará, a distance of one thousand miles, there were fourteen additions. Passing the mouth of the Madeira, the largest tributary to the Amazon, we anchored thirty miles below at Serpa, after nine hours' sailing. Serpa is a village of ninety houses, built on a high bank of variegated clay, whence its Indian name, *Ita-coatiara*, or painted rock. It was the most animated place we had seen on the river. The town is irregularly laid out and overrun with weeds, but there is a busy tile factory, and the port was full of canoes, montarias, and cubertas. The African element in the population began to show itself prominently here, and increased in importance as we neared Pará. The Negroes are very ebony, and are employed as stevedores. The Indians are well-featured, and wear a long gown of bark-cloth reaching to the knees.

Taking on board rubber and salt fish, the "Tapajos" steamed down stream, passing the perpendicular pink-clay cliffs of Cararaucú, arriving in ten hours at Villa Nova,* one hundred and fifty miles below Serpa. Villa Nova is a straggling village of mud huts standing on a conglomerate bank. The trade is chiefly in rubber, copaiba, and fish. The location is healthy, and in many respects is one of the most desirable places on the river. Here the Amazon begins to narrow, being scarcely three miles wide; but the channel, which has a rocky bed, is very deep. One hundred miles from Villa Nova is Obidos, airily situated on a bluff of pink and yellow clay one hundred feet above the river. The clay rests on a white calcareous earth, and this on red sandstone. It is a picturesque, substantially-built town, with a population, mostly white, engaged in raising cacao and cattle. Cacao is the most valuable product on the Amazon below Villa Nova. The soil is fertile, and the surrounding forest is alive with monkeys, birds, and insects, and abounds with precious woods and fruits. Obidos is blessed with a church, a school, and a weekly newspaper, and is defended by thirty-two guns. This is the Thermopylæ of the Amazon, the great river contracting to a strait not a mile in width, through which it rushes with tremendous velocity. The depth is forty fathoms, and the current 2.4 feet per second. As Bates remarks, however, the river valley is not contracted to this breadth, the southern shore not being continental land, but a low alluvial tract subject to inundation. Back of Obidos is an eminence which has been named *Mount Agassiz* in honor of the Naturalist. There is no mountain between it and Cotopaxi save the spurs from the Eastern Cordillera. Five miles above the town is the mouth of the Trombetas, where Orellana had his celebrated fight with the fabulous Amazons.

Adding to her cargo wood, hides, horses, and Paraguayan

* Otherwise called, on Brazilian maps, Villa Bella da Imperatriz.

Santarem.

prisoners (short, athletic men), the "Tapajos" sailed for Santarem. The river scenery below Obidos loses its wild and solitary character, and is relieved with scattered habitations, factories, and cacao plantations. We arrived at Santarem in seven hours from Obidos, a distance of fifty miles. This city, the largest on the Amazon save Pará, stands on a pretty slope at the mouth of the Rio Tapajos, and five hundred miles from the sea.* It mainly consists of three long rows of whitewashed, tiled houses, girt with green gardens. The citizens, made up of Brazilians, Portuguese, mulattoes, and blacks, number about two thousand five hundred. The surrounding country, which is an undulating campo, with patches of wood, is sparsely inhabited by Tapajocos. Cattle estates and cacao plantations are the great investments, but the soil is poor. Considerable sarsaparilla of superior quality, rubber, copaiba, Brazil nuts, and farina come down the Tapajos. The climate is delightful, the trade-winds tempering the heat and driving away all insect pests. Leprosy is somewhat common among the poorer class. At Santarem is one of the largest colonies which migrated from the disaffected Gulf States for Brazil. One hundred and sixty Southerners pitched their tents here. Many of them, however, were soon disgusted with the country, and, if we are to believe reports, the country was disgusted with them. On the 1st of January, 1868, only seventy-five remained. The colony does not fairly represent the United States, being made up in great part of the "roughs" of Mobile. A few are contented and are doing well. Amazonia will be indebted to them for some valuable ideas. Bates says: "Butter-making is unknown in this country; the milk, I was told, was too poor." But these Anglo-Saxon immigrants have no difficulty in making but-

* Herndon makes Santarem 460 miles from the Negro, and 650 from the sea. Bates calls it 400 miles from the Atlantic, and nearly 50 from Obidos.

ter. Santarem sends to Pará for sugar; but the cavaliers of Alabama are proving that the sugar-cane grows better than in Louisiana, attaining the height of twenty feet, and that it will yield for ten or twelve years without transplanting or cultivation. It is not, however, so sweet or juicy as the Southern cane. Some of the colonists are making tapioca and cashaça or Brazilian rum; others have gone into the pork business; while one, Dr. Jones, expects to realize a fortune burning lime. Here we met the rebel ex-General Dobbins, who had been prospecting on the Tapajos River, but had not yet located himself.

Below Santarem the Amazon vastly increases in width; at one point the southern shore was invisible from the steamer. The waves often run very high. At 10 A.M., eight hours from Santarem, we entered the romantic port of Monte Alégre. The road from the river to the village, just visible inland, runs through a pretty dell. Back of the village, beyond a low, swampy flat, rise the table-topped blue hills of Almeyrim. It was an exhilarating sight and a great relief to gaze upon a mountain range from three hundred to one thousand feet high, the greatest elevations along the Amazon east of the Andes. Agassiz considers these singular mountains the remnants of a plain which once filled the whole valley of the Amazon; but Bates believes them to be the southern terminus of the high land of Guiana. Their geological constitution—a pebbly sandstone—favors the Professor's theory. The range extends ninety miles along the north bank of the river, the western limit at Monte Alégre bearing the local name of Serra Ereré. Mount Agassiz, at Obidos, is a spur of the same table-land. The Amazon is here about five miles wide, the southern shore being low, uninhabited, and covered with coarse grass. Five schooners were anchored in the harbor of Monte Alégre, a sign of considerable trade for the Amazon. The place exports cattle, cacao, rubber, and fish.

In four hours we reached Prayinha, a dilapidated village of forty houses, situated on a low, sandy beach. The chief occupation is the manufacture of turtle-oil. In ten hours more we were taking in wood at Porto do Moz, situated just within the mouth of the Xingú, the last great tributary to the Amazon. Dismal was our farewell sail on the great river. With the highlands came foul weather. We were treated to frequent and furious showers, accompanied by a violent wind, and the atmosphere was filled with smoke caused by numerous fires in the forest. Where the Xingú comes in, the Amazon is ten miles wide, but it is soon divided by a series of islands, the first of which is Grand Island. Twenty miles below Porto do Moz is Gurupá, where we took in rubber. The village, nearly as inanimate as Pompeii, consists of one street, half deserted, built on an isolated site. Forty miles below Gurupá we left the Amazon proper, turning to the right down a narrow channel leading into the river Pará. The forest became more luxuriant, the palms especially increasing in number and beauty. At one place there was a forest of palms, a singularity, for trees of the same order are seldom associated. The forest, densely packed and gloomy, stands on very low, flat banks of hard river mud. Scarcely a sign of animal life was visible; but, as we progressed, dusky faces peered out of the woods; little shanties belonging to the *seringeros*, or rubber-makers, here and there broke the solitude, and occasionally a large group of half-clad natives greeted us from the shore. A labyrinth of channels connects the Amazon with the Pará; the steamers usually take the Tajapurú. This natural canal is of great depth, and from fifty to one hundred yards in width; so that, hemmed in by two green walls, eighty feet high, we seemed to be sailing through a deep gorge; in some places it was so narrow it was nearly overarched by the foliage. One hundred and twenty-five miles from Gurupá is Breves, a busy little town on the southwest corner of the great island of Marajó. The inhabitants, mostly Portuguese, are engaged in the rubber trade; the Indians in the vicinity manufacture fancy earthen-ware and painted cuyas or calabashes.

Soon after leaving Breves we entered the Pará River, which suddenly begins with the enormous width of eight miles. It is, however, shallow, and contains numerous shoals and islands. It is properly an estuary, immense volumes of fresh water flowing into it from the south. The tides are felt through its entire length of one hundred and sixty miles, but the water is only slightly brackish. It has a dingy orange-brown color. A narrow blue line on our left, miles away, was all that was visible, at times, of the island of Marajó; and as we passed the broad mouth of the Tocantíns, we were struck with the magnificent sea-like expanse, for there was scarcely a point of mainland to be seen.

At 4 P.M., eighteen hours from Breves, we entered the peaceful bay of Goajara, and anchored in front of the city of Pará. Beautiful was the view of the city from the harbor in the rays of the declining sun. The towering spires and cupolas, the palatial government buildings, the long row of tall warehouses facing a fleet of schooners, ships, and steamers, and pretty white villas in the suburbs, nestling in luxuriant gardens, were to us, who had just come down the Andes from mediæval Quito, the *ultima thule* of civilization. We seemed to have stepped at once from the Amazon to New York or London. We might, indeed, say *ne plus ultra* in one respect—we had crossed the continent, and Pará was the terminus of our wanderings, the

Pará.

end of romantic adventures, of privations and perils. We were kindly met on the pier by Mr. James Henderson, an elderly Scotchman, whom a long residence in Pará, a bottomless fund of information, and a readiness to serve an Anglo-Saxon, have made an invaluable cicerone. We shot through the devious, narrow streets to the Hotel Diana, where we made our toilet, for our habiliments, too, had reached their *ultima thule.* As La Condamine said on his arrival at Quito: "*Je me trouvai hors d'état de paroitre en public avec décence.*"

The same year which saw Shakspeare carried to his grave beside the Avon witnessed the founding of Pará, or, speaking more respectfully, of Santa Maria de Belém do Gram Pará. The city stands on a low elbow of land formed by the junction of the rivers Guamá and Pará, seventy-five miles from the ocean. The great forest comes close up to the suburbs; and, in fact, vegetation is so rapid the city fathers have a hard struggle to keep the jungle out of the streets. The river in front is twenty miles wide, but the vast expanse is broken by numerous islets. Ships of any size will float within one hundred and fifty yards of the shore. All passengers and goods are landed by boats at the custom-house wharf. The city is regularly laid out, there are several public squares, and many of the streets, especially in the commercial part, are well paved. Magnificent avenues, lined with silk-cotton trees, cocoa-palms, and almonds, lead out to beautiful *rocinhas*, or country residences, of one story, but having spacious verandas. The President's house, built in the Italian style, whose marble staircase is a wonder to Brazil; the six large churches, including the cathedral, after patterns from Lisbon; the post-office, custom-house, and convent-looking warehouses on the mole—these are the most prominent buildings. The architecture is superior to that of Quito. The houses, generally two-storied, are tiled, plastered, and whitewashed or painted; the popular colors are red, yellow, and blue. A few have porcelain facing. The majority have elegant balconies and glass windows, but not all the old projecting lattice casements have disappeared. Some of the buildings bear the marks of the cannonading in the Revolution of 1835. Instead of bedrooms and beds, the largest apartments and verandahs have hooks in the wall for hammocks. A carpeted, cushioned room is seldom seen, and is out of place in the tropics. Coaches and gas are supplanting ox-carts and candles. There are two hotels, but scant accommodations for travelers. Beef is almost the only meat used; the fish are poor and dear; the oysters are horrible. Bananas, oranges, and coffee are the best native productions on the table.

The population of Pará is thirty-five thousand, or double what it was when Wallace and Bates entered it twenty years ago. It is the largest city on the largest river in the world, and the capital of a province ten times the size of New York State. The enterprising, wealthy class consists of Portuguese and pure Brazilians, with a few English, Germans, French, and North Americans. The multitude is an amalgamation of Portuguese, Indian, and Negro. The diversity of races, and the mingled dialects of the Amazon and Europe, make an attractive street scene. Side by side we see the corpulent Brazilian planter, the swarthy Portuguese trader, the merry Negro porter, and the apathetic Indian boatman. Some of the more recent offspring are dressed *à la Adam* before the fall; numbers wear only a shirt or skirt; the negro girls who go about the streets with trays of sweetmeats on their heads are loosely yet prettily dressed in pure white, with massive gilded chains and earrings; but the middle and upper classes generally follow Paris fashions. The mechanic arts are in the hands of free Negroes and Indians, mulattoes and mamelucos.* Commerce is carried on almost exclusively by Portuguese and other foreigners. Dry-goods come chiefly from England and France; groceries from Portugal; flour and hardware from the United States. The principal exports are rubber, cacao, coffee,† sugar, cotton,

Fruit Peddlers.

Brazil nuts, sarsaparilla, vanilla, farina, copaiba, tobacco, rum, hides, fish, parrots, and monkeys.‡ Pará exceeds in the number of its indigenous commodities any other port in the world, but the trade at present is insignificant when we consider the vast extent and resources of the country. The city can never have a rival at the mouth of the Amazon, and is destined to become a great emporium. But Brazilian legislation stands in the way. Heavy import duties are charged—from 35 to 45 per cent.; and on the 1st of January, 1868, it was ordered that 15 per cent. must be paid in English gold. The consequence has been that gold has risen from 28 to 30 above par, creating an additional tax. Exportation is equally discouraging. There is a duty of nine per cent. to be paid at the custom-house, and seven

* We are inclined to doubt the assertion of Mansfield that Paraguay is the only country in eastern South America with an industrious peasantry.

† Brazil yields more than one half the quantity of coffee consumed by the world. That of Ceará is the best.

‡ In January, 1868, the current prices were as follows:

Refined Sugar, per arroba	....$3 00	Tapioca, per arroba		............$3 00
Rice	"	.... 1 40	Pure rubber	"	............11 50
Cacao	"	.... 3 20	Piassaba cord	"	.... 6 50
Coffee	"	.... 3 50	Tobacco	"	.... 1 50
Farina	"	 75	Sarsaparilla	"	............11 50

The Brazilian arroba is seven pounds heavier than the Spanish.

per cent. more at the consulado. But this is not the sum total. Those who live outside of the province of Pará, say above Obidos, must first pay an import of thirteen per cent. to get their produce into Pará. For example: up the river crude rubber can be bought for twenty-five cents a pound; the trader pays twenty-five cents an arroba (thirty-two pounds) for transportation to Pará from Santarem, exclusive of canoe hire and shipping; thirteen per cent. duty in entering Pará, ten per cent. to the commission merchant, and sixteen per cent. more as export tax; making a total loss on labor of about fifty per cent. Brazil abounds with the most valuable woods in the world, but is prevented from competing with other nations by this system of self-strangulation. In 1867 the import duty on timber was twelve per cent. Though situated on the edge of a boundless forest, Pará consumes large quantities of North American pine. There is not a grist-mill on the Amazon, and only two or three saw-mills. A dozen boards of red cedar (a very common timber) costs 60$000 per thousand (about thirty dollars) at Santarem. There is no duty on goods going to Peru. The current money, besides foreign gold, consists of copper coins and imperial treasury notes. The basis of calculation is the imaginary *rey*, equivalent to half a mill. The coins in use are the vintem (twenty reys), answering to our cent, the half vintem, and double vintem. The currency has so fluctuated in value that many of the pieces have been restamped. Fifty vintems make a *milrey*, expressed thus: 1$000. This is the smallest paper issue. Unfortunately, the notes may suddenly fall below par. As a great many counterfeits made in Portugal are in circulation, the government recalls the issue which has been counterfeited, notifying holders, by the provincial papers, that all such bills must be exchanged for a new issue within six months. Those not brought in at the end of that period lose ten per cent. of their value, and ten per cent. for each following month, until the value of the note is *nil.* The result has been that many persons trading up the river have lost heavily, and now demand hard money. Change is very scarce in Pará.

The province of Pará is governed by a president chosen at Rio, and every four years sends representatives to the Imperial Parliament. The Constitution of Brazil is very liberal; every householder, without distinction of race or color, has a vote, and may work his way up to high position. There are two drawbacks—the want of intelligence and virtue in the people, and the immense staff of officials employed to administer the government. There are also many formalities which are not only useless, but a hinderance to prosperity. Thus, the internal trade of a province carried on by Brazilian subjects is not exempt from the passport system. A foreigner finds as much trouble in getting his passport *en règle* in Pará as in Vienna. The religion of Pará is Romish, and not so tolerant as in Rio. We arrived during a *festa.* (When did a traveler enter a Portuguese town on any other than a feast day?) That night was made hideous with rockets, fire-crackers, cannon, and bells. "Music, noise, and fireworks," says Wallace, "are the three essentials to please a Brazilian populace." The most celebrated shrine in Northern Brazil is Our Lady of Nazareth. The little chapel stands about a mile out of the city, and is now rebuilding for the third time. The image is a doll about the size of a girl ten years old, wearing a silver crown and a dress of blue silk glittering with golden stars. Hosts of miracles are attributed to Our Lady, and we were shown votive offerings and models of legs, arms, heads, etc., etc., the grateful *in memoriam* of wonderful cures, besides a boat whose crew were saved by invoking the protection of Mary. The facilities for education are improving. There are several seminaries in Pará, of which the chief is the *Lyceo da Capital.* Too many youths, however, as in Quito, are satisfied with a little rhetoric and law. The city supports four newspapers.

Paráenses may well be proud of their delightful climate. Wallace says the thermometer ranges from 74° to 87°; our observation made the mean annual temperature 80.2°. The mean daily temperature does not vary more than two or three degrees. The climate is more equable than that of any other observed part of the New World.* The greatest heat is reached at two o'clock, but it is never so oppressive as in New York. The greater the heat, the stronger the sea-breeze; and in three hundred out of three hundred and sixty-five days, the air is farther cooled by an afternoon shower. The rainiest month is April; the dryest, October or November. Lying in the delta of a great river, in the middle of the tropics, and half surrounded by swamps, its salubrity is remarkable. We readily excuse the proverb, "*Quem vai para Pará para*" ("He who goes to Pará stops there"); and we might have made it good, had we not been tempted by the magnificent steamer "South America," which came up from Rio on the way to New York. On the moonlit night of the 7th of January, when the ice-king had thrown his white robes over the North, we turned our backs upon the glimmering lights of Pará, and noiselessly as a canoe glided down the great river. As the sun rose for the last time to us upon the land of perpetual verdure, our gallant ship was plowing the mottled waters on the edge of the ocean—mingled yellow patches of the Amazon

* "The traveler, in going from the equator toward the tropics, is less struck by the decrease of the mean annual temperature than by the unequal distribution of heat in different parts of the year."—*Humboldt.* The great German fixes the mean temperature of the equator at 81.5°; Brewster, at 82.8°; Kirwan, 83.9°; Atkinson, 84.5°.

and dark streaks from the Pará floating on the Atlantic green. Far behind us we could see the breakers dashing against the Braganza Banks; a moment after Cape Magoary dropped beneath the horizon, and with it South America vanished from our view.

CHAPTER XVIII.

The River Amazon.—Its Source and Magnitude.—Tributaries and Tints.—Volume and Current.—Rise and Fall.—Navigation.—Expeditions on the Great River.

NEAR the silver mines of Cerro Pasco, in the little Lake of Lauricocha, just below the limit of perpetual winter, rises the "King of Waters."* For the first five hundred miles it flows northerly, in a continuous series of cataracts and rapids, through a deep valley between the parallel Cordilleras of Peru. Upon reaching the frontier of Ecuador, it turns to the right, and runs easterly two thousand five hundred miles across the great equatorial plain of the continent.† No other river flows in the same latitude, and retains, therefore, the same climatic conditions for so great a distance. The breadth of the Amazon, also, is well proportioned to its extraordinary length. At Tabatinga, two thousand miles above its mouth, it is a mile and a half wide; at the entrance of the Madeira, it is three miles; below Santarem, it is ten; and if the Pará be considered a part of the great river, it fronts the Atlantic one hundred and eighty miles. Brazilians proudly call it the Mediterranean of the New World. Its vast expanse, presenting

* Herndon gives, for the altitude of Cerro Pasco, 13,802 feet; Rivero, 14,279. The lieutenant thus describes his first view from the rough hills surrounding this birthplace of the greatest of rivers: "I can compare it to nothing so fitly as looking from the broken and ragged edges of a volcano into the crater beneath."

† From Lauricocha to its mouth, the Amazon, following the main curves, is 2740 miles long, as estimated by Bates; in a straight line, 2050; from Pará to the head of the Ucayali, 3000. From north to south the tributaries stretch 1720 miles.

below Teffé magnificent reaches, with blank horizons, and forming a barrier between different species of animals; its system of back channels, joining the tributaries, and linking a series of lagunes too many ever to be named; its network of navigable waters stretching over one third of the continent; its oceanic fauna — porpoises and manatis, gulls and frigate-birds—remind the traveler of a great inland sea, with endless ramifications, rather than a river. The side-channels through the forest, called by the Indians *igarapés*, or canoe-paths, are one of the characteristic features

Igarapé, or Canoe-path.

of the Amazon.* They often run to a great distance parallel to the great river, and intersecting the tributaries, so that one can go from Santarem a thousand miles up the Amazon without once entering it. These natural highways will be of immense advantage for inter-communication.

But extraordinary as is this net-work of natural canals, the tributaries of the Amazon are still more wonderful. They are so numerous they appear on the map like a thousand ribbons streaming from a main mast, and many of the obscure affluents, though large as the Hudson, are unknown to geography. From three degrees north to twenty degrees south, every river that flows down the eastern slope of the Andes is a contributor—as though all the rivers between Mexico and Mount Hooker united their waters in the Mississippi. While the great river of the northern continent drains an area of one million two hundred thousand square miles, the Amazon (not including the Tocantíns) is spread over a million more, or over a surface equal to two thirds of all Europe. Let us journey around the grand trunk and take a glimpse of the main branches.

The first we meet in going up the left bank is the Rio Negro. It rises in the Sierra Tunuhy, an isolated mountain group in the llanos of Colombia, and enters the Amazon at Manáos, a thousand miles from the sea. The upper part, down to the parallel of one degree north, has a very rapid current; at San Gabriel are the first rapids in ascending; between San Gabriel and Barcellos the rate is not over two or three miles per hour; between Barcellos and Manáos it is a deep but sluggish river, and in the annual rise of the Amazon its waters are stagnant for several hundred miles

* *Igarapé* is sometimes limited to a creek filled with back-water; *paranamirim* is the proper term for a narrow arm of the main river; and *furos* are the diminutive mouths of the tributaries.

up, or actually flow back. Its extreme length is twelve hundred miles, and its greatest breadth is at Barcellos, where it is twelve or fifteen miles. Excepting this middle section, the usual breadth of the Negro below the equatorial line is about one mile. It is joined to the Orinoco by the navigable Cassiquiari,* a natural canal three fourths of a mile wide, and a portage of only two hours divides the head of its tributary, the Branco, from the Essequibo of Guiana. The Negro yields to commerce coffee, cacao, farina, sarsaparilla, Brazil nuts, pitch, piassaba, and valuable woods. The commerce of Brazil with Venezuela by the Rio Negro amounted in 1867 to $22,000, of which $9000 was the value of imports. The principal villages above Manáos are San Miguel and Moroa (which contain about fifty dwellings each), Tireguin, Barcellos, Toma, San Carlos, Coana, San Gabriel, and Santa Isabel.

The next great affluent is the Japurá. It rises in the mountains of New Granada, and, flowing southeasterly a thousand miles, enters the Amazon opposite Ega, five hundred miles above Manáos. Its principal mouth is three hundred feet wide, but it has a host of distributing channels, the extremes of which are two hundred miles apart. Its current is only three quarters of a mile an hour, and it has been ascended by canoes five hundred miles. A natural canal like the Cassiquiari is said to connect it with the Orinoco. The products of the Japurá are sarsaparilla, copaiba, rubber, cacao, farina, Brazil nuts, moira-piránga—a hard, fine-grained wood of a rich, cherry-red color—and carajurú, a brilliant scarlet dye.

Parallel to the Japurá is the Putumayo or Issá. Its source is the Lake of San Pablo, at the foot of the volcano

* The Cassiquiari belongs indifferently to both river systems, the level being so complete at one point between them as to obliterate the line of water-shed. —*Herschel.*

of Pasto; its mouth, as given by Herndon, is half a mile broad, and its current two and three fourths miles an hour.

Farther west are the Napo and Pastassa, starting from the volcanoes of Quito. The former is nearly seven hundred miles long, navigable five hundred. The latter is an unnavigable torrent. One of its branches, the Topo, is one continued rapid; "of those who have fallen into it, only one has come out alive." Another, the Patate, rises near Iliniza, runs through the plain to a little south of Cotopaxi, receives all streams flowing from the eastern side of the western Cordillera from Iliniza to Chimborazo, and unites near Tunguragua with the Chambo, which rises near Sangaí. Castelnau and Bates saw pumice floating on the Amazon; it was probably brought from Cotopaxi by the Pastassa.

Crossing the Marañon, and going eastward, we first pass the Huallaga, a rapid river of the size of the Cumberland, coming down the Peruvian Andes from an altitude of eight thousand six hundred feet, and entering the great river nearly opposite the Pastassa. Its mouth is a mile wide, and for a hundred miles up its average depth is three fathoms. In July, August, and September the steamers are not able to ascend to Yurimaguas. Canoe navigation begins at Tinga Maria, three hundred miles from Lima. The fertile plain through which the river flows is very attractive to an agriculturist. Cotton is gathered six months after sowing, and rice in five months. At Tarapoto a large amount of cotton-cloth is woven for export.

The next great tributary from the south is the Ucayali. This magnificent stream originates near ancient Cuzco, and has a fall of .87 of a foot per mile, and a length nearly equal to that of the Negro. For two hundred and fifty miles above its mouth it averages half a mile in width, and has a current of three miles an hour. At Sarayacu it is twenty feet deep. The Ucayali is navigable for at least seven hundred miles. The "Morona," a steamer of five hundred tons, has been up to the entrance of the Pachitéa in the dry season, a distance of six hundred miles, and in the wet season ascended that branch to Mayro. A small Peruvian steamer has recently ascended the Tambo to within sixty miles of Fort Ramon, or seven hundred and seventy-three miles from Nauta.

Leaving the Ucayali, we pass by six rivers rising in the unknown lands of Northern Bolivia: the Javarí, navigable by steam for two hundred and fifty miles; the sluggish Jutahí, half a mile broad and four hundred miles long; the Juruá, four times the size of our Connecticut, and navigable nearly its entire length; the unhealthy, little-known Teffé and Coary; and the Purus, a deep, slow river, over a thousand miles long, and open to navigation half way to its source. Soldan and Pinto claim to have ascended the Javarí, in a steamer, about one thousand miles, and it is said Chandless went up the Purus one thousand eight hundred miles. The Teffé is narrow, with a strong current. Of all these six rivers, the Purus is the most important. It is probably the Amaru-mayu, or "serpent-river," of the Incas, and its affluents enjoy the privilege of draining the waters of those beautiful Andes which formed the eastern boundary of the empire of Manco Capac, and fertilizing the romantic valley of Paucar-tambo, or "Inn of the Flowery Meadow." The banks of this noble stream are now held by the untamable Chunchos; but the steam-whistle will accomplish what the rifle can not. The Purus communicates with the Madeira, proving the absence of rapids and of intervening mountains.

Sixty miles below the confluence of the Negro, the mighty Madeira, the largest tributary of the Amazon, blends its milky waters with the turbid king of rivers.

It is about two thousand miles in length; one branch, the Beni, rising near Lake Titicaca, drains the fertile valleys of Yungus and Apollo, rich in cinchona, chocolate, and gold; the Marmoré springs from the vicinity of Chuquisaca, within fifteen miles of a source of the Paraguay, traversing the territory of the brave and intelligent Moxos; while the Itinez washes down the gold and diamonds of Matto Grosso. Were it not for the cascade four hundred and eighty miles from its mouth, large vessels might sail from the Amazon into the very heart of Bolivia. When full, it has a three-mile current, and at its junction with the Amazon it is two miles wide and sixty-six feet deep. Five hundred miles from its mouth it is a mile wide and one hundred feet deep. It contains numerous islands, and runs in a comparatively straight course. It received its name from the vast quantity of drift-wood often seen floating down. The value of Brazilian commerce with Bolivia by the Madeira was, in 1867, $43,000.*

At Santarem the Amazon receives another great tributary, the Tapajos (or Rio Preto, as the Portuguese call it), a thousand miles long, and, for the last eighty miles, from four to twelve miles in breadth. It rises amid the glittering mines of Matto Grosso, only twenty miles from the head-waters of the Rio Plata, and flows rapidly down through a magnificent hilly country to the last cataract, which is one hundred and sixty miles above Santarem, and is the end of navigation to sailing vessels. Thence to the Amazon it has little current and no great depth. From Santarem to Diamantino it is about twenty-six days' travel. Large quantities of sarsaparilla, rubber, tonka beans, mandioca, and guarana are brought down this river.

* In the map of Friar Fritz, published in 1707, the Madeira is one of the most insignificant of the tributaries, and the Ucayali and Putumayo are the largest.

Parallel to the Tapajos, and about two hundred miles distant, flows the Xingú. It rises in the heart of the empire, has the length of the Ohio and Monongahela, and can be navigated one hundred and fifty miles. This is the last great tributary of the Amazon proper; if, however, we consider the Pará as only one of the outlets of the great river, we may then add to the list the grand Tocantíns.* This splendid river has its source in the rich province of Minas (the source, also, of the San Francisco and Uruguay), not six hundred miles from Rio Janeiro—a region possessing the finest climate in Brazil, and yielding diamonds and rubies, the sapphire, topaz and opal, gold, silver, and petroleum. The Tocantíns is sixteen hundred miles long, and ten miles broad at its mouth; but, unfortunately, rapids commence one hundred and twenty miles above Cametá. The Araguaia, its main branch, is, according to Castelnau, one mile wide, with a current of three fourths of a mile an hour.

Here are six tributaries, all of them superior to any river in Europe, outside of Russia, save the Danube, and ten times greater than any stream on the west slope of the

* We are inclined to hold, with Bates and others, that the Pará River is not, strictly speaking, one of the mouths of the Amazon. "It is made to appear so on many of the maps in common use, because the channels which connect it with the main river are there given much broader than they are in reality, conveying the impression that a large body of water finds an outlet from the main river into the Pará. It is doubtful, however, if there be any considerable stream of water flowing constantly downward through these channels. There is a great contrast in general appearance between the Pará and the main Amazon. In the former the flow of the tide always creates a strong current upward, while in the Amazon the turbid flow of the mighty stream overpowers all tides, and produces a constant downward current. The color of the water is different; that of the Pará being of a dingy orange-brown, while the Amazon has an ochreous or yellowish-clay tint. The forests on their banks have a different aspect. On the Pará, the infinitely diversified trees seem to rise directly out of the water, the forest-frontage is covered with greenery, and wears a placid aspect; while the shores of the main Amazon are encumbered with fallen trunks, and are fringed with a belt of broad-leaved grasses."—*Naturalist on the Amazon*, i., p. 3–5.

Andes. While the Arkansas joins the Mississippi four hundred miles above New Orleans, the Madeira, of equal length, enters the Amazon nine hundred miles from Pará. But, vast as are these tributary streams, they seem to make no impression on the Amazon; they are lost like brooks in the ocean. Our ideas of the magnitude of the great river are wonderfully increased when we see the Madeira coming down two thousand miles, yet its enormous contribution imperceptible half way across the giant river; or the dark waters of the Negro creeping along the shore, and becoming undistinguishable five miles from its mouth. Though the Amazon carries a larger amount of sediment than any other river, it has no true delta, the archipelago in its mouth (for, like our own St. Lawrence, it has its Bay of a Thousand Isles) not being an alluvial formation, but having a rocky base. The great island of Marajó, in physical configuration, resembles the mainland of Guiana. The deltoid outlet is confined to the tributaries, nearly all of them, like "the disemboguing Nile," emptying themselves by innumerable embouchures. To several tributaries the Amazon gives water before it receives their tribute. Thus, by ascending the Negro sixty miles, we have the singular spectacle of water pouring in from the Amazon through the Guariba Channel.

The waters of this great river system are of divers tints. The Amazon, as it leaps from the Andes, and as far down as the Ucayali, is blue, passing into a clear olive-green; likewise the Pastassa, Huallaga, Tapajos, Xingú, and Tocantíns. Below the Ucayali it is of a pale, yellowish olive; the Madeira,* Purus, Juruá, Jutahí, Javarí, Ucayali, Napo, Içа, and Japurá are of similar color. The Negro, Coary, and Teffé are black. Humboldt observes that "a cooler

* The Madeira has often a milky color which it receives from the white clay along its banks.

atmosphere, fewer musquitoes, greater salubrity, and absence of crocodiles, as also of fish, mark the region of these black rivers." This is not altogether true. The Amazon throughout is healthy, being swept by the trade-winds. The branches, which are not so constantly refreshed by the ocean breezes, are occasionally malarious; the "white-water" tributaries, except when they have a slack current in the dry season, have the best reputation, while intermittent fevers are nearly confined to the dark-colored streams. Much of the sickness on these tropical waters, however, is due to exposure and want of proper food rather than to the climate. The river system of South America will favorably compare, in point of salubrity, with the river system of its continental neighbor.*

As we might expect, the volume of the Amazon is beyond all parallel. Half a million cubic feet of water pour through the narrows of Obidos every second, and fresh water may be taken up from the Atlantic far out of sight of land. The fall of the main easterly trunk of the Amazon is about six and a half inches per mile, equivalent to a slope of 21′—the same as that of the Nile, and one third that of the Mississippi. Below Jaen there are thirty cataracts and rapids; at the Pongo de Manseriche, at the altitude of 1164 feet (according to Humboldt), it bids adieu to mountain scenery. Between Tabatinga and the ocean the average current is three miles an hour. It diminishes toward Pará, and is every where at a minimum in the dry season; but it always has the "swing" of an ocean current.

* The average temperature of the water in the Lower Amazon is 81°, that of the air being a little less. The temperature of the Huallaga at Yurimaguas was 75° when the air was 88° in the shade; in another experiment both the river and air were 80°. The Marañon at Iquitos was 79° when the air was 90°. At the mouth of the Juruá, Herndon found both water and air 82°. In the tropics the difference between the temperature of the water and air is proportionally less than in high latitudes.

Though not so rapid as the Mississippi, the Amazon is deeper. There are seven fathoms of water at Nauta (2200 miles from the Atlantic), eleven at Tabatinga, and twenty-seven on the average below Manáos.*

The Amazon and its branches are subject to an annual rise of great regularity. It does not take place simultaneously over the whole river, but there is a succession of freshets. At the foot of the Andes the rise commences in January; at Ega it begins about the end of February. Coinciding with this contribution from the west, the October rains on the highlands of Bolivia and Brazil swell the southern tributaries, whose accumulated floods reach the main stream in February; and the latter, unable to discharge the avalanche of waters, inundates a vast area, and even crowds up the northern tributaries. As the Madeira, Tapajos, and Purus subside, the Negro, fed by the spring rains in Guiaña and Venezuela, presses downward till the central stream rolls back the now sluggish affluents from the south. There is, therefore, a rhythmical correspondence in the rise and fall of the arms of the Amazon, so that this great fresh-water sea sways alternately north and south; while the onward swell in the grand trunk is a progressive undulation eastward. As the Cambridge Professor well says: "In this oceanic river the tidal action has an annual instead of a daily ebb and flow; it obeys a larger orb, and is ruled by the sun and not the moon." As the southern affluents have the greatest volume, the Amazon receives its largest accession after the sun has been in the southern hemisphere. The rise is gradual, increasing to one foot per day. One lowland after another sinks beneath the flood; the forest stands up to its middle in the water, and

* The assertion of the *Ency. Metropolitana*, that "its current has great violence and rapidity, and its depth is unfathomable," must be received with some allowance.

shady dells are transformed into navigable creeks.* Swarms of turtles leave the river for the inland lakes; flocks of wading birds migrate to the banks of the Negro and Orinoco to enjoy the cloudless sky of the dry season; alligators swim where a short time before the jaguar lay in wait for the tapir; and the natives, unable to fish, huddle in their villages to spend the "winter of their discontent." The Lower Amazon is at its minimum in September or October. The rise above this lowest level is between seven and eight fathoms. If we consider the average width of the Amazon two miles, we shall have a surface of at least five thousand square miles raised fifty feet by the inundation. An extraordinary freshet is expected every sixth year.

The Atlantic tide is perceptible at Obidos, four hundred and fifty miles above Pará, and Bates observed it up the Tapajos, five hundred and thirty miles distant. The tide, however, does not flow up; there is only a rising and falling of the waters—the momentary check of the great river in its conflict with the ocean. The "bore," or *pirorôco*, is a colossal wave at spring tide, rising suddenly along the whole width of the Amazon to a height of twelve or fifteen feet, and then collapsing with a frightful roar.

The Amazon presents an unparalleled extent of water communication. So many and far reaching are its tributaries, it touches every country on the continent except Chile and Patagonia. South America is well nigh quartered by its river system: the Amazon starts within sixty miles of the Pacific; the Tapajos and Madeira reach down to the La Plata; while the Negro mingles its waters with those of the Orinoco. The tributaries also communicate with each other by intersecting canals, so numerous that central Amazonia is truly a cluster of islands. Wagons

* The flooded lands are called *gapos*.

and railroads will be out of the question for ages hence in this aquatic basin. No other river runs in so deep a channel to so great a distance. For two thousand miles from its mouth there are not less than seven fathoms of water. Not a fall interrupts navigation on the main stream for two thousand five hundred miles; and it so happens that while the current is ever east (for even the ocean can not send up its tide against it), there is a constant trade-wind westward, so that navigation up or down has always something in its favor. As a general rule, the breeze is not so strong during the rise of the river. There are at least six thousand miles of navigation for large vessels. It was lately said that the Mississippi carries more vessels in a month, and the Yang-tse-Kiang in a day, than the Amazon all the year round. But this is no longer true. Steamers already ascend regularly to the port of Moyabamba, which is less than twenty days' travel from the Pacific coast. The Amazon was opened to the world September 7, 1867; and the time can not be far distant when the exhaustless wealth of the great valley—its timber, fruit, medicinal plants, gums, and dye-stuffs—will be emptied by this great highway into the commercial lap of the Atlantic; when crowded steamers will plow all these waters—yellow, black, and blue—and the sloths and alligators, monkeys and jaguars, toucans and turtles, will have a bad time of it.

Officially free to the world, the great river is, however, for the present practically closed to foreign shipping, as it is difficult to compete with the Brazilian steamers. For, by the contract which lasts till 1877, the company is allowed an annual subsidy of $4,000,000, which has since been increased by 250 milreys per voyage. In 1867 the steamers and sailing vessels on the Amazon were divided as follows, though it must be remembered that few of the foreign ships, excepting Portuguese, ascended beyond Pará:

Nationality.	No.	Tonnage.	Nationality.	No.	Tonnage.
United States	37	39,901½	Holland	3	538
Brazil	49	28,639	Denmark	2	525
England	52	13,276½	Holstein	3	498
Portugal	24	7,871	Norway	1	135
France	18	5,344	Spain	1	90
Prussia	4	889½			

The vessels carrying the stars and stripes exported from Pará to the value of 3,235,073$950, or eight times the amount carried by Brazilian craft, and 50,000 milreys more than England. While, therefore, the Imperial Company has the monopoly of trade on the Amazon, our ships distribute one third of the products to the world. The United States is the natural commercial partner with Brazil; for not only is New York the half-way house between Pará and Liverpool, but a chip thrown into the sea at the mouth of the Amazon will float close by Cape Hatteras. The official value of exports from Pará in 1867 was 9,926,912$557, or about five millions of dollars, an increase of one million over 1866.

The early expeditions into the Valley of the Amazon, in search of the "Gilded King," are the most romantic episodes in the history of Spanish discovery. To the wild wanderings of these worshipers of gold succeeded the more earnest explorations of the Jesuits, those pioneers of geographical knowledge. Pinzon discovered the mouth of the river in 1500; but Orellana, who came down the Napo in 1541, was the first to navigate its waters. Twenty years later Aguirre descended from Cuzco; in 1637, Texeira ascended to Quito by the Napo; Cabrera descended from Peru in 1639; Juan de Palacios by the Napo in 1725; La Condamine from Jaen in 1744, and Madame Godin by the Pastassa in 1769. The principal travelers who preceded us in crossing the continent this century were Mawe (1828), Pœppig (1831), Smyth (1834), Von Tschudi (1845), Castelnau (1846), Herndon and Gibbon (1851), and Marcoy (1867), who came down through Peru, and a Spanish commission (Almagro, Spada, Martinez, and Isern), who made the Napo transit in 1865. To Spix and Martius (1820), Bates and Wallace (1848–1857), Azevedo and Pinto (1862–1864), and Agassiz (1865), the world is indebted for the most scientific surveys of the river in Brazil.

Such is the Amazon, the mightiest river in the world, rising amid the loftiest volcanoes on the globe, and flowing through a forest unparalleled in extent. "It only wants (wrote Father Acuña), in order to surpass the Ganges, Euphrates, and the Nile in felicity, that its source should be in Paradise." As if one name were not sufficient for its grandeur, it has three appellations: Marañon, Solimoens, and Amazon; the first applied to the part in Peru, the second to the portion between Tabatinga and Manáos, and the third to all below the Rio Negro.* We have no proper conception of the vast dimensions of the thousand-armed river till we sail for weeks over its broad bosom, be-

* The upper part of the Marañon, from its source to Jaen, is sometimes called the Tunguragua. Solimoens is now seldom heard; but, instead, Middle Amazon, or simply Amazon. The term Alto Amazonas or High Amazon is also applied to all above the Negro. Marañon, says Velasco, derives its name from the circumstance that a soldier, sent by Pizarro to discover the sources of the Rio Piura, having beheld the mighty stream from the neighborhood of Jaen, and, astonished to behold a sea of fresh water, exclaimed, "*Hac mare an non?*" Orellana's pretended fight with a nation of female warriors gave rise to the Portuguese name of the river, Amazonas (anglicized Amazon), after the mythical women in Cappadocia, who are said to have burnt off their right breasts that they might use the bow and javelin with more skill and force, and hence their name, Ἀμαζόνες, from α and μαζος. Orellana's story probably grew out of the fact that the men wear long tunics, part the hair in the middle, and, in certain tribes, alone wear ornaments. Some derive the name from the Indian word *amassona*, boat-destroyer. The old name, Orellana, after the discoverer, is obsolete, as also the Indian term Parana-tinga, or King of Waters. In ordinary conversation it is designated as *the* river, in distinction from its tributaries. "In all parts of the world (says Humboldt), the largest rivers are called by those who dwell on their banks, *The River*, without any distinct and peculiar appellation."

holding it sweeping disdainfully by the great Madeira as if its contribution was of no account, discharging into the sea one hundred thousand cubic feet of water per second more than our Mississippi, rolling its turbid waves thousands of miles exactly as it pleases,—plowing a new channel every year, with tributaries twenty miles wide, and an island in its mouth twice the size of Massachusetts.

CHAPTER XIX.

The Valley of the Amazon.—Its Physical Geography.—Geology.—Climate.—Vegetation.

FROM the Atlantic shore to the foot of the Andes, and from the Orinoco to the Paraguay, stretches the great Valley of the Amazon. In this vast area the United States might be packed without touching its boundaries. It could contain the basins of the Mississippi, the Danube, the Nile, and the Hoang-Ho. It is girt on three sides by a wall of mountains: on the north are the highlands of Guiana and Venezuela; on the west stand the Andes; on the south rise the table-lands of Matto Grosso. The valley begins at such an altitude, that on the western edge vegetation differs as much from the vegetation at Pará, though in the same latitude, as the flora of Canada from the flora of the West Indies.

The greater part of the region drained by the Amazon, however, is not a valley proper, but an extensive plain. From the mouth of the Napo to the ocean, a distance of eighteen hundred miles in a straight line, the slope is one foot in five miles.* At Coca, on the Napo, the altitude is 850 feet, according to our observations; at Tinga Maria, on the Huallaga, it is 2200 according to Herndon; at the junction of the Negro with the Cassiquiari, it is 400 according to Wallace; at the mouth of the Marmoré, it is 800 according to Gibbon; at the Pongo de Manseriche, below

* Professor Agassiz gives the average slope as hardly more than a foot in ten miles, which is based on the farther assertion that the distance from Tabatinga to the sea-shore is more than 2000 miles in a straight line. The distance is not 1600, or exactly 1500, from Pará.—See *A Journey in Brazil*, p. 349.

all rapids, it is 1160 according to Humboldt; and at the junction of Araguaia with the Tocantíns, it is 200 according to Castelnau. These barometrical measurements represent the basin of the Amazon as a shallow trough lying parallel to the equator, the southern side having double the inclination of the northern, and the whole gently sloping eastward. Farthermore, the channel of the great river is not in the centre of the basin, but lies to the north of it: thus, the hills of Almeyrim rise directly from the river, while the first falls on the Tocantíns, Xingú, and Tapajos are nearly two hundred miles above their mouths; the rapids of San Gabriel, on the Negro, are one hundred and seventy-five miles from the Amazon, while the first obstruction to the navigation of the Madeira is a hundred miles farther from the great river.

Of the creation of this valley we have already spoken. No region on the face of the globe of equal extent has such a monotonous geology. Around the rim of the basin are the outcroppings of a cretaceous deposit; this rests on the hidden mezozoic and palæozoic strata which form the ribs of the Andes. Above it, covering the whole basin from New Granada to the Argentine Republic,* are the following formations: first, a stratified accumulation of sand; second, a series of laminated clays, of divers colors, without a pebble; third, a fine, compact sandstone; fourth, a coarse, porous sandstone, so ferruginous as to resemble bog iron-ore. This last was, originally, a thousand feet in thickness, but was worn down, *perhaps*, in some sudden escape of the

* Messrs. Myers and Forbes found this red clay on the Negro, most abundantly near Barcellos; also in small quantities on the Orinoco above Maipures. The officers of the "Morona" assured us that the same formation was traceable far up the Ucayali and Huallaga. This clay from the Amazon, as examined microscopically by Prof. H. James Clark, contains fragments of gasteropod shells and bivalve casts. The red earth of the Pampas, according to Ehrenberg, contains eight fresh-water to one salt-water animalcule.

pent-up waters of the valley. The table-topped hills of Almeyrim are almost the sole relics.* Finally, over the undulating surface of the denuded sandstone an ochraceous, unstratified sandy clay was deposited.

It is a question to what period this great accumulation is to be assigned. Humboldt called it "Old Red Sandstone;" Martius pronounced it "New Red;" Agassiz says "Drift"—the glacial deposit brought down from the Andes and worked over by the melting of the ice which transported it.† The Professor farther declares that "these deposits are fresh-water deposits; they show no sign of a marine origin; no sea-shells nor remains of any marine animal have as yet been found throughout their whole extent; tertiary deposits have never been observed in any part of the Amazonian basin." This was true up to 1867. Neither Bates, Wallace, nor Agassiz found any marine fossil on the banks of the great river. But there is danger in building a theory on negative evidence. These explorers ascended no farther than Tabatinga. Two hundred miles west of that fort is the little Peruvian village of Pebas, at the confluence of the Ambiyacu. We came down the Napo and Marañon, and stopped at this place. Here we discovered a fossiliferous bed intercalated between the variegated clays so peculiar to the Amazon. *It was crowded with marine tertiary shells!* This was Pebas *vs.* Cambridge. It was unmistakable proof that the formation was not drift, but tertiary; not of fresh, but salt water origin. The species,

* "On the South American coast, where tertiary and supra-tertiary beds have been extensively elevated, I repeatedly noticed that the uppermost beds were formed of coarser materials than the lower; this appears to indicate that, as the sea becomes shallower, the force of the waves or currents increased."—Darwin's *Observations*, pt. ii., 131. "Nowhere in the Pampas is there any appearance of much superficial denudation."—Pt. iii., 100.

† *A Journey in Brazil*, p. 250, 411, 424. Again, in his Lecture before the Lowell Institute, 1866: "These deposits could not have been made by the sea, nor in a large lake, as they contain no marine nor fresh-water fossils."

as determined by W. M. Gabb, Esq., of Philadelphia, are: *Neritina pupa, Turbonilla minuscula, Mesalia Ortoni, Tellina Amazonensis, Pachydon obliqua*, and *P. tenua*.* All of these are new forms excepting the first, and the last is a new genus. It is a singular fact that the *Neritina* is now living in the West India waters, and the species found at Pebas retains its peculiar markings. So that we have some ground for the supposition that not many years ago there was a connection between the Caribbean Sea and the Upper Amazon; in other words, that Guiana has only very lately ceased to be an island. There is no mountain range on the water-shed between the Orinoco and the Negro and Japurá, but the three rivers are linked by natural canals.† Interstratified with the clay deposit are seams of a highly bituminous lignite; we traced it from near the mouth of the Curaray on the Rio Napo to Loreto on the Marañon, a distance of about four hundred miles. It occurs also at Iquitos. This is farther testimony against the glacial theory of the formation of the Amazonian Valley. The paucity of shells in such a vast deposit is not astonishing. It is as remarkable in the similar accumulation of reddish argillaceous earth, called "Pampean mud," which overspreads the Rio Plata region.‡ Some of the Pampa shells, like those at Pebas, are proper to brackish water, and occur only on the highest banks. The Pampean formation is believed by Mr. Darwin to be an estuary or delta deposit. We will mention, in this connection, that silicified wood is found at the

* These interesting fossils are figured and described in the *Am. Journal of Conchology*.

† "The whole basin between the Orinoco and the Amazon is composed of granite and gneiss, slightly covered with débris. There is a total absence of sedimentary rocks. The surface is often bare and destitute of soil, the undulations being only a few feet above or below a straight line."—Evan Hopkins, in *Quart. Jour. Geol. Soc.*, vol. vi.

‡ See Darwin on the absence of extensive modern conchiferous deposits in South America, *Geological Observations*, pt. iii., ch. v.

head waters of the Napo; the Indians use it instead of flint (which does not occur there) in striking a light. Darwin found silicified trees on the same slope of the Andes as the Uspallata Pass.

The climatology of the Valley of the Amazon is as simple as its physical geography. There is no circle of the seasons as with us—nature moves in a straight line. The daily order of the weather is uniform for months. There is very little difference between the dry and hot seasons; the former, lasting from July to December, is varied with showers, and the latter, from January to June, with sunny days, while the daily temperature is the same within two or three degrees throughout the year. On the water-shed between the Orinoco and Negro it rains throughout the year, but most water falls between May and November, the coolest season in that region. On the Middle Negro the wet season extends from June 1st to December 1st, and is the most sultry time.

Comparatively few insects, birds, or beasts are to be seen in summer; but it is the harvest-time of the inhabitants, who spend the glorious weather rambling over the plaias and beaches, fishing and turtle-hunting. The middle of September is the midsummer of the valley. The rainy season, or winter, is ushered in by violent thunder-storms from the west. It is then that the woods are eloquent with buzzing insects, shrill cicadas, screaming parrots, chattering monkeys, and roaring jaguars. The greatest activity of animal and vegetable life is in June and July. The heaviest rains fall in April, May, and June. Scarcely ever is there a continuous rain for twenty-four hours. Castelnau witnessed at Pebas a fall of not less than thirty inches in a single storm. The greatest amount noticed in New York during the whole month of September was 12.2 inches. The humidity of the atmosphere, as likewise the luxuriance of vegetation and the abundance and beauty of animal forms, increases from the Atlantic to the Andes. At the foot of the Andes, Pœppig found that the most refined sugar in a few days dissolved into sirup, and the best gunpowder became liquid even when inclosed in canisters. So we found the Napo steaming with vapor. Fogs, however, are rarely seen on the Amazon.

The animals and plants are not all simultaneously affected by the change of seasons. The trees retain their verdure through the dry *veraõ*, and have no set time for renewing their foliage. There are a few trees, like Mongruba, which drop their leaves at particular seasons; but they are so few in number they create the impression of a few dead leaves in a thick-growing forest. Leaves are falling and flowers drooping all the year round. Each species, and, in some cases, each individual, has its own particular autumn and spring. There is no hibernation nor æstivation (except by land shells); birds have not one uniform time for nidification; and moulting extends from February to May.

Amazonia, though equatorially situated, has a temperate climate. It is cooler than Guinea or Guiana. This is owing to the constant evaporation from so much submerged land, and the ceaseless trade winds. The mean annual temperature of the air is about 81°.* The nights are always cool. There are no sudden changes, and no fiery "dog days." Venereal and cutaneous affections are found among the people; but they spring from an irregular life. A traveler on the slow black tributaries may take the tertiana, but only after weeks of exposure. Yellow fever and cholera seldom ascend the river above Pará; and on the Middle Amazon there are neither endemics nor epidemics,

* Agassiz calls the average temperature 84°, which, it seems to us, is too high. The mean between the temperatures of Pará, Manáos, and Tabatinga is 80.7°.

though the trades are feebly felt there, and the air is stagnant and sultry. According to Bates, swampy and weedy places on the Amazon are generally more healthy than dry ones. Whatever exceptions be taken to the branches, the main river is certainly as healthy as the Mississippi: the rapid current of the water and the continual movement of the air maintaining its salubrity. The few English residents (Messrs. Hislop, Jeffreys, and Hauxwell), who have lived here thirty or forty years, are as fresh and florid as if they had never left their native country. The native women preserve their beauty until late in life. Great is the contrast between the gloomy winters and dusty summers, the chilly springs and frosty autumns of the temperate zone, and the perennial beauty of the equator! No traveler on the Amazon would exchange what Wallace calls "the magic half-hour after sunset" for the long gray twilight of the north. "The man accustomed to this climate (wrote Herndon) is ever unwilling to give it up for a more bracing one."

The mineral kingdom is represented only by sand, clay, and loam. The solid rock (except the sandstone already mentioned) begins above the falls on the tributaries. The precious gems and metals are confined to the still higher lands of Goyaz, Matto Grosso, and the slopes of the Andes. The soil on the Lower Amazon is sandy; on the Solimoens and Marañon it is a stiff loam or vegetable mould, in many places twenty feet deep.

Both in botany and zoology, South America is a natural and strongly-marked division, quite as distinct from North America as from the Old World; and as there are no transverse barriers, there is a remarkable unity in the character of the vegetation. No spot on the globe contains so much vegetable matter as the Valley of the Amazon. From the grassy steppes of Venezuela to the treeless Pampas of Buenos

Ayres, expands a sea of verdure, in which we may draw a circle of eleven hundred miles in diameter, which shall include an ever green, unbroken forest. There is a most bewildering diversity of grand and beautiful trees — a wild, unconquered race of vegetable giants, draped, festooned, corded, matted, and ribboned with climbing and creeping plants, woody and succulent, in endless variety. The exuberance of nature displayed in these million square acres of tangled, impenetrable forest offers a bar to civilization nearly as great as its sterility in the African deserts. A *macheta* is a necessary predecessor: the moment you land (and it is often difficult to get a footing on the bank), you are confronted by a wall of vegetation. Lithe lianas, starred with flowers, coil up the stately trees, and then hang down like strung jewels; they can be counted only by myriads, yet they are mere superfluities. The dense dome of green overhead is supported by crowded columns, often branchless for eighty feet. The reckless competition among both small and great adds to the solemnity and gloom of a tropical forest. Individual struggles with individual, and species with species, to monopolize the air, light, and soil. In the effort to spread their roots, some of the weaker sort, unable to find a footing, climb a powerful neighbor, and let their roots dangle in the air; while many a full-grown tree has been lifted up, as it were, in the strife, and now stands on the ends of its stilt-like roots, so that a man may walk upright between the roots and under the trunk.*

The mass of the forest on the banks of the great river is composed of palms (about thirty species†), leguminous or

* Buttress roots are not peculiar to any one species, but common to most of the large trees in the crowded forest, where the lateral growth of the roots is made difficult by the multitude of rivals. The Paxiuba, or big-bellied palm, is a fine example.

† Von Martius, in his great work on the Brazilian Palms, enumerates in all 582 species.

pod-bearing trees, colossal nut-trees, broad-leaved Musaceæ or bananas, and giant grasses. The most prominent palms are the architectural Pupunha, or "peach-palm," with spiny stems, drooping, deep green leaves, and bunches of mealy, nutritious fruit; the slender Assaï, with a graceful head of delicate green plumes; the Ubussú, with mammoth, undivided fronds; the stiff, serrated-leaved Bussú, and gigantic Mirití. One of the noblest trees of the forest is the Massaranduba, or "cow-tree" (*Brosimum galactodendron*), often rising one hundred and fifty feet. It is a hard, fine-grained, durable timber, and has a red bark, and leathery, fig-like foliage. The milk has the consistency of cream, and may be used for tea, coffee, or custards. It hardens by exposure, so as to resemble gutta-percha. Another interesting tree, and one which yields the chief article of export, is the Caucho, or India-rubber tree* (*Siphonia Brasiliensis*), growing in the lowlands of the Amazon for eighteen hundred miles above Pará. It has an erect, tall trunk, from forty to eighty feet high, a smooth, gray bark, and thick, glossy leaves. The milk resembles thick, yellow cream, and is colored by a dense smoke obtained by burning palm-nuts. It is gathered between August and December. A man can collect six pounds a day, though this is rarely done. It is frequently adulterated with sand. The tree belongs to the same apetalous family as our castor-oil and the mandioca; while the tree which furnishes the caoutchouc of the East Indies and Africa is a species of Ficus, and yields an inferior article to the rubber of America. Other characteristic trees are the Mongruba, one of the few which shed their foliage

* The Portuguese and Brazilians call it *seringa*, or syringe, in which form it is still used extensively, injections forming a great feature in the popular system of cures. The tree mentioned above yields most of the rubber of commerce, and is considered distinct from the species in Guiana, *S. elastica*; while the rubber from the Upper Amazon and Rio Negro comes from the *S. lutea* and *S. brevifolia*. Agassiz puts milk-weed in the same family!

before the new leaf-buds expand; the giant Samaüma, or silk-cotton tree (called *huimba* in Peru); the Calabash, or *cuieira*, whose gourd-like fruit furnishes the cups used throughout the Amazon; the Itauba, or stone-wood, furnishing ship-timber as durable as teak; the red and white Cedar, used for canoes (not coniferous like the northern evergreen, but allied to the mahogany); the Jacarandá, or rosewood, resembling our locust; Palo de sangre, one of the most valuable woods on the river; Huacapú, a very common timber; Capirona, used as fuel on the steamers; and Tauarí, a heavy, close-grained wood, the bark of which splits into thin leaves, much used in making cigarettes. The Piassaba, a palm yielding a fibre extensively manufactured into cables and ropes, and exported to foreign countries for brushes and brooms, being singularly elastic, strong, and more durable than hemp; and the Moira-pinima, or "tortoise-shell wood," the most beautiful wood in all Amazonia, if not in the world, grow on the Upper Rio Negro. A small willow represents the great catkin family.

The valley is as remarkable for the abundance, variety, and value of its timber as for any thing else. Within an area of half a mile square, Agassiz counted one hundred and seventeen different kinds of woods, many of them eminently fitted, by their hardness, tints, and beautiful grain, for the finest cabinet-work. Enough palo de sangre or moira-pinima is doubtless wasted annually to veneer all the palaces of Europe.

While most of our fruits belong to the rose family, those of the Amazon come from the myrtle tribe. The delicious flavor, for which our fruits are indebted to centuries of cultivation, is wanting in many of the torrid productions. We prefer the sweetness of Pomona in temperate climes to her savage beauty in the sunny south. It is a curious fact, noticed by Herndon, that nearly all the valuable fruits of the valley are inclosed in hard shells or acid pulps. They also reach a larger size in advancing westward. The common Brazil nut is the product of one of the tallest trees in the forest (*Bertholletia excelsa*). The fruit is a hard, round shell, resembling a common ball, which contains from twenty to twenty-four nuts. Eighteen months are required for the bud to reach maturity. This tree, says Humboldt, offers the most remarkable example of high organic development. Akin to it is the Sapucaya or "chickens' nuts" (*Lecythis sapucaya*), whose capsule has a natural lid, and is called "monkey's drinking-cup." The nuts, about a dozen in number, are of irregular shape and much richer than the preceding. But they do not find their way to market, because they drop out of the capsule as soon as ripe, and are devoured by peccaries and monkeys. The most luscious fruit on the Amazon is the atta of Santarem. It has the color, taste, and size of the chirimoya; but the rind, which incloses a rich, custardly pulp, frosted with sugar, is scaled. Next in rank are the melting pine-apples of Pará, and the golden papayas, fully equal to those on the western coast. This is the original home of the cacao. It grows abundantly in the forests of the upper river, and particularly on the banks of the Madeira. The wild nut is smaller but more oily than the cultivated. The Amazon is destined to supply the world with the bulk of chocolate. The aromatic tonka beans (Cumarú) used in flavoring snuff, and the Brazilian nutmegs (Puxiri), inferior to the Ceylon, grow on lofty trees on the Negro and Lower Amazon. The Guaraná beans are the seeds of a trailing plant; from these the Mauhés prepare the great medicine, on the Amazon, for diarrhœa and intermittent fevers. Its active principle, caffeine, is more abundant than in any other substance, amounting to 5.07 per cent.; while black tea contains only 2.13. Coffee, rice, tobacco, and sugar-cane are grown to a limited extent. Rio Negro coffee, if put into the market, would probably eclipse that of Ceará, the best Brazilian. Wild rice grows abundantly on the banks of the rivers and lakes. The cultivated grain is said to yield forty fold. Most of the tobacco comes down from the Marañon and Madeira. It is put up in slender rolls from three to six feet long, tapering at each end, and wound with palm fibre. The sugar-cane is an exotic from Southeastern Asia, but grows well. The first sugar made in the New World was by the Dutch in the island of St. Thomas, 1610. Farina is the principal farinaceous production of Brazil. The mandioca or cassava (*Manihot utilissima*) from which it is made is supposed to be indigenous, though it is not found wild. It does not grow at a higher altitude than 2000 feet. Life and death are blended in the plant, yet every part is useful. The cattle eat the leaves and stalks, while the roots are ground into pulp, which, when pressed and baked, forms farina, the bread of all classes. The juice is a deadly poison: thirty-five drops were sufficient to kill, in six minutes, a negro convicted of murder; but it deposits a fine sediment of pure starch that is the well-known tapioca; and the juice, when fermented and boiled, forms a drink. On the upper waters grow the celebrated coca, a shrub with small, light-green leaves, having a bitter, aromatic taste. The powdered leaves, mixed with lime, form *ypadú*. This is to Peruvians what opium is to the Turk, betel to the Malay, and tobacco to the Yankee. Thirty million pounds are annually consumed in South America. It is not, however, an opiate, but a powerful stimulant. With it the Indian will perform prodigies of labor, traveling days without fatigue or food. Von Tschudi considers its moderate consumption wholesome, and instances the fact that one coca-chewer attained the good old age of one hundred and thirty years; but when used to excess it leads to idiocy. The signs of intemperance are an uncertain step, sallow complexion, black-rimmed, deeply-sunken eyes, trembling lips, incoherent speech, and stolid apathy. Coca played an important part in the religious rights of the Incas, and divine honors were paid to it. Even to-day the miners of Peru throw a quid of coca against the hard veins of ore, affirming that it renders them more easily worked; and the Indians sometimes put coca in the mouth of the dead to insure them a welcome in the other world. The alkaloid cocaïne was discovered by Wöhler.

Flowers are nearly confined to the edges of the dense forest, the banks of the rivers and lagunes. There are a greater number of species under the equator, but we have brighter colors in the temperate zone. "There is grandeur and sublimity in the tropical forest (wrote Wallace, after four years of observation), but little of beauty or brilliancy of color." Perhaps the finest example of inflorescence in the world is seen in the *Victoria Regia*, the magnificent water-lily discovered by Schömberg in 1837. It inhabits the tranquil waters of the shallow lakes which border the Amazon. The leaves are from fifteen to eighteen feet in circumference, and will bear up a child twelve years old; the upper part is dark, glossy green, the under side violet or crimson. The flowers are a foot in diameter, at first pure white, passing, in twenty-four hours, through successive hues from rose to bright red. This queen of water-plants was dedicated to the Queen whose empire is never at once shrouded in night.

Coca-plant.

CHAPTER XX.

Life within the Great River.—Fishes.—Alligators.—Turtles.—Porpoises and Manatís.

THE Amazon is a crowded aquarium, holding representatives of every zoological class—infusoria, hydras, fresh-water shells (chiefly Ampullaria, Melania, and Unios), aquatic beetles (belonging mostly to new genera), fishes, reptiles, water birds, and cetaceans. The abundance and variety of fishes are extraordinary; so also are the species. This great river is a peculiar ichthyic province, and each part has its characteristics. According to Agassiz, the whole river, as well as its tributaries, is broken up into numerous distinct fauna.* The *pirarucú*, or "red-fish" (the *Sudis gigas* of science), is at once the largest, most common, and most useful fish. The Peruvian Indians call it *payshi.* It is a powerful fish, often measuring eight feet in length and five in girth, clad in an ornamental coat-of-mail, its large scales being margined with bright red. It ranges from Peru to Pará. It is usually taken by the arrow or spear. Salted and dried, the meat will keep for a year, and forms, with farina, the staple food on the Amazon. The hard, rough tongue is used as a grater. Other fishes most frequently seen are the prettily-spotted catfish, Pescada, Piranha, Acará, which carries its young in its mouth, and a long, slender needle-fish. There are ganoids in the river, but no sturgeons proper. Pickerel, perch, and trout are also wanting. The sting-ray rep-

* We await the Professor's examination of his "more than 80,000 specimens" before we give the number of new species.

resents the shark family. As a whole, the fishes of the Amazon have a marine character peculiarly their own.

The reptilian inhabitants of this inland sea are introduced by numerous batrachians, water-snakes (*Heliops*), and anacondas. But alligators bear the palm for ugliness, size, and strength. In summer the main river swarms with them; in the wet season they retreat to the interior lakes and flooded forests. It was for this reason that we did not see an alligator on the Napo. At low water they are found above the entrance of the Curaray. About Obidos, where many of the pools dry up in the fine months, the alligator buries itself in the mud, and sleeps till the rainy season returns. "It is scarcely exaggerating to say (writes Bates) that the waters of the Solimoens are as well stocked with large alligators in the dry season as a ditch in England is in summer with tadpoles." There are three or four species in the Amazon. The largest, the Jacaré-uassú of the natives, attains a length of twenty feet. The Jacaré-tinga is a smaller kind (only five feet long when full grown), and has the long, slender muzzle of the extinct teleosaurus. The South American alligators are smaller than the crocodiles of the Nile or Ganges, and they are also inferior in rank. The head of the Jacaré-uassú (the ordinary species) is broad, while the gavial of India has a long, narrow muzzle, and that of the Egyptian lizard is oblong. The dentition differs: while in the Old World saurian the teeth interlock, so that the two jaws are brought close together, the teeth in the upper jaw of the Amazonian cayman pass by the lower series outside of them. The latter has therefore much less power. It has a ventral cuirass as well as dorsal, and it is web-footed, while the crocodile has the toes free—another mark of inferiority. Sluggish on land, the alligator is very agile in its element. It never attacks man when on his guard, but it is cunning enough to know when it may do this with safety. It lays its eggs (about twenty) some distance from the river bank, covering them with leaves and sticks. They are larger than those of Guayaquil, or about four inches long, of an elliptical shape, with a rough, calcareous shell. Negro venders sell them cooked in the streets of Pará.

Turtles are, perhaps, the most important product of the Amazon, not excepting the pirarucú. The largest and most abundant species is the Tortaruga grande. It measures, when full grown, nearly three feet in length and two in breadth, and has an oval, smooth, dark-colored shell. Every house has a little pond (called *currál*) in the back yard to hold a stock of turtles through the wet season. It furnishes the best meat on the Upper Amazon. We found it very tender, palatable, and wholesome; but Bates, who was obliged to live on it for years, says it is very cloying. Every part of the creature is turned to account. The entrails are made into soup; sausages are made of the stomach; steaks are cut from the breast; and the rest is roasted in the shell.* The turtle lays its eggs (generally between midnight and dawn) on the central and highest part of the plaias, or about a hundred feet from the shore. The Indians say it will lay only where itself was hatched out. With its hind flippers it digs a hole two or three feet deep, and deposits from eighty to one hundred and sixty eggs (Gibbon says from one hundred and fifty to two hundred). These are covered with sand, and the next comer makes another deposit on the top, and so on until the pit is full. Egg-laying comes earlier on the Amazon than on the Napo, taking place in August and September. The tracajá, a smaller species, lays in July and August; its eggs are smaller and oval, but richer than those of the great turtles.

* The natives have this notion about the land-tortoise, that by throwing it three times over the head, the liver (the best part) will be enlarged.

The mammoth tortoise of the Galápagos lays an egg very similar in size and shape to that of the Tortaruga, but a month later, or in October. The hunting of turtle eggs is a great business on the Amazon. They are used chiefly in manufacturing oil (mantéca) for illumination. Thrown into a canoe, they are broken and beaten up by human feet; water is then poured in, and the floating oil is skimmed off, purified over the fire in copper kettles, and finally put up in three-gallon earthen jars for the market. The turtles are caught for the table as they return to the river after laying their eggs. To secure them, it suffices to turn them over on their backs. The turtles certainly have a hard time of it. The alligators and large fishes swallow the young ones by hundreds; jaguars pounce upon the full-grown specimens as they crawl over the plaias, and vultures and ibises attend the feast. But man is their most formidable foe. The destruction of turtle life is incredible. It is calculated that fifty millions of eggs are annually destroyed. Thousands of those that escape capture in the egg period are collected as soon as hatched and devoured, "the remains of yolk in their entrails being considered a great delicacy." An unknown number of full-grown turtles are eaten by the natives on the banks of the Marañon and Solimoens and their tributaries, while every steamer, schooner, and little craft that descends the Amazon is laden with turtles for the tables of Manáos, Santarem, and Pará. When we consider, also, that all the mature turtles taken are females, we wonder that the race is not well-nigh extinct. They are, in fact, rapidly decreasing in numbers. A large turtle which twenty years ago could be bought for fifty cents, now commands three dollars. One would suppose that the males, being unmolested, would far outnumber the other sex, but Bates says "they are immensely less numerous than the females."

The male turtles, or *Capitaris*, "are distinguishable by their much smaller size, more circular shape, and the greater length and thickness of their tails." Near the Tapajos we met a third species, called *Matá-matá*. It has a deeply-keeled carapax, beautifully bossed, and a hideous triangular head, having curious, lobed, fleshy appendages, and nostrils prolonged into a tube. It is supposed to have great virtues as a remedy for rheumatism. But the most noticeable feature of the Amazonian fauna, as Agassiz has remarked, is the abundance of cetaceans through its whole extent. From the brackish estuary of Pará to the clear, cool waters at the base of the Andes, these clumsy refugees from the ocean may be seen gamboling and blowing as in their native element. Four different kinds of porpoises have been seen. A black species lives in the Bay of Marajó. In the Middle Amazon are two distinct porpoises, one flesh-colored;* and in the upper tributaries is the *Inia Boliviensis*, resembling, but specifically different from the sea-dolphin and the soosoo of the Ganges. "It was several years (says the Naturalist on the Amazon) before I could induce a fisherman to harpoon dolphins (*Boutos*) for me as specimens, for no one ever kills these animals voluntarily; the superstitious people believe that blindness would result from the use of the oil in lamps." The herbivorous manati (already mentioned, Chap. XV.) is found throughout the great river. It differs slightly from the Atlantic species. It rarely measures over twelve feet in length. It is taken by the harpoon or nets of chambiri twine. Both Herndon and Gibbon mention seals as occurring in the Peruvian tributaries; but we saw none, neither did Bates, Agassiz, or Edwards. They probably meant the manati.

* *Delphinus pallidus*. Bates observed this species at Villa Nova; we saw it at Coary, 500 miles west; and Herndon found it in the Huallaga.

CHAPTER XXI.

Life around the Great River.—Insects.—Reptiles.—Birds.—Mammals.

THE forest of the Amazon is less full of life than the river. Beasts, birds, and reptiles are exceedingly scarce; still there is, in fact, a great variety, but they are widely scattered and very shy. In the animal, as in the vegetable kingdom, diversity is the law; there is a great paucity of individuals compared with the species.* Insects are rare in the dense forest; they are almost confined to the more open country along the banks of the rivers. Ants are perhaps the most numerous. There is one species over an inch long. But the most prominent, by their immense numbers, are the dreaded saübas. Well-beaten paths branch off in every direction through the forest, on which broad columns may be seen marching to and fro, each bearing vertically a circular piece of leaf. Unfortunately they prefer cultivated trees, especially the coffee and orange. They are also given to plundering provisions; in a single night they will carry off bushels of farina. They are of a light red color, with powerful jaws. In every formicarium or ant colony there are three sets of individuals—males, females, and workers; but the saübas have the singularity of possessing three classes of workers. The light-colored mounds often met in the forest, sometimes

* Amazonia is divided into four distinct zoological districts: those of Ecuador, Peru, Guiana, and Brazil; the limits being the Amazon, Madeira, and Negro. The species found on one side of these rivers are seldom found on the other.

measuring forty feet in diameter by two feet in height, are the domes which overlie the entrances to the vast subterranean galleries of the saüba ants. These ants are eaten by the Rio Negro Indians, and esteemed a luxury; while the Tapajos tribes use them to season their mandioca sauce. Akin to the vegetable-feeding saübas are the carnivorous ecitons, or foraging ants, of which Bates found ten distinct species. They hunt for prey in large organized armies, almost every species having its own special manner of marching and hunting. Fortunately the ecitons choose the thickest part of the forest. The fire-ant is the great plague on the Tapajos. It is small, and of a shiny reddish color; but its sting is very painful, and it disputes every fragment of food with the inhabitants. All eatables and hammocks have to be hung by cords smeared with copaiba balsam.

The traveler on the Amazon frequently meets with conical hillocks of compact earth, from three to five feet high, from which radiate narrow covered galleries or arcades. The architects of these wonderful structures are the termites, or "white ants," so called, though they belong to a higher order of insects, widely differing from the true ants. The only thing in common is the principle of division of labor. The termite neuters are subdivided into two classes, soldiers and workers, both wingless and blind. Their great enemy is the ant-eater; but it is a singular fact, noticed by Bates, that the soldiers only attach themselves to the long worm-like tongue of this animal, so that the workers, on whom the prosperity of the termitarum depends, are saved by the self-sacrifice of the fighting caste. The office of the termites in the tropics seems to be to hasten the decomposition of decaying vegetation. But they also work their way into houses, trunks, wardrobes, and libraries. "It is principally owing to their destructiveness" (wrote Humboldt) "that it is so rare to find papers in tropical America older than fifty or sixty years."

Dragon-flies are conspicuous specimens of insect life on the Amazon. The largest and most brilliant kinds are found by the shady brooks and creeks in the recesses of the forest, some of them with green or crimson bodies seven inches long, and their elegant lace-like wings tipped with white or yellow. Still more noticeable are the butterflies. There is a vast number of genera and species, and great beauty of dress, unequaled in the temperate zone. Some idea of the diversity is conveyed by the fact mentioned by Mr. Bates that about 700 species are found within an hour's walk of Pará, and 550 at Ega; while the total number found in the British Islands does not exceed 66, and the whole of Europe supports only 390. After a shower in the dry season the butterflies appear in fluttering clouds (for they live in societies), white, yellow, red, green, purple, black, and blue, many of them bordered with metallic lines and spots of a silvery or golden lustre. The sulphur-yellow and orange-colored kinds predominate. A colossal morpho, seven and a half inches in expanse, and visible a quarter of a mile off, frequents the shady glades; splendid swallow-tailed papilios, green, rose, or velvety-black, are seen only in the thickets; while the *Hetaira esmeralda*, with transparent wings, having one spot of a violet hue, as it flies over the dead leaves in the dense forest looks "like a wandering petal of a flower." Very abundant is the *Heliconius*, which plays such an important figure, by its variations, in Wallace's theory of the origin of species. On the Marañon we found *Callidryas eubule*, a yellow butterfly common in Florida. The most brilliant butterflies are found on the Middle Amazon, out of reach of the strong trade winds. The males far outnumber the other sex, are more richly colored, and generally lead a sunshiny life.

The females are of dull hues, and spend their lives in the gloomy shadows of the forest. Caterpillars and nocturnal moths are rare.

There are no true hive-bees (*Apides*) in South America,* but instead there are about one hundred and fifty species of bees (mostly social *Moliponas*), smaller than the European, stingless, and constructing oblong cells. Their colonies are much larger than those of the honey-bee. The *Trigona* occurs on the Napo. Unlike the *Melipona*, it is not confined to the New World. A large sooty-black Bombus represents our humble-bee. Shrill cicadas, bloodthirsty mantucas, piums, punkies, and musquitoes are always associated in the traveler's memory with the glorious river. Of the last there are several kinds. "The forest musquito belongs to a different species from that of the town, being much larger and having transparent wings. It is a little cloud that one carries about his person every step on a woodland ramble, and their hum is so loud that it prevents one hearing well the notes of birds. The town musquito has opaque, speckled wings, a less severe sting, and a silent way of going to work. The inhabitants ought to be thankful the big noisy fellows never come out of the forest" (Bates, ii., 386). There are few musquitoes below Ega; above that point a musquito net is indispensable. Beetles abound, particularly in shady places, and are of all sizes, from that of a pin's head to several inches in length. The most noticeable are the gigantic *Megalosoma* and *Enema*, armed with horns. Very few are carnivorous. "This is the more remarkable," observes Darwin, "when compared to the case of carnivorous quadrupeds, which are so abundant in hot countries." Very few are terrestrial, even the carnivorous species being found clinging to branches and leaves. In going from the pole to the equator we find

* The honey-bee of Europe was introduced into South America in 1845.

that insect life increases in the same proportion as vegetable life. There is not a single beetle on Melville Island; eleven species are found in Greenland; in England, 2500; in Brazil, 8000. Here lives the king of spiders, the *Mygale Blondii*, a monstrous hairy fellow, five inches long, of a brown color, with yellowish lines along its stout legs. Its abode is a slanting subterranean gallery about two feet in length, the sides of which are beautifully lined with silk. Other spiders barricade the walks in the forest with invisible threads; some build nests in the trees and attack birds; others again spin a closely-woven web, resembling fine muslin, under the thatched roofs of the houses.

Of land vertebrates, lizards are the first to attract the attention of the traveler on the equator. Great in number and variety, they are met every where—crawling up the walls of buildings, scampering over the hot, dusty roads, gliding through the forest. They stand up on their legs, carry their tails cocked up in the air, and run with the activity of a warm-blooded animal. It is almost impossible to catch them. Some of them are far from being the unpleasant-looking animals many people imagine; but in their coats of many colors, green, gray, brown, and yellow, they may be pronounced beautiful. Others, however, have a repulsive aspect, and are a yard in length. The iguana, peculiar to the New World tropics, is covered with minute green scales banded with brown (though it changes its color like the chameleon), and has a serrated back and gular pouch. It grows to the length of five feet, and is arboreal. Its white flesh, and its oblong, oily eggs, are considered great delicacies. We heard of a lady who kept one as a pet. Frogs and toads, the chief musicians in the Amazonian forest, are of all sizes, from an inch to a foot in diameter. The *Bufo gigas* is of a dull gray color, and is covered with warts. Tree-frogs (*Hyla*) are

Iguana.

very abundant; they do not occur on the Andes or on the Pacific coast. Their quack-quack, drum-drum, hoo-hoo, is one of our pleasant memories of South America. Of snakes there is no lack; and yet they are not so numerous as imagination would make them. There are one hundred and fifty species in South America, or one half as many, on the same area, as in the East Indies. The diabolical family is led by the boa, while the rear is brought up by the Amphisbænas, or "double-headed snakes," which progress equally well with either end forward, so that it is difficult to make head or tail of them. The majority are harmless. The deadly corál is found on both sides of the Andes, and wherever there is a cacao plantation. One of the most beautiful specimens of the venomous kind is a new species (*Elaps imperator*, Cope), which we discovered on the Marañon. It has a slender body more than two feet in length, with black and red bands margined with yellow, and a black and yellow head, with permanently erect fangs.

We have already mentioned the most common birds. Probably, says Wallace, no country in the world contains a greater variety of birds than the Amazonian Valley.

But the number does not equal the expectations of the traveler; he may ramble a whole day without meeting one. The rarity, however, is more apparent than real; we forget, for the moment, the vastness of their dwelling-place. The birds of the country, moreover, are gregarious, so that a locality may be deserted and silent at one time and swarming with them at another. Parrots and toucans are the most characteristic groups. To the former belong true parrots, parroquets, and macaws. The first are rarely seen walking, but are rapid flyers and expert climbers. On the trees they are social as monkeys, but in flight they always go in pairs. The parroquets go in flocks. The Hyacinthine macaw (the Araruna of the natives) is one of the finest and rarest species of the parrot family. It is found only on the south side of the Amazon. The macaw was considered sacred by the Maya Indians of Yucatan, and dedicated to the sun. The Quichuans call it guacamayo, guaca meaning sacred. Of toucans there are many species; the largest is the toco, with a beak shaped like a banana; the most beautiful are the curb-crested, or Beauharnais toucans, and the *P. flavirostris*, whose breast is adorned with broad belts of red, crimson, and black. "Wherefore such a beak?" every naturalist has asked; but the toucan still wags his head, as much as to say, "you can not tell." There must be some other reason than adaptation. Birds of the same habits are found beside it—the ibis, pigeon, spoonbill, and toucan are seen feeding together. "How astonishing are the freaks and fancies of Nature! (wrote the funny Sidney Smith). To what purpose, we say, is a bird placed in the woods of Cayenne with a bill a yard long, making a noise like a puppy-dog, and laying eggs in hollow trees? The toucan, to be sure, might retort, to what purpose are certain foolish, prating members of Parliament created, pestering the

House of Commons with their ignorance and folly, and impeding the business of the country? There is no end to such questions; so we will not enter into the metaphysics of the toucan."

Toucans.

On the flooded islands of the Negro and Upper Amazon is found the rare and curious umbrella bird, black as a crow, and decorated with a crest of hairy plumes and a long lobe suspended from the neck, covered with glossy blue feathers. This latter appendage is connected with the vocal organs, and assists the bird in producing its deep, loud, and lengthy fluty note. There are three species. Another rare bird is the Uruponga, or Campanéro, in English the tolling-bell bird, found only on the borders of Guiana. It is of the size of our jay, of a pure white color, with a black tubercle on the upper side of the bill. "Orpheus himself (says Waterton) would drop his lute to listen to him, so sweet, so novel, and romantic is the toll of the pretty, snow-white Campanéro." "The Campanéro may be heard three miles! (echoes Sidney Smith). This single little bird being more powerful than the belfry of a cathedral ringing for a new dean! It is impossible to contradict a gentleman who has been in the forests of Cayenne, but we are determined, as soon as a Campanéro is brought to England, to make him toll in a public place, and have the distance measured."* But the most remarkable songster of the Amazonian forest is the Realejo, or organ-bird. Its notes are as musical as the flageolet. It is the only songster, says Bates, which makes any impression on the natives. Besides these are the Jacamars, peculiar to equatorial America, stupid, but of the most beautiful golden, bronze, and steel colors; sulky Trogons, with glossy green backs and rose-colored breasts; long-toed Jaçanas, half wader, half fowl; the rich, velvety purple and black *Rhamphocoelus Jacapa*, having an immense range from Archidona to Pará; the gallinaceous yet arboreal Ciganas; scarlet ibises, smaller, but more beautiful than their sacred cousins of the Nile; stilted flamingoes, whose awkwardness is atoned for by their brilliant red plumage; glossy black Mutums, or curassow turkeys; ghostly storks, white egrets, ash-colored herons, black ducks, barbets, kingfishers, sandpipers, gulls, plovers, woodpeckers, oreoles; tanagers, essentially a South American family, and, excepting three or four species, found only east of the Andes; wagtails, finches, thrushes, doves, and hummers. The last, "by western Indians *living sunbeams* named," are few, and not to be compared with the swarms in the Andean valleys. The birds of the Amazon have no

* Review of Waterton's *Wanderings in South America.*

Brazilian Hummers.

uniform time for breeding. The majority, however, build their nests between September and New Year's, and rarely lay more than two eggs.

Amazonia, like Australia, is poor in terrestrial mammals, and the species are of small size. Nearly the only game a hunter can depend upon for food, besides toucans and macaws, is peccari. One species of tapir, to represent the elephants and rhinoceroses of the Old World; three small species of deer, taking the places of deer, antelopes, buffaloes, sheep, and goats of the other continent; three species of large Felidæ; one peccari, and a wild dog, with opossums, ant-eaters, armadilloes, sloths, squirrels (the only rodents which approach ours),* capybaras, pacas, agoutis, and monkeys, comprise all the quadrupeds of equatorial America. The last two are the most numerous. Marsupial rats take the place of the insectivorous mammals. Of ant-eaters, there are at least four distinct species; but they are scattered sparingly, and are seldom found on the low

* Large rats abound on the Marañon, but they are not American.

flooded lands. Four or five species of armadillo inhabit the valley. These little nocturnal burrowing edentates are the puny representatives of the gigantic Glyptodon of Pleistocene times, and the sloths are the dwindling shadows of the lordly Megatherium. There are two species of three-toed sloths—one inhabiting the swampy lowlands, the other confined to the terra-firma land. They lead a lonely life, never in groups, harmless and frugal as a hermit. They have four stomachs, but not the long intestines of ruminating animals. They feed chiefly on the leaves of the trumpet-tree (*Cecropia*), resembling our horse-chestnut. The natives, both Indian and Brazilian, hold the common opinion that the sloth is the type of laziness. The capybara or ronsoco, the largest of living rodents, is quite common on the river side. It is gregarious and amphibious, and resembles a mammoth guinea-pig. Pacas and agoutis are most abundant in the lowlands, and are nocturnal. These semi-hoofed rodents, like the Toxodon of old, approach the Pachyderms. The tapir, or gran-bestia, as it is called, is a characteristic quadruped of South America. It is a clumsy-looking animal, with a tough hide of an iron-gray color, covered with a coat of short coarse hair. Its flesh is dry, but very palatable. It has a less powerful proboscis than the Malay species. M. Roulin distinguishes another species from the mountains, which more nearly resembles the Asiatic. The tapir, like the condor, for an unknown reason, is not found north of 8° N., though it wanders as far south as 40°. We met but one species of peccari, the white-lipped (*D. labiatus*). It is much larger than the "Mexican hog," and, too thick-

Capybara.

headed to understand danger, is a formidable antagonist. The raposa is seen only on the Middle Amazon, and very rarely there. It has a long tapering muzzle, small ears, bushy tail, and grayish hair. It takes to the water, for the one we saw at Tabatinga was caught while crossing the Amazon. Fawn-colored pumas, spotted jaguars, black tigers, tiger-cats—all members of the graceful feline family—inhabit all parts of the valley, but are seldom seen. The puma, or panther, is more common on the Pacific side of the Andes. The jaguar* is the fiercest and most powerful animal in South America. It is marked like the leopard—roses of black spots on a yellowish ground; but they are

Jaguar.

angular instead of rounded, and have a central dot. There are also several black streaks across the breast, which easily distinguish it from its transatlantic representative. It is also longer than the leopard; indeed, Humboldt says he saw a jaguar "whose length surpassed that of any of the tigers

* The Tupi word for dog is *yaguara*, and for wolf, *yagua-men*, or old dog.

of India which he had seen in the collections of Europe." The jaguar frequents the borders of the rivers and lagunes, and its common prey is the capybara. It fears the peccari. The night air is alive with bats of many species, the most prominent one being the *Dysopes perotis*, which measures two feet from tip to tip of the wings. If these Cheiropters are as impish as they look, and as bloodthirsty as some travelers report, it is singular that Bates and Waterton, though residing for years in the country, and ourselves, though sleeping for months unprotected, were unmolested.

About forty species of monkeys, or one half of the New World forms, inhabit the Valley of the Amazon. Wallace, in a residence of four years, saw twenty-one species—seven with prehensile and fourteen with non-prehensile tails. They all differ from the apes of the other hemisphere. While those of Africa and Asia (Europe has only one) have opposable thumbs on the fore feet as well as hind, uniformly ten molar teeth in each jaw, as in man, and generally cheek-pouches and naked collosities, the American monkeys are destitute of the two latter characteristics. None of them are terrestrial, like the baboon; all (save the marmosets) have twenty-four molars; the thumbs of the fore-hands are not habitually opposed to the fingers (one genus, Ateles, "the imperfect," is thumbless altogether); the nostrils open on the sides of the nose instead of beneath it, as in the gorilla, and the majority have long prehensile tails. They are inferior in rank to the anthropoids of the Old World, though superior to the lemurs of Madagascar. They are usually grouped in two families—Marmosets and Cebidæ. The former are restless, timid, squirrel-like lilliputs (one species is only seven inches long), with tails not prehensile—in the case of the scarlet-faced, nearly wanting. The Barigudos, or gluttons (*Lagothrix*), are the largest of American monkeys, but are not so tall as the Coaitas. They are found west of Manáos. They have more human features than the other monkeys, and, with their woolly gray fur, resemble an old negro. There are three kinds of howlers (*Mycetes*)—the red or mono-colorado of Humboldt, the black, and the *M. beelzebub*, found only near Pará. The forest is full of these surly, untamable guaribas, as the natives call them. They are gifted with a voice of tremendous power and volume, with which they make night and day hideous. They represent the baboons of the Old World in disposition and facial angle (30°), and the gibbons in their yells and gregarious habits.* The Sapajous (*Cebus*) are distributed throughout Brazil, and have the reputation of being the most mischievous monkeys in the country. On the west coast of South America there are at least three or four species of monkeys, among them a black howler and a *Cebus capucinus*. The Coitas, or spider-monkeys, are the highest of American quadrumana. They are slender-legged, sluggish, and thumbless, with a most perfectly prehensile tail, terminating in a naked palm, which answers for a fifth hand. The Indians say they walk under the limbs like the sloth. They are the most common pets in Brazil, but they refuse to breed in captivity. Both Coitas and Barigudos are much persecuted for their flesh, which is highly esteemed by the Indians.

Mr. Bates has called our attention to the arboreal character of a large share of the animals in the Amazonian forest. All the monkeys and bats are climbers, and live in the trees. Nearly all the carnivores are feline, and are therefore tree-mounters, though they lead a terrestrial life. The plantigrade Cercoleptes has a long tail, and is entirely arboreal. Of the edentates, the sloth can do nothing on

* Rütimeyer has found a fossil howler in the Swiss Jura—middle eocene.

the ground. The gallinaceous birds, as the cigana and curassow—the pheasant and turkey of the Amazon—perch on the trees, while the great number of arboreal frogs and beetles is an additional proof of the adaptation of the fauna to a forest region. Even the epiphytous plants sitting on the branches suggest this arboreal feature in animal life.

CHAPTER XXII.

Life around the Great River.—Origin of the Red Man.—General Characteristics of the Amazonian Indians.—Their Languages, Costumes, and Habitations.—Principal Tribes.—Mixed Breeds.—Brazilians and Brazil.

WE come now to the genus Homo. Man makes a very insignificant figure in the vast solitudes of the Amazon. Between Manáos and Pará, the most densely-peopled part of the valley, there is only one man to every four square miles; and the native race takes a low place in the scale of humanity. As the western continent is geologically more primitive than the eastern, and as the brute creation is also inferior in rank, so the American man, in point of progress, seems to stand in the rear of the Old World races. Both the geology and zoology of the continent were arrested in their development. Vegetable life alone has been favored. "The aboriginal American (wrote Von Martius) is at once in the incapacity of infancy and unpliancy of old age; he unites the opposite poles of intellectual life."*

We will not touch the debatable ground of the red man's origin, nor inquire whether he is the last remains of a people once high in civilization. But we are tempted to express the full belief that tropical America is not his "centre of creation." He is not the true child of the tropics; and he lives as a stranger, far less fitted for its climate than

* "I think I discover in the Americans (said Humboldt) the descendants of a race which, early separated from the rest of mankind, has followed up for a series of years a peculiar road in the unfolding of its intellectual faculties and its tendency toward civilization." The South American Indian seems to have a natural aptitude for the arts of civilized life not found in the red man of our continent.

the Negro or Caucasian. Yet a little while, and the race will be as extinct as the Dodo. He has not the supple organization of the European, enabling him to accommodate himself to diverse conditions. Among the Andean tribes there are seldom over five children, generally but one, in a family; and Bates, speaking of Brazilian Indians, says "their fecundity is of a low degree, and it is very rare to find a family having so many as four children."*

While it is probable that Mexico was peopled from the north, it is very certain that the Tupi and Guarani, the long-headed hordes that occupied eastern South America, came up from the south, moving from the Paraguay to the banks of the Orinoco. From the Tupi nation (perhaps a branch of the Guarani) sprung the multitudinous tribes now dwelling in the vast valley of the Amazon. In such a country—unbroken by a mountain, uniform in climate—we need not look for great diversity. The general characters are these: skin of a brown color, with yellowish tinge, often nearly the tint of mahogany; thick, straight, black hair; black, horizontal eyes; low forehead, somewhat compensated by its breadth; beardless; of the middle height, but thick-set; broad, muscular chest; small hands and feet; incurious; unambitious; impassive; undemonstrative; with a dull imagination and little superstition; with no definite idea of a Supreme Being, few tribes having a name for God, though one for the "Demon;" with no belief in a future state; and, excepting civility, with virtues all negative. The semi-civilized along the Lower Amazon, called *Tupuyos*, seem to have lost (in the language of Wallace) the good qualities of savage life, and gained only the vices of civilization.

There are several hundred different tribes in Amazonia,

* We do not infer, however, from this fact alone, that the race is exotic, for the Negroes of Central Africa multiply very slowly.

each having a different language; even the scattered members of the same tribe can not understand each other.* This segregation of dialects is due in great part to the inflexibility of Indian character, and his isolated and narrow round of thought and life. When and where the Babel existed, whence the many branches of the great Tupi family separated, we know not. We only know that though different in words, these languages have the same grammatical construction. In more than one respect the polyglot American is antipodal to the Chinese. The language of the former is richest in words, that of the latter the poorest. The preposition follows the noun, and the verb ends the sentence. Ancient Tupi is the basis of the Lingoa Geral, the inter-tribal tongue on the Middle Amazon. The semi-civilized Ticunas, Mundurucus, etc., have one costume—the men in trowsers and white cotton shirts, the women in calico petticoats, with short, loose chemises, and their hair held in a knot on the top of the head by a comb, usually of foreign make, but sometimes made of bamboo splinters. The wild tribes north and south go nearly or quite nude, while those on the western tributaries wear cotton or bark togas or ponchos. The habitations are generally a frame-work of poles, thatched with palm-leaves; the walls sometimes latticed and plastered with mud, and the furniture chiefly hammocks and earthen vessels.

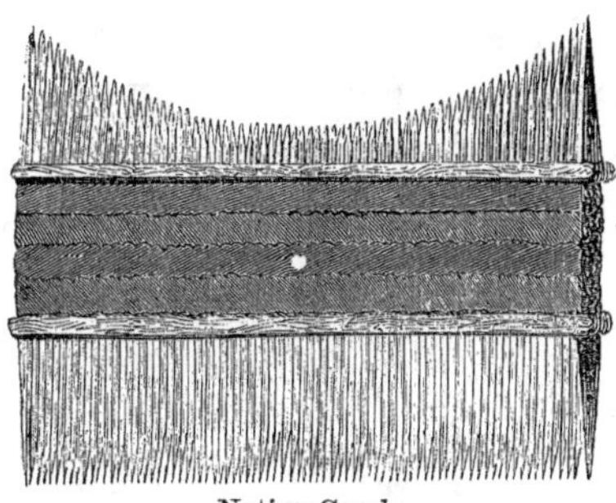

Native Comb.

* Authors compute in South America from 280 to 700 languages (Abbé Royo said 2000), of which four fifths are composed of idioms radically distinct.

The Mundurucus are the most numerous and warlike tribe in Amazonia. They inhabit both banks of the Tapajos, and can muster, it is said, 2000 fighting men. They are friendly to the whites, and industrious, selling to traders large quantities of farina, sarsaparilla, rubber, and tonka beans. Their houses are conical or quadrangular huts, sometimes open sheds, and generally contain many families. According to Wallace, the Mundurucus are the only perfectly tattooed nation in South America. It takes at least ten years to complete the tattooing of the whole person. The skin is pricked with spines, and then the soot from burning pitch rubbed in. Their neighbors, the Parárauátes, are intractable, wandering savages, roaming through the forest and sleeping in hammocks slung to the trees. They have delicately-formed hands and feet, an oval face, and glistening black eyes. On the west side of the Tapajos, near Villa Nova, are the Mauhés, an agricultural tribe, well formed, and of a mild disposition. On the Lower Madeira are the houseless, formidable Aráras, who paint their chins red with achote (anatto), and usually have a black tattooed streak on each side of the face. They have long made the navigation of the great tributary hazardous. Above them dwell the Parentintíns, light colored and finely featured, but nude and savage. In the labyrinth of lakes and channels at the mouth of the Madeira live the lazy, brutal Múras, the most degraded tribe on the Amazon. They have a darker skin than their neighbors, an extraordinary breadth of chest, muscular arms, short legs, protuberant abdomens, a thin beard, and a bold, restless expression. They pierce the lips, and wear peccari tusks in them in time of war. The Indians on the Purus live generally on the communal principle, and are unwarlike and indolent. The Puru-purús bury in sandy beaches, go naked, and have one wife.

On the great northwest tributary of the Rio Negro, the Uacaiari, there are numerous tribes, collectively known as the Uaupés. They have permanent abodes, in shape a parallelogram, with a semicircle at one end, and of a size to contain several families, sometimes a whole tribe. One of them, Wallace informs us, was 115 feet long by 75 broad, and about 30 high. The walls are bullet-proof. Partitions of palm-leaves divide it into apartments for families, the chief occupying the semicircular end. The men alone wear clothes and ornaments, but both sexes paint their bodies with red, black, and yellow colors in regular patterns. The men have a little beard, which they pull out, as also the eyebrows, and allow the hair to grow unshorn, tying it behind with a cord and wearing a comb; while the women cut theirs and wear no comb. They are an agricultural people—peaceable, ingenious, apathetic, diffident, and bashful.

The Catauishés inhabit the banks of the Teffé. They perforate the lips, and wear rows of sticks in the holes. At the mouth of the Juruá are the uncivilized, but tall, noble-looking Marauás. They pierce the ears and lips, and insert sticks. They live in separate families, and have no common chief. Above them live the treacherous Arauás.* On the opposite side of the Amazon are the nearly extinct Passés and Jurís, the finest tribes in central South America. They are peaceable and industrious, and have always been friendly to the whites. The Passés are a slenderly-built, light-colored, dignified, superior race, distinguished by a large square tattooed patch in the middle of the face. The Jurís tattoo in a circle round the mouth. Near by are the Uænambeus, or "Humming-birds," distinguished by

* Near the sources of this river Castlenau locates the Canamas and Uginas; the former dwarfs, the latter having tails a palm and a half long—a hybrid from an Indian and Barigudo monkey.

a small blue mark on the upper lip. Higher up the Japurá is the large cannibal tribe of Miránhas, living in isolated families; and on the Tocantíns dwell the low Caishánas, who kill their first-born children. Along the left bank of the Amazon, from Loreto to Japurá, are the scattered houses and villages of the Tucúnas. This is an extensive tribe, leading a settled agricultural life, each horde having a chief and a "medicine-man," or priest of their superstitions. They are good-natured and ingenious, excelling most of the other tribes in the manufacture of pottery; but they are idle and debauched, naked except in the villages, and tattooed in numbers of short, straight lines on the face. The Marúbos, on the Javarí, have a dark complexion and a slight beard; and on the west side of the same river roam the Majerónas—fierce, hostile, light colored, bearded cannibals. In the vicinity of Pebas dwell the inoffensive Yaguas. The shape of the head (but not their vacant expression) is well represented by Catlin's portrait of "Black Hawk," a Sauk chief. They are quite free from the encumbrance of dress, the men wearing a girdle of fibrous bark around the loins, with bunches looking like a mop hanging down in front and rear, and similar bunches hung around the neck and arms. The women tie a strip of brown cotton cloth about the hips. They paint the whole body with achote.* They sometimes live in communities. One large structure, with Gothic roof, is used in common; on the inside of which, around the walls, are built family sleeping-rooms. The Yaguas are given to drinking and dancing. They are said to bury their dead inside the house of the deceased, and then set fire to it; but this conflicts with their communal life. Perhaps, with the other tribes on the Japurá, Iça, and Napo, they are

* Query: Is the name Yagua (blood) derived from the practice of coloring the body red?

fragments of the great Omágua nation; but the languages have no resemblance. Of the Oriente Indians we have already spoken. The tall, finely-built Cucámas near Nauta are shrewd, hard-working canoe-men, notorious for the singular desire of acquiring property; and the Yámeos, a white tribe, wander across the Marañon as far as Sarayacú. On the Ucayali are numerous vagabond tribes, living for the most part in their canoes and temporary huts. They are all lazy and faithless, using their wives (polygamy is common) as slaves. Infanticide is practiced, *i. e.*, deformed children they put out of the way, saying they belong to the devil. They worship nothing. They bury their dead in a canoe or earthen jar under the house (which is vacated forever), and throw away his property.* The common costume is a long gown, called *cushma*, of closely-twilled cotton, woven by the women. Their weapons are two-edged battle-axes of hard wood, as palo de sangre, and bows and arrows. The arrows, five or six feet long, are made from the flower-stalk of the arrow-grass (*Gynerium*), the head pointed with the flinty chonta and tipped with bone, often anointed with poison. At the base two rows of feathers are spirally arranged, showing the Indian's knowledge of the rifle principle. When they have fixed abodes several families live together under one roof, with no division separating the women, as among the Red Indians on the Pastassa. The roof is not over ten feet from the ground. The Piros are the highest tribe; they have but one wife. The Conibos are an agricultural people, yet cannibals, stretching from the Upper Ucayali to the sources of the Purus. They are a fair-looking, athletic

* Compare the ancient burial custom on the Andes: "On the decease of the Inca his palaces are abandoned; all his treasures, except those that were employed in his obsequies, his furniture and apparel, were suffered to remain as he left them, and his mansions, save one, were closed up forever."—*Prescott.*

peoplė, and, like the Shipibos, often wear a piece of money under the lip. The Campas are the most numerous and warlike.* They are little known, as travelers give them a wide berth. Herndon fancied they were the descendants of the Inca race. They are said to be cannibals, and from the specimen we saw we should judge them uncommonly sharp. He was averse to telling us any thing about his tribe, but turned our questions with an equivocal repartee and a laugh. The Cashíbos, on the Pachitéa, is another cannibal tribe. They are light colored and bearded. The dwarfish, filthy Rimos alone of the Ucayali Indians tattoo, though not so perfectly as the Mundurucus, using black and blue colors. The other tribes simply paint. It was among these wild Indians on the Ucayali that the Franciscan friars labored so long and zealously, and with a success far greater and more lasting than that which attended any other missionary enterprise in the valley.

The remaining inhabitants of the Amazon are mixed-breeds, Negroes, and whites. The amalgamations form the greater part of the population of the large towns. Von Tschudi gives a catalogue of twenty-three hybrids in Peru, and there are undoubtedly as many, or more, in Brazil. The most common are Mamelucos (offspring of white with Indian), Mulattoes (from white and Negro), Cafuzos or Zambos (from Indian and Negro), Curibocos (from Cafuzo and Indian); and Xibaros (from Cafuzo and Negro). "To define their characteristics correctly," says Von Tschudi, "would be impossible, for their minds partake of the mixture of their blood. As a general rule, it may be said that they unite in themselves all the faults without any of the

* The women circumcise themselves, and a man will not marry a woman who is not circumcised. They perform the singular rite upon arriving at the age of puberty, and have a great feast at the time. Other tribes flog and imprison their daughters when they reach womanhood.

virtues of their progenitors. As men they are generally inferior to the pure races, and as members of society they are the worst class of citizens." Yet they display considerable talent and enterprise, as in Quito; a proof that mental degeneracy does not necessarily result from the mixture of white with Indian blood. "There is, however," confesses Bates, after ten years' experience, "a considerable number of superlatively lazy, tricky, and sensual characters among the half-castes, both in rural places and in the towns." Our observations do not support the opinion that the result of amalgamation is "a vague compound, lacking character and expression." The moral part is perhaps deteriorated; but in tact and enterprise they often excel their progenitors.

Negroes are to be seen only on the Lower Amazon. By the new act of emancipation, such as are slaves continue so, but their children are free. Negroes born in the country are called creoles.

Of the white population, save a handful of English, French, and German, the Portuguese immigrants are the most enterprising men on the river. They are willing to work, trade, or do any thing to turn a penny. Those who acquire a fortune generally retire to Lisbon. The Brazilians proper are the descendants of the men who declared themselves "free and independent" of the mother country. Few of them are of pure Caucasian descent, for the immigration from Portugal for many years has been almost exclusively of the male sex. "It is generally considered bad taste in Brazil to boast purity of descent" (Bates, i, 241). Brazilians are stiff and formal, yet courteous and lively, communicative and hospitable, well-bred and intelligent. They are not ambitious, but content to live and enjoy what nature spontaneously offers. The most a Brazilian wants is farina and coffee, a hammock and cigar. Brazilian ladies have led a dreary life of constraint and silence, without education or society, the husband making a nun of his wife after the old bigoted Portuguese notion; but during the last twenty years the doors have been opened. Brazil attained her independence in 1823; Brazilian women in 1848.

Here, in this virgin valley, where every plant is an evergreen, possessing the most agreeable and enjoyable climate in the world, with a brilliant atmosphere, rivaled only by that of Quito, and with no changes of seasons—here we may locate the paradise of the lazy. Life may be maintained with as little labor as in the Garden of Eden. Perhaps no country in the world is capable of yielding so large a return for agriculture. Nature, evidently designing this land as the home of a great nation, has heaped up her bounties of every description—fruits of richest flavors, woods of finest grain, dyes of gayest colors, and drugs of rarest virtues; and left no sirocco or earthquake to disturb its people. Providence, moreover, has given the present emperor a wise and understanding heart; and the government is a happy blending of imperial dignity and republican freedom. White, Negro, half-caste, and Indian may be seen sitting side by side on the jury-bench. Certainly "the nation can not be a despicable one whose best men are able to work themselves up to positions of trust and influence."

God bless the Empire of the South!

CHAPTER XXIII.

How to Travel in South America.—Routes.—Expenses.—Outfit.—Precautions.—Dangers.

THE most vague and incorrect notions prevail in respect to traveling in South America. The sources of trustworthy and desirable information are very meagre. Murray has not yet published a "Hand-book for the Andes;" routes, methods, and expenses of travel are almost unknown; and the imagination depicts vampires and scorpions, tigers and anacondas, wild Indians and fevers without end, impassable rivers and inaccessible mountains as the portion of the tourist. The following statements, which can be depended upon, may therefore be acceptable to those who contemplate a trip on the Andes and the Amazon.

The shortest, cheapest, most feasible, and least interesting route across the continent is from Valparaiso to Buenos Ayres. The breadth of South America is here only eight hundred miles. By railroad from Valparaiso to the foot of the Andes; thence a short mule-ride by the Uspallata Pass (altitude 12,000 feet), under the shadow of Aconcagua to Mendoza; thence by coach across the pampas to the Rio Plata. The Portillo Pass (traversed by Darwin) is nearer, but more lofty and dangerous.

Bolivia offers the difficult path of Gibbon: From the coast to Cochabamba; thence down the Marmoré and Madeira. There are three routes through Peru: First, from Lima to Mayro, by way of Cerro Pasco and Huánaco, by mule, ten days; thence down the Pachitea, by canoe, six days; thence down the Ucayali to Iquitos, by steamer, six days (forty-five hours' running time). When the road from Lima to Mayro is finished the passage will be shortened four days. No snow is met in crossing the Andes in summer, but in winter it is very deep. Second (Herndon's route), from Lima to Tinga Maria, by way of Huánaco, by mule, fifteen days, distance three hundred miles (the passage is difficult in the rainy season); thence by canoe fifteen days down the Huallaga to Yurimaguas. Third and best, by mule from Truxillo to Caximárca, five days (note the magnificent ruins); thence to Chachapoyas, seven days (here are pre-Incarial relics); thence to Moyabamba, eight days; thence on foot to Balsa Puerto, four days; thence by canoe to Yurimaguas, two days. Price of a mule from Truxillo to Moyabamba is $30; canoe-hire, $10. The Peruvian steamers arrive at Yurimaguas the fifth of every month and leave the seventh; reach Nauta the ninth and Iquitos the tenth; leave Iquitos the sixteenth and arrive at Tabatinga the nineteenth, to connect with the Brazilian line. Going up, they leave Tabatinga the twenty-first and arrive at Iquitos the twenty-fourth, stopping six days. Running time from Yurimaguas to Tabatinga, forty-eight hours; fare, $70, gold; third-class, $17. La Condamine's route, *via* Loxa and the Marañon, is difficult; and Md. Godin's, *via* the Pastassa, is perilous on account of rapids and savages. The transit by the Napo we will now give in detail.

Six hundred dollars in gold will be amply sufficient for a first-class passage from New York to New York across the continent of South America, making no allowance for stoppages. For necessary expenses in Ecuador, take a draft on London, which will sell to advantage in Guayaquil; so will Mexican dollars. American gold should be taken for expenses on the Amazon in Brazil; at Pará it commands a premium. On the Marañon it is below par; Peruvian gold should therefore be bought at Guayaquil for that part of the route. Also French *medios*, or quarter francs; they will be very useful every where on the route, especially on the Upper Amazon, where change is scarce. Fifty dollars' worth will not be too many; for, as the Scotchman said of sixpences, "they are canny little dogs, and often do the work of shillings." Take a passport for Brazil. Leave behind your delicacies and superfluities of clothing; woolen clothes will be serviceable throughout. A trunk for mountain travel should not exceed 24 by 15 by 15 inches—smaller the better. Take a rubber air-pillow and mattress: there is no bed between Guayaquil and Pará. A hammock for the Amazon can be bought on the Napo.

The Pacific Mail steamships, which leave New York on the first and sixteenth of each month, connect at Panama without delay with the British Steam Navigation line on the South Pacific. Fare, first-class, from New York to Guayaquil, by way of Panama and Paita, $215, gold; second-class, $128. Time to Panama, eight days; to Paita, four days; to Guayaquil, one day. A coasting steamer leaves Panama for Guayaquil the thirteenth of each month. There are two so-called hotels in Guayaquil. "Los tres Mosqueteros," kept by Sr. Gonzales, is the best. Take a front room ($1 per day), and board at the Fonda Italiana or La Santa Rosa ($1 per day). Here complete your outfit for the mountains: saddle, with strong girth and crupper; saddle-bags, saddle-cover, sweat-cloth, and bridle ($40, paper), woolen poncho ($9), rubber poncho ($4), blanket ($6), leggins, native spurs and stirrups, knife, fork, spoon, tea-pot, chocolate (tea, pure and cheap, should be purchased at Panama), candles, matches, soap, towels, and tarpaulin for wrapping up baggage. Convert your draft into paper, *quantum sufficit* for Guayaquil; the rest into silver.

Besides this outer outfit, an inner one is needed—of patience without stint. You will soon learn that it is one thing to plan and quite another to execute. "To get out of the inn is one half of the journey" is very appropriately a Spanish proverb. Spaniards do nothing *d'appressado* (in a hurry), but every thing *mañana* (to-morrow). You will find fondas, horses, and roads divided into the bad, the worse, and the worst, and bad is the best. But fret not thyself. "Serenity of mind," wrote Humboldt, "almost the first requisite for an undertaking in inhospitable regions, passionate love for some class of scientific labor, and a pure feeling for the enjoyment which nature in her freedom is ready to impart, are elements which, when they meet together in an individual, insure the attainment of valuable results from a great and important journey."

The journey to Quito must be made between May and November; in the rainy season the roads are impassable. From Guayaquil to Bodegas by Yankee steamer; fare, $2; time, eight hours. At Bodegas hire beasts at the *Consignacion* for Guaranda; price for riding and cargo beasts, $4 each. No extras for the *arriero*. A mule will carry two hundred and fifty pounds. Buy bread at Bodegas and Guaranda. The Indians on the road are very loth to sell any thing; buy a fowl, therefore, at the first opportunity, or you will have to live on dirty potato soup, and be glad of that. At the tambos, or wayside inns, you pay only for *yerba* (fodder). Never unsaddle your beast till it is cool; an Indian will even leave the bridle on for a time. To Guaranda, three full days. There take mules (safer than horses in climbing the mountains) for Quito; $6 25, silver, per beast; time, five days. Be sure to leave Guaranda by 4 A.M., for in the afternoon Chimborazo is swept by furious winds. Also start with a full stomach; you will get nothing for two days. Drink sparingly of the snow-water which dashes down the mountain. You will be tempted to curse Chuquipoyo; but thank heaven it is no worse.

There are two hotels in Quito, French and American; the former has the better location, the latter the better rooms. Best front room, furnished, half a dollar a day; cheaper by the month. Meals (two), twenty-five cents each. The beef is excellent, but the *cuisine*—oh, onions! "God sends the meat, and the evil one cooks." You can hire a professional male cook (Indian) for $5 a month, but you can't teach him any thing. Fish is not to be had in Quito. Gibbon speaks of having some in Cuzco, but does not tell us where it came from.* Price of best flour, $3 60 per quintal; butter, thirty cents a pound; beef, $1 an arroba (twenty-five pounds); refined sugar, $3 50 an arroba; brown sugar (*rapidura*),† five cents a pound; cigars, from six to sixteen for a dime; cigarettes, five cents a hundred. Horse hire, from fifty cents to $1 per day. If you are to remain some time, buy a beast: a good mule costs $40; an ordinary horse, $50. The Post-office Department is a swindle. If you "pay through" you will find on your arrival home that your letters have been paid at both ends. Ask our consul at Guayaquil to forward them.

The necessary preparations for the Napo journey have been given in a previous chapter (Chap. XI). We might add to the list a few cans of preserved milk from New York, for you will not see a drop between the Andes and the Atlantic. Fail not to take plenty of lienzo; you must have it to pay the Indians, and any surplus can be sold to advantage. A bale of thirty varas costs about five dollars.

* The Guayaquil market is well supplied with fish of a fair quality. Usually the fish of warm tropical waters are poor, but the cold "Humboldt current," which passes along the west coast of Ecuador, renders them as edible as those of temperate zones.

† Called *chancaca* in Peru. In flavor it is very nearly equal to maple-sugar.

Rely not at all on game; a champion sharpshooter could not live by his rifle. Santa Rosa and Coca will be represented to you as small New Yorks; but you will do well if you can buy a chicken between them.

From Quito to Papallacta, two days and a half; riding beast, $2 silver, and $1 20 for each cargo of three arrobas. At Papallacta hire Indians for Archidona; each carries three arrobas, and wants $5 silver in advance. You take to your feet; time, nine days, including one day of rest at Baeza. At Archidona you take a new set of peons for Napo at twenty-five cents apiece; time, one day. From Napo down the river to Santa Rosa, one day. You give two and a half varas of lienzo to each Indian, and the same for the canoe. From Santa Rosa to Pebas, on the Marañon, fifteen days; cost of an Indian, twenty-five varas; ditto for a canoe. We advise you to stop at Coca and rig up a raft or craft of some kind; we ascribe our uninterrupted good health to the length and breadth of our accommodations. The Peruvian steamer from the west arrives at Pebas on the sixteenth of each month; fare to Tabatinga, $15 gold; time, four days; running time, eleven hours. Brazilian steamer leaves Tabatinga the twentieth of each month; fare to Manáos, $44 44 gold; time, five days; distance, one thousand miles. From Manáos to Pará, $55 55 gold; time, six days; distance, one thousand miles. The Brazilian steamers make semi-monthly trips. We found two hotels in Pará—the "Italiana," dear and poor; the "Diana," unpretending but comfortable. Charges at the latter for room and board, $2 a day. The best time for traveling on the Amazon is between July and December. The United States and Brazilian steamships on their homeward voyage call at Pará the seventh of each month; fare to New York, $150 gold (the same as down the whole length of the Amazon); second class, $75; time, fourteen days; distance by way of St. Thomas, 1610+1400 miles. Steamer for Rio the ninth of each month; fare, $125; time, twelve days; distance, 2190 miles. Fare from Rio to New York, $200. Fare by sailing vessel from Pará to New York, from $50 to $75; time, three weeks. A British steamer from Rio stops at Pará and Lisbon.

A word about health. First, take one grain of commonsense daily; do as the natives do, keep out of the noonday sun, and make haste slowly. Secondly, take with you quinine in two-grain pills, and begin to take them before leaving New York, as the great African traveler, Du Chaillu, recommended us. As preventive against the intermittent fevers on the lowlands and rivers, nothing is better than Dr. Copeland's celebrated pills—quinine, twelve grains; camphor, twelve grains; cayenne pepper, twelve grains. Mix with mucilage, and divide into twelve pills; take one every night or morning as required. On the Amazon carry guarana. Woolen socks are recommended by those who have had much experience of tropical fevers. Never bathe when the air is moist; avoid a chill; a native will not bathe till the sun is well up. Rub yourself with *aguardiente* (native rum) after a bath, and always when caught in a shower. Freely exercise in Quito to ward off liver complaints. Drink little water; coffee or chocolate is better, and tea is best. Avoid spirits with fruit, and fruit after dinner. The sickliest time in Guayaquil is at the breaking up of the rainy season.

As to dangers: First, from the people. Traveling is as safe in Ecuador as in New York, and safer than in Missouri. There are no Spanish banditti, though some places, as Chambo, near Riobamba, bear a bad name. It is not wise to tempt a penniless footpad by a show of gold; but no more so in Ecuador than any where. We have traveled from Guayaquil to Damascus, but have never had occasion to use a weapon in self-defense; and only once for offense, when we threatened to demolish an Arab sheik with an umbrella. Secondly, from brutes. Some travelers would have us infer that it is impossible to stir in South America without being "affectionately entwined by a serpent, or sprung upon by a jaguar, or bitten by a rattlesnake; jiggers in every sand-heap and scorpions under every stone" (*Edinburgh Review*, xliii, 310). Padre Vernazza speaks of meeting a serpent two yards in diameter! But you will be disappointed at the paucity of animal life. We were two months on the Andes (August and September) before we saw a live snake. They are plentiful in the wet season in cacao plantations; but the majority are harmless. Dr. Russel, who particularly studied the reptiles of India, found that out of forty-three species which he examined not more than seven had poisonous fangs; and Sir E. Tennent, after a long residence in Ceylon, declared he had never heard of the death of an European by the bite of a snake. It is true, however, that the number and proportion of the venomous species are greater in South America than in any other part of the world; but it is some consolation to know that, zoologically, they are inferior in rank to the harmless ones; "and certainly," adds Sidney Smith, "a snake that feels fourteen or fifteen stone stamping on his tail has little time for reflection, and may be allowed to be poisonous." If bitten, apply ammonia externally immediately, and take five drops in water internally; it is an almost certain antidote. The discomforts and dangers arising from the animal creation are no greater than one would meet in traveling overland from New York to New Orleans.

Finally, of one thing the tourist in South America may be assured—that dear to him, as it is to us, will be the remembrance of those romantic rides over the Cordilleras amid the wild magnificence of nature, the adventurous walk through the primeval forest, the exciting canoe-life on the Napo, and the long, monotonous sail on the waters of the Great River.

CHAPTER XXIV.

IN MEMORIAM.

"A life that all the Muses decked
 With gifts of grace that might express
 All comprehensive tenderness,
All-subtilizing intellect."—TENNYSON.

ON the east of the city of Quito is a beautiful and extensive plain, so level that it is literally a *table-land.* It is the classic ground of the astronomy of the eighteenth century: here the French and Spanish academicians made their celebrated measurement of a meridian of the earth. As you stand on the edge of this plain just without the city, you see the dazzling summit of Cayambi looking down from the north; on your left are the picturesque defiles of Pichincha; on your right the slopes of Antisana. Close by you, standing between the city and the plain, is a high white wall inclosing a little plot, like the city above, "four square." You are reminded by its shape, and also by its position relative to Quito and Pichincha, of that other sacred inclosure just outside the walls of Jerusalem and at the foot of Olivet, the Garden of Gethsemane. This is the Protestant Cemetery.

Through the efforts of our late representative—now also numbered with the dead—this place was assigned by the government for the interment of foreigners who do not die in the Romish faith. And there we buried our fellow-traveler, COLONEL PHINEAS STAUNTON, the artist of the expedition, and Vice-Chancellor of Ingham University, New York. On the 8th of September, 1867, we bore him through

P. Stanton

the streets of Quito to this quiet resting-place, without parade and in solemn silence—just as we believe his unobtrusive spirit would have desired, and just as his Savior was carried from the cross to the sepulchre. No splendid hearse or nodding plumes; no long procession, save the unheard tread of the angels; no requiem, save the unheard harps of the seraphs. We gave him a Protestant Christian burial, such as Quito never saw. In this corner of nature's vast cathedral, the secluded shrine of grandeur and beauty not found in Westminster Abbey, we left him. We parted with him on the mount which is to be the scene of his transfiguration.

It would be difficult for an artist to find a grave whose surroundings are so akin to his feelings. He lies in the lofty lap of the Andes, and snow-white pinnacles stand around him on every side, just as we imagine the mountains are around the city of God. We think we hear him saying, as Fanny Kemble Butler said of another burial-ground: "I will not rise to trouble any one if they will let me sleep here. I will only ask to be permitted, once in a while, to raise my head and look out upon this glorious scene." No dark and dismal fogs gather at evening about that spot. It lies nearer to heaven than any other Protestant cemetery in the world. "It is good (says Beecher) to have our mortal remains go upward for their burial, and catch the earliest sounds of that trumpet which shall raise the dead." And the day is coming when that precious vein of gold that now lies in the bosom of the mighty Andes shall leave its rocky bed and shine in seven-fold purity. Indeed, the artist is already in that higher studio among the mountains of Beulah.

A simple sculptured obelisk of sorrow stands over the dust of Colonel Staunton: his most fitting monument is his own life-work. He was the very painter Humboldt longed for in his writings—"the artist, who, studying in nature's great hot-house bounded by the tropics, should add a new and more magnificent kingdom of nature to art." Colonel Staunton, true and lovely in his own character, was ever seeking in nature for whatsoever things are lovely, whatsoever things are pure, and now was about to add whatsoever things are grand. He was a *Christian* artist, in sympathy with such men as Raphael and Leonardo de Vinci. "The habitual choice of sacred subjects (says Ruskin) implies that the painter has a natural disposition to dwell on the highest thoughts of which humanity is capable." No shallow or false person could have conceived his *Ascension.* Only the highest qualities of the intellect and heart—a soul already half ascended—could have given such ethereal lightness to those "two men in white apparel." Only the pure in heart see God. As we revisit in imagination the spot where he sleeps so well, we behold, in the calm sublimity of the mountains that surround his grave, an image of the undisturbed repose of his spirit on the Rock of Ages.

APPENDICES.

APPENDICES.

APPENDIX A.

Barometrical Measurements across South America.*

Locality.	Altitude.	Barometer.	Boiling Point.	Regnault's Equiv.	Difference.	Other Estimates.
Pacific Ocean......	0	29.930	212.01°			*Bar.* of Visse, 29.904; Boussingault, 29.867.
Guayaquil..........	10	29.899	211.95	29.891	—.008	*B. P.* of Visse, 211.8°.
Guaranda..........	8,840	21.976				*Alt.* of Visse, 8872; Hall, 8928.
Arenal............	14,250	18.123				*Alt.* of Visse, 13,917. Hall, 14,268.
Mocha.............	10,900	20.393				
Ambato............	8,490	22.241				*Alt.* of Visse, 8541; Boussingault, 8787. *Bar.* of Jameson, 22.218.
Tacunga...........	9,181	21.693				*Alt.* of Visse, 9180; Boussingault, 9384. *Bar.* of Jameson, 21.700.
Tiupullo...........	11,662	19.858				*Alt.* of Visse, 11,702.
Machachi..........	9,900	21.212				*Alt.* of Visse, 9823.
Quito.............	9,520	21.530	195.8	21.485	—.045	*Alt.* of La Condamine, 9596; Humboldt, 9570; Caldas, 8947; Boussingault, 9567; Aguilar, 9496; Visse, 9307; Bureau des Longs., 9540; Tramblay's *Ann.*, 9538; Jameson, 9513. *Bar.* of La Condamine, 21.404; Humboldt, 21.403; Aguilar, 21.465; Jameson, 21.566. *B. P.* of Visse, 195.6°; Tramblay, 184.18°.
Panecillo..........	10,101	21.043				*Alt.* of Humboldt, 10,244; Aguilar, 10,135. *Bar.* of Jameson, 21.207. *B. P.* of Visse, 194.7°.
Pichincha, top......	15,827	17.038	184.5	17.030	—.008	*Alt.* of La Condamine, 15,606; Humboldt, 15,922; Boussingault, 15,676; Visse, 16,200: Hall, 15,380; Jameson, 15,704. *Bar.* of Visse, 16.942.
Pichincha, crater...	13,300		189.2	18.672		*Alt.* of Visse and Moreno, 13,600.
Antisana H.........	13,300	18.583				*Alt.* of Humboldt, 13,465; Boussingault, 13,356. *Bar.* of Aguirre, 18.573; Jameson, 18.630.
On Antisana.......	16,000	16.782				
Pinatura..........	10,410	20.791				*Alt.* of Boussingault, 10,348.
Padregal..........	11,860	19.817				
On Cotopaxi.......	12,860	19.004				
Riobamba..........	9,200	21.705				*Alt.* of Visse, 9157; Boussingault, 9413.
Cajabamba.........	10,918	20.512				*Alt.* of La Condamine, 11,000.
Itulcache..........	8,885	22.006				
Tablon.............	10,516	20.800				
Papallacta..........	10,511	20.803	193.8	20.598	—.205	

* First published in the *American Journal of Science* for September, 1868, to which the reader is referred for other physical observations. The barometric anomaly, noticed particularly on the Lower Amazon, was also observed by Herndon, Castelnau, Chandless, Spruce, and Wallace.

Locality.	Altitude.	Barometer.	Boiling Point.	Regnault's Equiv.	Difference.	Other Estimates.
Guila..............	8,622	22.206				
Pachamama........	7,920	22.751				
Baeza..............	6,625	23.793				
Chinipleia..........	6,200	24.145				
Cochachimbamba..	4,252	25.832				
Curi-urcu..........	3,247	26.746				
Archidona..........	2,115	27.816	209° 00	28.180	+.364	
Napo..............	1,450	28.419	209.4	28.407	—.012	
Santa Rosa.........	1,100	28.814	210.4	28.982	+.168	
Coca..............	858	29.022	210.65	29.127	+.105	
Mouth of the River Aguarico.........	586	29.321	211 00	29.331	+.010	
Do. River Curaray..	500	29.408	210.8	29.215	—.193	
Do. River Napo....	385	29.526	211.4	29.566	+.040	*Alt.* at Nauta, by Castelnau, 365.
Pebas..............	345	29.510	211.1	29.390	—.120	*Alt.* of Herndon, 537. *B. P.* of Herndon, 211.1°.
Loreto.............			211.4	29.566		
San Antonio.......	256	29.655				
Tabatinga..........	255	29.656	211.5	29.625	—.041	*Alt.* of Spix and Martius, 670; Azevedo and Pinto, 150; Agassiz, 200.
Tunantins..........	138?	29.770				*Alt.* of Azevedo and Pinto, 124.
Ega................	100?	29.813	211.9	29.862	+.049	*Alt.* of Herndon, 2052; Azevedo and Pinto, 120. *B. P.* of Herndon, 208.2°.
Manáos............	199?	29.705				*Alt.* of Herndon, 1475; Castelnau, 293; Spix and Martius, 556; Azevedo and Pinto, 92. *B. P.* of Herndon, 209.3°; Gibbon, 210°.87; Wallace, 212°.5.
Serpa..............	158?	29.752				*Alt.* of Azevedo and Pinto, 84.
Obidos.............	114	29.802				*Alt.* of Azevedo and Pinto, 58; Agassiz, 45.
Santarem..........	107	29.808	211.5	29.625	—.183	*Alt.* of Herndon, 846; Azevedo and Pinto, 50. *B. P.* of Herndon, 210.5°.
Mount Alégre......	83	29.834				
Gurupá............	38	29.890				*Alt.* of Azevedo and Pinto, 42.
Pará...............	15	29.889	211.95	29.891	+.002	*Alt.* of Herndon, 320; Azevedo and Pinto, 35; Dewey, 35. *Bar.* of Herndon, 29.708; Dewey, 29.941; Orton (reduced to level of river), 29.914. *B.P.* of Herndon, 211.5°.
Atlantic Ocean.....	—2	29.932	212.16			*Bar.* of Dewey, 29.977.

APPENDIX B.

VOCABULARIES FROM THE QUÍCHUA, ZÁPARO, YÁGUA, AND CÁMPAS LANGUAGES.

[SPANISH PRONUNCIATION.]

English.	*Quíchua.*	*Záparo.*	*Yágua.*
Father,	Yáya,	Apochójo,	Yen.
Mother,	Máma,	Ańno,	Nihuá.
Son (said by father),	Chúri,	Niáto,	Poén.
Son (said by mother),	Cári huáhua,	Tauquí,	Poén.
Daughter (said by father),	Ushúshi,	Coniát *or* cuniató.	
Daughter (said by mother),	Huármi huáhua,	Itúm.	
Own father,	Quíquin yáya,	Cuqu máno.	
Own mother,	Quíquin máma,	Ia cuáno.	
Step-father,	La yáya,	Táma quíra.	
Step-mother,	La máma,	Táma quíra (máma?).	
Own son,	Quíquin chúri,	Ia cuniána.	
Step-son,	Quípai chúri,	Saquína cuniána.	
Elder son (said by father),	Cúra (*or* ñáupa) chúri,	Cuniapíra.	
Elder son (said by mother),	Cúra (*or* ñáupa, huáhua,	Cuniapíra.	
Younger son (said by mother),	Súllca (*or* quípa) chúri,	Nunoé.	
Younger daughter (said by father),	Súllca (*or* quípa) ushúshi,	Nunoé cuniató.	
Only son (said by father),	Zapálla (*or* zapaí) chúri,	Noquí cunián,	Tíqui rai (huahua).
Only son (said by mother),	Zapálla (*or* zapaí) cári huáhua,	Noquí táuco cunián,	Tíqui rai (huahua).
Grandson,	Cári huáhuay,	Cuajenáño.	
Granddaughter,	Huármi huáhuay,		
Great-grandson,	Cári víllca.	Cuajenáño.	
Great-great-grandson,	Cári chupúllu.		

Grandfather,	Hátun yáya,	Quirraíto piátzo,	Yen.
Grandmother,	Hátun máma,	Quirraíto ocuáje.	
Great-grandfather,	Machúi yáya,	Quirishepúi.	
Great-grandmother,	Páya (*or* ápa) máma,	Pára.	
Great-great-grandfather,	Apúsqui (*or* apúnche) yáya,	Piátzo.	
Ancestors,	Apúsqui cúna,	Idasipóa.	
Brother (said by male),	Hauaúqui,	Cuquihúño,	Rai taíre.
Brother (said by female),	Túri,	Cuáuuo,	Rai puipuín.
Sister (said by male),	Páni,	Cuirimáto,	Rai pópo.
Sister (said by female),	Náña,	Taquí,	Rai taíre tu.
Elder brother,	Cúrac huaúqui,	Irishía cuquíño.	
Younger brother,	Súllca huaúqui,	Noquí.	
Cousin (said by male),	Chíspa huaúqui,	Cuaneráno,	Primoíne.
Cousin (said by female),	Chíspa páni,	Cuaneráno,	Primaíne.
Second cousin,	Caílla chíspa huaúqui,	Cuaneráno (*or* cuaramá, *relation*).	
Third cousin,	Cáru chíspa huaúqui,	Cuaneráno (*or* cuaramá, *relation*).	
Uncle (father's brother),	Yayapác huaúqui (*or* háchi),*	Táuco.	
Uncle (mother's brother),	Mamapác (*or* caca) túri,	Cuánoro.	
Aunt (father's sister),	Ypa (*on Marañon*, tiaíne),	Cuiquíña.	
Aunt (mother's sister),	Mamapác ñáña,	Cuáno cuíño.	
Father-in-law,	Cacáy (*of male*); quihuachí (*of female*).		
Mother-in-law,	Quihuác (*of male*); quihuachí (*of female*).		
Son-in-law,	Másha,	Acamía,	Quiria.
Daughter-in-law,	Kachún,	Cuarí ráno.	
Brother-in-law,	Masaní (*or* catáy),	Cuajinojóno.	
Sister-in-law,	Ypa (*or* kachún púra).		

* *Quichua on Marañon*, tiuiúi.

VOCABULARIES FROM THE QUÍCHUA, ZÁPARO, YÁGUA, AND CÁMPAS LANGUAGES.—*Continued.*

English.	*Quíchua.*	*Záparo.*	*Yágua.*
God-son,	Chúri cáshcai (*or* cháscai),	(*Not used*).	
God-father,	Shutichíc (*or* shutíshca) yáya,	Na achiatáno.	
God-mother,	Shutichíc (*or* shutíshca) máma,	Noaichozáno.	
Relation,	Aíllu,	Cuaramá,	(*Same as brother*).
Husband,	Cúsa,	Cuirán,	Rai-huáno.
Wife,	Huármi,	Cuirichán,	Rai-huaturá.
Widower,	Huáccha cári,	Machícho.	
Widow,	Huáccha huármi,	Machícho.	
Twins,	Yshcai huacháshca (*or* huachác),	Sárro.	
Hand,	Maquí,	Cuichoác,	Samutú.
Foot,	Chaquí,	Cuiñocá,	Nimutú.
Fingers,	Maquí pálca,	Canasú,	(*No terms for fingers and toes*).
Toes,	Chaquí pálca,	Cuiñocá canasú.	
Thumb,	(*No separate terms for thumb and big toe*).	Cumacaná.	
Nails,	Silhú,	Anahuachá.	
God,	Apúnchi-yáya (*God our Father*),	Piátzo,	Tupana.
One,	Shuc (*or* Shug),	Noquí,	Tiquí.
Two,	Ishcay,	Ammasaniquí,	Nanoíjoi.
Three,	Quínsa,	Imucú maraquí (*above three they have no names, but show their fingers; do not count above ten*).	Momuhí.
Four,	Chúscu,		Nañunjúia.
Five,	Píshca (*or* pítchca),		Tanaíjo.
Six,	Sócta,		Tiquí ñiháte.
Seven,	Cánchis,		Nañoujaiáte.
Eight,	Púsac (*or* pusag),		Momunhuaiáte.

Nine,	Iscún,	Nañauyuía-áte.
Ten,	Chúnga,	Nanjui. (*Go no higher.*)
Eleven,	Chúnga shug.	
Twelve,	Chúnga íshcay, *etc.*	
Twenty,	Ishcay-chúnga.	
Twenty-one,	Ishcay-chúnga shug, *etc.*	
Thirty,	Quínsa chúnga.	
One hundred,	Páchac (*or* pátzag).	
One thousand,	Guaránga.	
Ten thousand,	(*Would be* chúnga-guaránga; *but they never go over* 1000).	
Ordinal numbers,	(Niquí *is joined to the number:* e.g., *first is* shug niquí; *second*, ishcáy niquí).	

(*The Conibos count by twos. Thus, one is* avícho; *two*, rabói. *Above two, so many twos, as four is* rabói-rabói; *and six*, rabói-rabói-rabói. *Ten is expressed by spreading both hands, and twenty by bringing fingers and toes together. Thus the Caribs. Decimal numeration is found among all the American aborigines, ancient and modern, juxtaposition usually designating multiplication.*)

CAMPAS WORDS.

Mother,	Ina.	Nose,	Aquíry.	Leg,	Aítse.	Curasson,	Choichítes.	Rope,	Piaminíta.
Brother (said		Mouth,	Apa-anti.	Belly,	Amútse.	Turtle,	Tutá.	Twine,	Quiritarí.
by male),	Incho.	Hand,	Náco.	Wrist,	Acú.	Monkey,	Tsepé.	Maize,	Chínque.
Brother (said		Foot,	Aítse-cunída.	Knee,	Airitú.	Cocoa,	Quinbíto.	One,	Paníro.
by female),	Iga.	Lips,	Achíra.	Ankle,	Atúnque.	Clay,	Quipateí.	Two,	Pitiní.
Sister (said by		Teeth,	Aiquí.	Nails,	Achíte.	Shirt,	Pápani.	Three,	Pariotohuáy.
by male),	Incho.	Hair,	Quísti.	Fly,	Chimbóque.	Fire,	Pamarí.	Four,	Pariopatóta.
Head,	Aítu.	Neck,	Aquínce.	Musquito,	Chítu.	Hammock,	Quio-ots.	Five,	Pariotohuaygae.
Eyes,	Oquí.	Arm,	Acú.	Armadillo,	Pícha.				

(*My informant on numerals, a boy, though quite intelligent, could go no farther; but the tribe undoubtedly count ten.*)

APPENDIX C.

COMMERCE OF THE AMAZON.

I.—Value of Products Exported from different Towns on the Amazon by the Imperial Steamers in 1867.*

Products.	Cametá.	Breves.	Macapá.	Gurupá.	Porto do Moz.	Pra-inha.	Mt. Alégre.	Santa-rem.	Obidos.	Villa Nova.	Serpa.	Manáos.	Cuda-jaz.	Coary.	Ega.	Fonte Boa.	Tonan-tins.	S. Paulo.	Taba-tinga.	Quantity.	Mean Price.	Total Value.
Brazil Nuts...	....	$600	$400	$290	$10	$16	....	$1,334	$6,938	$2,564	$6,886	$15,010	$1,442	$498	$325	....	....	....	....	18,397 alq.	$2 00	$36,794
Cacao.........	$44,054	1,615	6,429	1,345	257	1,677	$86	69,111	172,421	28,907	34,462	38,802	1,945	5,192	4,907	$957	$365	$310	$227	314,327 arr.	3 00	942,981
Cattle.........	....	....	....	....	....	1,575	600	550	25	....	....	....	....	....	....	....	....	....	....	110	25 00	2,750
Coffee	....	....	....	....	....	....	....	56	33	7	....	172	....	....	....	....	....	....	25	79 arr.	3 70	292
Copaiba	....	....	....	....	....	....	....	18	1,422	4,383	8,631	5,175	132	....	1,559	123	....	....	....	72,030 lbs.	30	2,160
Cotton, raw...	....	....	100	90	....	....	....	....	....	....	103	293	....	....	....	1	6	....	232	653 arr.	1 25	816
Dried Meat ...	....	....	....	....	....	145	....	2,744	15,699	167	....	....	....	....	....	....	....	....	....	6,821 "	2 75	18,757
Farina........	....	....	....	....	....	....	....	....	....	....	....	....	....	80	37	15	105	10	....	99 alq.	2 50	247
Guarana......	....	....	....	....	....	....	....	1,620	750	24,240	14,550	60	....	....	....	....	....	....	....	1,374 arr.	30 00	41,220
Hides	138	800	3,302	858	271	152	....	2,426	4,087	5,787	6,296	2,163	....	....	....	....	....	....	....	11,871	2 00	23,742
Horses........	....	75	600	....	....	375	3,225	3,975	2,100	....	....	300	....	....	....	....	....	....	....	142	75 00	10,650
India-rubber..	123,460	128,440	306,880	85,110	85,780	1,430	....	22,670	8,640	20,100	209,400	219,340	30,468	7,644	6,308	5,460	2,252	9,155	15,054	128,955 arr.	10 00	1,289,550
Piassaba......	....	....	....	....	....	....	....	....	....	....	....	7,612	....	....	....	....	....	....	....	7,612 "	1 00	7,612
Pirarucu......	....	10	20	....	200	1,805	525	18,902	31,525	40,827	21,025	79,055	8,273	5,944	6,205	7,572	6,768	2,018	920	94,316 "	2 50	235,790
Sarsaparilla...	....	....	....	....	....	60	....	2,376	1,392	108	372	33,708	207	943	5,163	4,876	5,209	2,334	3,703	5,119 "	11 80	60,442
Tallow........	....	12	212	....	....	60	....	200	1,484	1,368	4,164	16	....	....	....	....	....	....	....	1,893 "	4 00	7,572
Tobacco	....	50	....	25	....	25	....	....	....	225	1,187	237	....	48	360	....	....	12	360	205 "	12 23	2,525
Tonka Beans .	....	....	....	43	....	....	....	....	120	1,070	5	9	....	....	....	....	....	....	....	260 "	4 80	1,248
Turtles	....	....	....	....	....	....	....	....	76	....	2	76	136	39	33	10	50	3	3	331	1 80	596
Turtle-oil.....	....	....	....	....	....	....	....	....	100	....	5	8,220	216	2,382	3,123	1,693	1,646	298	335	3,762 j'rs.	4 75	17,769

* This Table is taken from the *Relatoria da Companhia de Navegaçao e Commercio do Amazonas*, and includes only the commerce by the Brazilian steamers and the staple products. The vast amount carried by sailing craft and by Peruvian steamers on the Marañon is unknown to us. The number of passengers transported by the steamers in 1867 was 13,886; receipts from passage, $75,744; from freight, $210,654. In the reduction, the milrey has been taken at 50 cts. U. S. currency, which was the rate very nearly in 1867. The alquiere (alq.) = .988 of a bushel; arr. = arroba of 32 lbs.

II. ARTICLES EXPORTED FROM PARÁ TO THE UNITED STATES IN 1860.

Annatto	lbs.	64,832
Balsam Copaiba	"	89,670
Cacao	"	145,888
Copper, old	"	1,171
Hides, wet	"	616,172
" dry	"	4,503
Nuts, Brazil	"	23,582
" " unshelled	"	19,481
Piassaba	lbs.	3,488
Rubber, fine	"	2,394,656
" mixed	"	69,120
" coarse	"	420,000
Skins, Deer	"	64,406
Tapioca	"	118,080
Tonka Beans	"	18,298

III. ARTICLES IMPORTED FROM THE UNITED STATES TO PARÁ IN 1860.

Axes	dozens,	1,826
Candles	boxes,	594
Chairs	dozens,	333
Codfish	drums,	1,943
Clocks	number,	660
Combs	dozens,	7,353
Domestics	packages,	2,370
Drugs	"	435
Flour	barrels,	16,755
Fire-crackers	boxes,	1,800
Gunny-bags	number,	13,000
Gunpowder	kegs,	2,150
Hams	tierces,	38
Hardware	packages,	201
Hats, Palm-leaf	cases,	506
Knives	dozens,	2,195
Lard	packages,	2,709
Lumber	feet,	75,955
Nails	kegs,	588
Matches	cases,	174
Oars	number,	592
Pepper	bags,	190
Rosin	barrels,	1,556
Rubber and other Shoes	pairs,	3,398
Shooks (box)	number,	16,428
Soap	boxes,	6,891
Specie, in Gold	dollars,	113,827
Straw Paper	reams,	12,903
Soda-biscuit	12-lb. tins,	5,954
Saltpetre	kegs,	95
Tea	chests,	235
Tea	boxes,	533
Tar and Pitch	barrels,	329
Tobacco	boxes,	257
Twine, Cotton	pounds,	13,322
Tortoise-shell	"	299½

IV. DUTIES ON PRINCIPAL IMPORTS FROM UNITED STATES AT PARÁ.

Axes and Hatchets	30	reys per	pound.
Biscuit, Soda	400	"	arroba.
Brooms	600	"	dozen.
Chairs, cane-seat	1,000	"	article.
" rocking	3,000	"	"
" " extra	6,000	"	"
Cinnamon, Ceylon	500	"	pound.
Combs, rubber	600	"	"
" ivory	2,000	"	"
Cotton Goods	90	"	sq. vara.
" " colored twills	150	"	"

Candles	240	reys per	pound.
Cigars	1,200	"	"
Cordage	50	"	"
Dirks, ordinary	6,000	"	article.
" extra	12,000	"	"
Flour	150	"	arroba.
Hats, Palm-leaf	180	"	article.
Hams	70	"	pound.
Homœopathic Medicine	300	"	ounce.
Knives	250	"	article.
Lard	1,500		
Matting, India,	240	"	pound.
Nails, to two inches	40	"	"
" over "	20	"	"
Padlocks, brass	250	"	"
" iron	180	"	"
Pearl Barley	400	"	arroba.
Pepper, India	70	"	pound.
Plows	free.		
Pork	600	"	arroba.
Powder	200	"	pound.
Paper, Straw	30	"	"
Pilot Bread	150	"	arroba.
Roman Cement	50	"	"
Rosin	1,200		
Sieves, iron wire	30	"	pound.
" brass	50	"	"
Shoes, Rubber	400	"	"
Store Trucks	900	"	article.
Shooks, boxes	400	"	arroba.
Soap, Yellow	30	"	pound.
Scales, simple	120	"	"
Tar and Pitch	200	"	arroba.
Tortoise-shell	2,500	"	pound.
Tea	450	"	"
Twine, Cotton	300	"	"
Trunks, 2 to 4 palms	2,700	"	article.
" over 4 "	3,600	"	"
Tobacco, chewing	4,800	"	arroba.
" cut	9,600	"	arroba.

☞ This Tariff went into operation February 23, 1861.

ADDENDA.

Orchilla, page 29.—This valuable lichen comes chiefly from Tumbez. It is not found on the rocks, like the orchilla of the Old World, but grows on various trees. The foliage of a tree disappears when the orchilla commences. The sea air is indispensable to its production, as it is found only near the coast.

Religious Intolerance, p. 91.—The expression "Protestant dogs" has since been publicly repeated by a priest in a sermon, who told the people to confess, or they would be treated in a similar way. It called forth a remonstrance from Mr. Hamilton, the British Minister, directed to the archbishop, declaring such conduct inhuman and unchristian. The Pope's Nuncio left Quito for good in July, 1869.

Fish in the Quito Valley, p. 107.—Dr. Gill informs me that the true name of this little fish is *Cyclopium Humboldtii*, Swainson. It belongs to the subfamily Trachelypterinæ, under Siluridæ.

Hummers' Nests, p. 108.—They are not always of a lengthened form, as the text would imply, but are sometimes quite shallow. They are invariably lined with the softest vegetable materials and covered with moss. The nests are not as compact as those of our Northern hummer, and, so far as we observed, are never shingled with flat lichens.

Humboldt in 1802, p. 156.—He spent five months in the valley of Quito.

Pebas Fossils, p. 282.—In a letter to the author, Mr. Darwin says: "Your discovery of marine shells high up the Amazon possesses *extreme* interest, not only in itself, but as one more most striking instance how rash it is to assert that any deposit is not a marine formation because it does not contain fossils. As for myself, I never believed for a moment in Agassiz's idea of the origin of the Amazonian formation." Agassiz "candidly confesses (Lyell's *Principles*, i., 468) that he failed to discover any of those proofs which we are accustomed to regard, even in temperate latitudes, as essential for the establishment of the former existence of glaciers where they are now no more. No glaciated pebbles, or far-transported angular blocks with polished and striated sides; no extensive surface of rock, smooth, and traversed by rectilinear furrows, were observed." The fossiliferous bed at Pebas is as plainly *in situ* as the Medina sandstone at Genesee Falls.

Tropical Flowers, p. 292.—"During twelve years spent amid the grandest tropical vegetation, I have seen nothing comparable to the effect produced on our landscapes by gorse, broom, heather, wild hyacinths, hawthorns, purple orchises, and buttercups."—Wallace's *Malay Archipelago.*

Coca-plant, p. 293.—The engraving conveys the impression that the leaves are parallel-veined; but the coca is a dicotyledon, with the under surface of the leaf strongly marked with veins, of which two, in addition to the midrib, run parallel with the margin.

Pedrero, Map.—This town on the Rio Negro is also written *Pedreira.*

INDEX.

Adobe dwellings, page 46.
Agassiz, Mount, 250.
" Prof., on the geology of the Amazonian valley, 280, 282, 347.
Agriculture on the Amazon, 243.
" " Andes, 75.
Aground on the Amazon, 239.
Aguano, 201.
Aguardiente, 175.
Alcalde's house, 202.
Alligators, 35, 296.
Almeyrim Hills, 252.
Aloe, American, 100.
Alpargates, 70.
Altar, volcano of, 150.
Amazon River, annual rise, 274.
" " birds on, 306.
" " cetaceans, 299.
" " climate, 273, 284.
" " commerce, 277.
" " current, 273.
" " delta, 272.
" " depth, 274.
" " etymology, 278.
" " expeditions, 277.
" " first view of, 226.
" " fishes, 295.
" " foreign vessels on, 276.
" " insects, 300.
" " life within, 295.
" " magnitude, 264, 272, 278.
" " natural canals, 265.
" " navigation, 276.
" " reptiles, 296.
" " scenery, 236.
" " source, 264.
" " tints, 272.
" " tributaries, 266, 271.
" " volume, 273.
" Valley, 280.
" " creation of, 117.
" " forest, 287.
Amazon Valley, fruits, 289.
" " geology, 281, 347.
" " minerals, 286.
" " slope, 280.
" " soil, 286.
" " trees, 289.
" " zoology, 284.
Amazonian Indians, 316.
Ambato, 52, 153.
America, the continent of vegetation, 103.
America, South, geology of, 114.
Amphisbœna, 194.
Amusements in Quito, 80.
Anacondas, 222.
Andean chain, 119.
Andes, as a geological boundary, 207.
" birds on the, 105, 146.
" equipped for the, 37.
" first sight of the, 33.
" heart of the, 48.
" last view of the, 214.
" of Ecuador, 121.
" reptiles on the, 107.
" rise of the, 115.
" sinking of the, 138.
" summit of the, 49, 134.
" valleys of the, 130.
" views from the, 45, 134, 141.
Anguteros Indians, 222.
Animal life, dearth of, 188.
Animals on the Napo, 207.
Antisana, volcano of, 144, 180.
" hacienda, 144.
Ants, battle with, 225.
" on the Amazon, 300.
" on the Napo, 194.
Apothecaries in Quito, 93.
Archidona, 191.
Architecture in Quito, 78.
Arenal, 49.
Armadillo, 310.
Army of Ecuador, 87.

Arrieros, 36.
Arrows, Indian, 321.
Arts in Quito, 78.
Ascending the Andes, 43, 96, 144.
Astronomy on the Andes, 97.
Atahuallpa, 56.
Atmosphere of Quito, 97.

Baeza, 187.
Balsas, 32.
Bamboos on the Napo, 220.
Banana, 34.
Baños, 149.
Barometric measurements, 337.
" anomaly, 241, 226.
" variations at Quito, 92.
Barra, 243.
Bartholomew, St., 54.
Bats, 205, 312.
Bears, 105.
Bed, Andean, 181.
Bees on the Amazon, 303.
" of Quito, 108.
" on the Napo, 207.
Beetles on the Amazon, 303.
" on the Napo, 206.
Bells of Quito, 89.
"Big-ear" Indians, 222.
Birds on the Amazon, 306.
" coloration of, in the tropics, 105.
" moulting of, 285.
" of South America, 105.
Blow-guns, 170.
Boa-constrictor, 223.
Bodegas, 35.
Botany of South America, 286.
Brazilian etiquette, 235, 246.
" frontier, 233.
" steamers, 234.
Brazilians, 323.
Brazil-nut trees, 290.
Bread-tree, 34.
Breves, 254.
Buildings, Andean, 46.
Bull-baits, 80.
Burial customs, 91, 321.
" at Quito, 91.
Butter, 251.
Butterflies on the Amazon, 302.
" on the Napo, 206.
Buzzards, 29.

Caballococha, 232.
Cacao, 30, 290.
Cajabamba, 153.
Calabash-tree, 289.
Camino Real, 45.
Camellones, 43.
Camindo on the Napo, 226.
Campas Indians, 322.
Canélos, 172.
Canoe-life on the Napo, 213.
Canoe-paths, 265.
Canoes on the Napo, 200.
Capybara, 310.
Caraguairazo, 132.
Carnival, 81.
Carranqui, 157.
Cassiquari Canal, 267.
Cathedral of Guayaquil, 26.
" of Quito, 66.
Cattle on the Andes, 145.
Caucho-tree, 288.
Cayambi, 143.
Cedar on the Amazon, 289.
Cemetery, Protestant, 91.
Century-plant, 100.
Cerro, 33.
Cetaceans in the Amazon, 299.
Chicha, 167, 210.
Chillo hacienda, 155.
Chimbo, Valley of, 46.
Chimborazo, 33, 44, 49, 127.
Chimneys, absence of, 44.
Chirimoya, 101.
Chuquipoyo, 51.
Chuquiragua, 100.
Cigána, 206, 308.
Cinchona, 47.
Cinnamon, American, 172.
Circumcision, 322.
Civility, Ecuadorian, 35, 71.
Civilization on the Amazon, 236.
Clay-eating, 229.
" formation of the Amazon, 225.
Climate of Guayaquil, 28.
" of Quito, 91.
" of the Amazon, 238, 251.
Coary, River, 242, 269.
Coca-chewing, 291, 348.
Coca village, 207.
Cochineal, 108.
Cock-fighting, 35, 80.
Cocoa-palm, 35.
Coffee, 31, 259, 290.
Colleges of Ecuador, 79.
Combativeness on the Andes, 95.
Commerce on the Amazon, 342.
Compressed heads, 171.
Compulsory commerce, 195.
Condor, 106, 131.
Cones of volcanoes, 122.

Conibos Indians, 321.
Cookery in Quito, 44, 84.
Copal-gum, 193.
Cordillera, 33, 126.
Cosanga River, 189.
Costumes of Amazonian Indians, 239, 241.
Cotocachí, village, 154.
" volcano, 142.
Cotopaxi, 55, 146.
" eruptions of, 125.
Cotton-mills, 77, 155.
Cow-tree, 288.
Craft on the Napo, 209.
Craters, deep, 133.
Crocodiles, 296.
Cudajá, 242.
Cuenca, 152.
Cunchebamba, 53.
Curaray River, 224.
Curassow, 308.
Curi-urcu, 191.
Currency of Pará, 260.
" " Quito, 75.
Cuzco ladies, 82.

Dangers in South America, 331.
Darwin on the geology of the Pampas, 282.
Darwin on the geology of the Amazon, 347.
Debt of Ecuador, 87.
Deer on the Napo, 226.
" fossil, 154.
Descent into Pichincha, 139.
Discipline on the Napo, 204.
Diseases on the Andes, 93, 331.
Dogs on the Andes, 95.
Dolphins, 299.
Dragon-flies, 302.
Dress in Quito, 69.
Drunkenness at Quito, 146.

Earthquake at Ibarra, 157.
" at Riobamba, 153.
" effect of, on climate, 91.
" experience of, 163.
" theories of, 161.
Eastern Cordillera, 179.
Eciton ants, 301.
Ecuador, army, 87.
" Congress, 86.
" debt, 87.
" extent, 85.
" flora and fauna, 103.
" government, 86.
Ecuador, population, 85.
" religion, 89.
" repudiation, 86.
" revenue, 87.
" revolutions, 86.
" supreme court, 87.
" volcanoes, 122, 148.
Ecuadorian cooking, 44, 84.
Education on the Andes, 79.
Edwards, George, 195.
Ega, 239.
Eggs of the alligator, 297.
" of the turtle, 297.
El Dorado, 183.
Elephant at high altitudes, 155.
Equator, mean temperature, 262.
Expenses of travel, 327.

Farina, 235, 291.
Ferns, tree, 38.
Fever remedies, 331.
Fire-flies, 25.
Fish in the Napo, 226.
" in Quito Valley, 107, 347.
" in the tropics, 329.
Fishes ejected from volcanoes, 107, 132, 143.
" of the Amazon, 295.
Fishing with barbasco, 169.
Flamingoes, 308.
Flowers on the Amazon, 292, 347.
" on the Andes, 50, 102, 136.
Fonte Boa, 239.
Forest on the Napo, 216, 219.
" trail, 182, 186.
" tropical, 36, 38, 287.
Fossil bones on the Andes, 154.
Fossils in the Amazon Valley, 282, 347.
Frogs in Quito Valley, 107.
" of the Amazon, 304.
Fruits of Quito, 101.
" on the Amazon, 289.

Galapagos Islands, 105, 124.
Gentians, 103.
Geology of South America, 114.
" of the Amazon Valley, 225, 347.
Glacial theory of Agassiz, 282, 347.
Glaciers, absence of, 131.
Glimpse of the Andes, 33.
Goître, 94.
Gold on the Napo, 196.
Grapes on the Amazon, 234.
Grebe on the Andes, 146.

Guacamayo Mountain, 190.
Guamani, 144, 179.
Guápulo, 178.
Guarani race, 316.
Guarana, 290.
Guaranda, 46.
Guayaquil, city and people, 25.
" climate, 28.
" commerce, 29.
" history, 28.
" market, 30.
Guayas River, scenes on, 32.
Guayusa tea, 193.
Gurupá, 253.
Gypsy-birds, 223.

Hammocks, 202.
Hats of Guayaquil, 31.
Hatuntaqui, battle of, 56, 154.
Hauxwell, Mr., 227, 229.
Health in the tropics, 331.
" on the Andes, 93.
Heart of the Andes, 48.
High altitudes, experience at, 96, 142.
Himalayas, vegetation on, 50, 100.
Horns, blowing of, 209.
Horses, extinct species of, 154.
" for the Andes, 36.
Hospitality, Ecuadorian, 35, 71.
Hotels, Andean, 40, 53.
" in Guayaquil, 328.
" in Quito, 329.
Howling monkeys, 223, 313.
Huallaga River, 268.
Humboldt, 136, 156, 348.
Hummers in Quito, 107, 347.
" on the Amazon, 303.
Hybrids, 43.
Hypsometric zones, 50.

Ibarra, 157.
Ibis, 308.
Ida Pfeiffer, 53.
Iguana, 304.
Imbabura, 143, 154.
Immorality of priests, 89.
Incarial relics, 109, 112, 124.
Incas in Quito, 56.
Indian character, 153, 203, 243.
" dwellings, 78.
" peons, 36, 183.
" savages, 221.
" villages, 237.
Indians, Amazonian, 315.
" Andean, 69, 109, 111.
" as travelers, 186.
India-rubber-tree, 288.
In memoriam, 334.
Insect pests, 224.
Insects, Amazon, 206, 300.
" in Quito, 108.
Iquitos, 231.
Itulcachi, 178.

Jacamars, 308.
Jaçanas, 308.
Jacapas, 308.
Jaguars, 311.
Japurá River, 267, 320.
Javarí River, 269, 320.
Jesuits, 89, 321.
Jiggers, 108.
Jívaros Indians, 165, 171.
Jurís Indians, 319.
Juruá River, 269, 319.
Jutahí River, 269.

Lady travelers on the Amazon, 236.
La Mona, 38.
Language of Ecuador, 71.
Latacunga, 53.
Lava, absence of, 122.
" streams, 144.
Lepers, 55, 94.
Lianas, 188.
Lice-eating, 181.
Life within the Amazon, 295.
" around the Amazon, 300.
Lignite on the Amazon, 225, 283.
Lion, American, 105.
Living on the Amazon, 235.
Lizards of the Amazon, 304.
Llama, 104.
" fossil, 154.
Llanganati Mountains, 149.
Locro, 44.
Loja, 152.
Longevity on the Andes, 92.
Loreto, 232.
Lotteries in Quito, 90.
Lungs of mountaineers, 95.
Lyell on the Valley of the Amazon, 347.

Macaws, 306.
Machachi, 55.
Madeira River, 269.
Mamaï, 234.
Mamelucos, 239.
Mammals on the Amazon, 309.
Manáos, 243.
Manati, 215, 299.

Mandioca, 291.
Mango, 34.
Manufactures of Quito, 77.
Marañon River, 227.
" steamers, 230.
Maravilla, 48.
Market of Quito, 77.
Mashka, 36.
Maspa, 186.
Masquerade, Indian, 110.
Mastodon, Andean, 154.
Matá-matá turtle, 299.
Maucallacta, 232.
Mauhés Indians, 318.
Mazan River, 226.
Meat, preservation of, 222.
Merchants of Quito, 74.
Mica Lake, 146.
Milk on the Andes, 179.
Milky Way at Quito, 98.
Mixed races, 68, 322.
Mocha, 52.
Mongruba-tree, 288.
Monkey meat, 203.
Monkeys, 223, 313.
Montaña of Peru, 231.
Monte Alégre, 252.
Montúca flies, 224.
Moreno, President, 54, 86, 138.
Mountaineers, 43, 69, 95.
Mountains on the Amazon, 252.
Moyabamba, 231.
Mules, 43.
Muleteers, 36.
Mundurucus Indians, 318.
Múras Indians, 318.
Music in the forest, 205.
Musquitoes, 224, 228, 303.

Napo country, 164.
" diseases, 198.
" fish, 226.
" Indians, 165, 197, 180, 210.
" journey, 174.
" navigation, 197, 209.
" productions, 196.
" rapids, 200.
" river, 197, 199, 227, 268.
" scenery, 216, 220.
" tea, 193.
" turtles, 226.
" village, 194.
" wilderness, 188, 191.
Nauta, 231.
Negroes on the Amazon, 247, 323.
Negro River, 242, 266, 319.
Newspapers in Ecuador, 27, 80.
Nocturnal music, 205.

Obidos, 248.
Obsidian, 124, 148.
Orchids, 216.
Orchilla, 347.
Orejones, 222.
Orellana's expedition, 183, 207.
Organ-bird, 308.
Oriente, 164.
Otovalo, 157.
Outfit for travel, 327.

Paita, raised beach at, 115.
Paja, or Paramo grass, 49.
Palms, cocoa, 35.
" on the Amazon, 287.
" on the Napo, 219.
Palo de cruz, 228.
Pampas, geology of, 282.
Panama hats, 31.
Pañuelon, 69.
Papallacta, 177, 181.
Papaya-tree, 202, 234.
Pará City, buildings, 257.
" climate, 262.
" commerce, 259.
" currency, 260.
" government, 261.
" people, 258.
" view of, 254.
Para River, 254, 271.
Paramo, 33.
Parrots, 206, 306.
Passés Indians, 319.
Pastassa River, 150, 268.
Pebas, 227.
" fossils, 282, 347.
Peccaries, 221, 310.
Peons, 36, 183.
Peruvian bark, 47.
" steamers, 230.
Pfeiffer, Ida, 53.
Piassaba palm, 289.
Pichincha volcano, 124, 133, 140.
Pigs, mode of dressing, 49.
Pirarucú fish, 295.
Piums, 224.
Pizarro at Coca, 183, 207.
Plantain, 34.
Poison antidote, 332.
Politeness, Ecuadorian, 35, 71.
Politics in Quito, 86.
Polylepis-trees, 50, 179.
Poncho, 69.

Porphyroid trachytes, 124.
Porpoises, 299.
Porto do Moz, 253.
Potatoes on the Andes, 101.
Potato soup, 44, 50.
Prayinha, 253.
President's order, 176.
Priests of Quito, 89.
Protestant cemetery, 90, 334.
Puma, 105.
Pumice, 148.
" on the Amazon, 268.
Puna, 96.
Purus Indians, 318.
" River, 269.

Quadrupeds on the Amazon, 309.
Quartz, paucity of, 122.
Quito agriculture, 75.
" amusements, 80.
" architecture, 78.
" arts, 78.
" atmosphere, 96.
" bells, 89.
" birds, 106.
" bull-baits, 80, 94.
" butterflies, 108.
" capital, 66.
" carnival, 81.
" climate, 91.
" cock-fights, 81.
" cookery, 84.
" currency, 75.
" diseases, 93.
" dress, 69.
" drunkenness, 142.
" education, 79.
" fashions, 70.
" fish, 108.
" flour, 98, 101.
" history, 56, 152.
" insects, 108.
" ladies, 70, 81.
" manufactures, 77.
" market, 77.
" masquerades, 81.
" merchants, 74.
" newspapers, 80.
" politics, 86.
" population, 68.
" potatoes, 101.
" prices, 329.
" Protestant cemetery, 90.
" religion, 87.
" reptiles, 107.
" scenery, 178.
Quito servants, 83.
" situation, 55, 59, 62.
" streets and buildings, 64, 65.
" street scene, 60.
" suburbs, 55, 59.
" under the Incas, 56.
" under the Spaniards, 57.
" Valley, 51, 55, 73, 149, 152.
" " archæology of, 109, 112.
Quitonians, character of the, 71, 86.
" primeval, 109.

Rain-fall at Quito, 93.
" line on the Andes, 45.
Raposa, 233, 311.
Regularity of nature, 92.
Religion of Ecuador, 87.
Religious intolerance, 91, 347.
Reptiles at Quito, 107.
" on the Amazon, 296.
Revenue of Ecuador, 87.
Ride down the Andes, 180.
Rimos Indians, 322.
Riobamba, 150, 153.
River systems of South America, 118, 275.
Roads on the Andes, 43, 53, 74.
Rodents on the Amazon, 309.
Romanism on the Andes, 88.
Rose of the Andes, 103.
Routes across South America, 325.
Rumiñagui, 146.

Salt on the Andes, 193.
San Antonio, 233.
Sand-flies, 224.
Sangai volcano, 150.
San Paulo, 237.
Santarem, 251.
Santa Rosa, 201.
Sapucaya nut, 290.
Sarsaparilla, 224.
Saüba ants, 194, 300.
Savages on the Napo, 221.
Savaneta, 40.
Scenery on the Amazon, 253.
Sea-cows, 215.
Serpa, 247.
Shells in Quito Valley, 109.
" in the Amazon Valley, 295.
Sierra, 33.
Silk-cotton-tree, 220, 289.
Sincholagua, 146.
Sloths, 310.
Slow-worm on the Napo, 194.
Snakes, scarcity of, 195, 332.

Snakes on the Amazon, 305.
Snow at high altitudes, 138.
" limit in the Andes, 125.
Soil in the Amazon Valley, 286.
Solimoens, 237.
South America, geology of, 114.
" American fauna and flora, 103.
" American Indians, 315.
Southerners on the Amazon, 246, 251.
Spanish character, 328.
" language, 71.
" Republicanism, 58.
Spiders on the Amazon, 304.
Stars at Quito, 97.
Staunton, Col., burial of, 91, 334.
Steam on the Amazon, 230, 234, 330.
Storm on the Napo, 213.
Sugar on the Amazon, 252.
" on the Andes, 329.
Sugar-cane on the Amazon, 291.
Suno, 205.
Superstition, 54.

Tabatinga, 233.
Table-lands of the Old World, 152.
Tablon, 178.
Tacunga, 53.
Tambillo ridge, 55.
Tambo on the mountains, 40.
Tapajos River, 270.
Tapir, 104, 310.
Teffe River, 269.
Temperature, correspondence of altitude and latitude as to, 145.
Termite ants, 301.
Thermometer, variations of, 92.
Tide on the Amazon, 275.
Timber on the Amazon, 289.
Tiupullo, 54.
Toads of the Amazon, 304.
Tobacco on the Amazon, 291.
" use of, by the Napos, 197.
Tocantíns River, 271.
Tolling-bell bird, 307.
Tortoise-shell wood, 289.
Toucan, 206, 306.
Trade wind, 118.
Trail in the forest, 182.
Trapiche, 207.
Traveling in South America, 325.
Trees in Quito Valley, 100.
" on the Amazon, 288.
Trogon, 308.
Tropical flowers, 292, 347.
" forest, 287.
Tropical vegetation, 34, 38, 188, 190, 219.
Tucúna Indians, 320.
Tucker, Admiral, 232.
Tunantíns, 237.
Tunguragua volcano, 149.
Tupi race, 316.
Turtles in the Amazon, 297.
" in the Napo, 215, 226.

Uaupés Indians, 319.
Ucayali Indians, 321.
" River, 268.
Umbrella bird, 307.
Upper Amazon towns, 231.
Urarí poison, 228.

Valediction on the Napo, 204.
Valley of the Amazon, 280.
" of the Andes, 130.
" of the Chimbo, 46.
" of Quito, 51, 55, 73, 149, 151, 155.
Vanilla on the Napo, 196.
Vegetation in the tropics, 34, 38.
" on the Amazon, 287.
" zones of, on the Andes, 50.
Verdure on the Amazon, 285.
Veta, 96.
Victoria Regia, 292.
Views from the Andes, 45.
Villa Nova, 248.
Vocabularies, Indian, 339.
Volcanoes of Ecuador, 122, 125, 151.

Washerwomen of Quito, 83.
Water-beetles, 295.
" carriers, 61.
Water-shed of the Atlantic and Pacific, 54.
Water-snakes, 296.
Wayside inn, 40.
White ants, 301.
Wisse, M., descent into Pichincha, 138.
Wool, Andean, 104.

Xingú River, 271.

Yagua Indians, 320.
Yana-urcu, 142.
Ypadú, 291.
Yuca, 167.
Yurimaguas, 231.

Záparo Indians, 165, 170.
Zodiacal light, 98.
Zones of vegetation, 50.
Zoology of the Napo, 206.
Zoology of South America, 286.
Zoological provinces of Amazonia, 300.

THE END.

www.ingramcontent.com/pod-product-compliance
Lightning Source LLC
LaVergne TN
LVHW010156110826
845151LV00002B/532
9781425536756